Pre-Communist Indochina

This book explores the history of pre-communist Indochina, from the fourteenth century to the 1940s. It examines the early state of Vietnam, comparing and contrasting its political and social systems, with both those of neighbouring states such as Thailand and those prevalent at the time in Europe. It identifies the forces that shaped Indochina before the arrival of European colonial powers, in particular the impact of China, which was not only a military threat and extracted payments of tribute, but was also an important commercial and cultural influence, not least through the export of Confucianism. It demonstrates clearly that the events and transformations of the late sixteenth and early seventeenth centuries are the starting point of developments which by around 1800 established the broad pattern of political and economic relations that existed before the nineteenth century 'impact of the West' began. It goes on to consider the impact of European colonialism in Indochina, focusing especially on French Indochina. It explores the ways in which the French occupiers groomed a new indigenous colonial elite to replace the existing elites who refused to co-operate with the authorities, and examines the growing opposition to French rule, including the role played by the often misunderstood religious and political movement of Caodaism. It analyses the different avenues of expression of Vietnamese nationalism, including the emergence of the Constitutionalist Party – the nearest French Indochina had to a democratic party in the Western sense. It shows how it sought to seek, through the actions of the French themselves, reforms that would lead to the modernisation of the country and more liberty for its inhabitants; and explains why it ultimately failed to achieve its objectives. Written by the late Ralph Smith, a highly respected historian of Asia, this book is essential reading for anyone seeking to understand the history of Indochina.

R.B. Smith was Professor of the International History of South-East Asia at the School of Oriental and African Studies, University of London, where he taught from 1962–2000. His works include *Vietnam and the West* (1971) and the three–volume *An International History of the Vietnam War* (1983, 1985, 1990).

Beryl Williams is Emeritus Reader in History, University of Sussex, UK. She taught at Sussex from 1963–2003, and her publications include *The Russian Revolution 1917–1921* (1987) and *Lenin* (2000).

Routledge studies in the modern history of Asia

Pre-Communist Indochina

R.B. Smith
Edited by Beryl Williams

Routledge
Taylor & Francis Group

LONDON AND NEW YORK

First published 2009
by Routledge
2 Park Square, Milton Park, Abingdon, Oxon, OX14 4RN

Simultaneously published in the USA and Canada
by Routledge
711 Third Avenue, New York, NY 10017

*Routledge is an imprint of the Taylor & Francis Group,
an informa business*

First issued in paperback 2012

© 2009 Editorial selection and matter, Beryl Williams; individual chapters,
R.B. Smith; introduction, A.J. Stockwell

Typeset in Times New Roman by Keyword Group Ltd

British Library Cataloguing in Publication Data
A catalogue record for this book is available from the British Library

Library of Congress Cataloguing in Publication Data

p. cm. – (Routledge studies in the modern history of Asia ; 53)

The foundation of the Indochinese Communist Party, 1929–1930 –
The Japanese period in Indochina and the coup of 9 Mar. 1945 –
The Vietnamese revolution of Aug.-Sept. 1945 : a South-East Asian
perspective – The work of the provisional government of Vietnam,
Aug.–Dec., 1945 – China and Southeast Asia : the revolutionary
perspective, 1951 – The Tet crisis of 1967–68 in perspective – The
international setting of the Cambodia crisis, 1969–1970 – Cambodia in
the context of Sino-Vietnamese relations – Vietnam from the 1890s to
the 1990s : continuity and change in the longer perspective.

Includes bibliographical references and index.
ISBN 978-0-415-46805-3 (hardback : alk. paper)
1. Indochina–History–20th century. I. Williams, Beryl, 1940- II. Title.
DS549.S65 2008
959.704–dc22   2008026415

ISBN 13: 978-0-415-46805-3 (hbk)
ISBN 13: 978-0-415-54306-4(pbk)

In memory of Judy Stowe

Contents

Preface

Professor Ralph Smith died suddenly in London in December 2000, leaving a number of unfinished projects. The most important of these was later edited by one of his former research students and published by Routledge as: R. B. Smith, edited by Chad J. Mitcham, *Changing Visions of East Asia, 1943–93, Transformations and Continuities* (Routledge, 2007). Dr Mitcham also kindly agreed to compile the indexes for the two current volumes. An unfinished work on historiography has also led to the publishing of two articles in the journal *History of European Ideas* (no. 33, 2007 and forthcoming). The idea for a collected volume of Professor Smith's essays on Indochina, including a number of unpublished conference papers, was first put forward in 2003 by the late Judy Stowe. Assisted then by Professor Kevin Ruane of Canterbury Christchurch University, she selected items for a one-volume collection, but problems with finding a publisher and her own declining health led to the project being put to one side. These two volumes are dedicated to her memory. I am most grateful to Peter Sowden of Routledge for enabling me to resurrect the project and for insisting that the material available justified two volumes rather than one. I am also grateful to Professor Anthony Stockwell for agreeing to write the introduction and to the various journals involved for permissions to reprint.

Beryl Williams
University of Sussex

Acknowledgements

The editor and publishers would like to thank the following for granting permission to reproduce material in this work:

Oxford University Press for the reproduction of

'The development of opposition to French rule in Southern Vietnam 1880–1940', in *Past and Present* 54, Feb. 1972.

Cambridge University Press for the reproduction of

'The Vietnamese élite of French Cochinchina 1943', in *Modern Asian Studies* 6, 1972.

'An introduction to Caodaism: 1. origins and early history; 2. beliefs and organization, in *Bulletin of the School of Oriental and African Studies* 33, 1970.

'Bui Quang Chiêu and the Constitutionalist Party in French Cochinchina 1917–30', in *Modern Asian Studies* 3, 1969.

University of Hawaii Press for reproduction of:

'The cycle of Confucianization in Vietnam', in W.F. Vella (ed.) *Aspects of Vietnamese History* (Honolulu: University of Hawaii Press, 1973).

The Siam Society for the reproduction of:

'Thailand and Vietnam: some thoughts towards a comparative historical analysis', *Journal of the Siam Society* 60, 1972.

Cornell University Press for reproduction of:

England and Vietnam in the Fifteenth and Sixteenth Centuries: An Essay in Historical Comparison, in C.D. Cowan and O.W. Wolters (ed.),

Southeast Asian History and Historiography (Ithaca, NY: Cornell University Press, 1976).

Introduction

Ralph Bernard Smith was born, an only child, in 1939 in the Yorkshire town of Bingley. He attended Burnley Grammar School and proceeded to the University of Leeds where he read History. Having graduated with first-class honours in 1959, he proceeded to research and completed his doctorate in 1963. The subject of his thesis was Yorkshire during the Henrician Reformation and it remained for years the single, authoritative work on the Pilgrimage of Grace. A subsequently revised version was published in 1970 as *Land and Politics in the England of Henry VIII: the West Riding of Yorkshire, 1530–46* (Oxford, Clarendon Press). By then, however, Ralph's career had taken an unexpected turn. In 1962, while a post-graduate student at London's Institute of Historical Research, he had successfully applied to the nearby School of Oriental and African Studies for a part-time job that held out the prospect of an established lectureship. He had two principal duties: to teach Early Modern European History to students majoring in non-European subjects, and to learn the history and language of a country on the South East Asian mainland.

Having selected Vietnam almost at random and in virtual ignorance, Ralph immersed himself in a new culture. He stayed with the Vietnamese community in Paris while working at the Bibliothèque Nationale. Then, in January 1966, he flew to Saigon with Beryl Williams (lecturer and later Reader in Modern Russian History at Sussex University) whom he had married in 1964. Bilingual in French, Ralph learned Vietnamese and, notwithstanding the war, Beryl and he travelled extensively in Indo-China and elsewhere in the region (including Hong Kong and Malaya) although they were barred from North Vietnam. Smitten by the world east of Suez and with £5 between them, they returned to the United Kingdom in September. Ralph went to Vietnam at least one more time before 1975 but thereafter his exclusion from the country until the mid-1990s must have been a factor in the expansion of his interests from the national history of Vietnam to the international history of East Asia. He continued to visit other parts of Asia, and regularly presented papers at conferences there as well as in continental Europe and the United States.

A year after his field trip to Vietnam and now established at SOAS, Ralph published in the *Bulletin of the School of Oriental and African Studies* (30 (3), 1967) an introduction to Sino-Vietnamese sources for the Nguyen period.

Then *Viet-Nam and the West* (London, Heinemann, 1968) appeared. Full of insight and wisdom, this book had an immediate and enduring impact. After forty years it is still obligatory reading for undergraduates and a delight for all. The range of his interests is reflected in *Early South East Asia: Essays in Archaeology, History, and Historical Geography* (New York, OUP, 1979), a large volume of papers which he edited in collaboration with the scholar of ancient China, William Watson, and which had originally been presented to the colloquy on early South East Asia at SOAS in September 1973. His own research, however, came to focus on the rise of the Indo-Chinese Communist Party during the period of French colonial rule and on its struggle for supremacy after 1945.

It is as an historian of Vietnam and of the international dimension of the Vietnam War that Ralph Smith became best known. His purpose was to explain the origins and course of the conflict. His approach was to cut through the propaganda surrounding it – as a student his own political views had had an affinity with those of the Bow Group on the Conservative left. Using American and British archives as well as the media and monitored broadcasts from the Communist world, and demonstrating his mastery of great power strategy, he examined decision-making on both sides and situated the conflict in a wider context than either area-study or bipolar US–Vietnamese relations. The first volume of *An International History of the Vietnam War* (London, Macmillan) came out in 1983 and was followed in 1985 and 1990 by the second and third. Between them they covered the years 1955–66. Ralph had planned four volumes to take the story to its dénouement in 1976 and one may surmise why he did not reach the fall of Saigon in 1975 or even the Paris Peace Accords of 1973. Perhaps he felt that the release of Soviet archives in the 1990s had changed the methodological assumptions of his project, but, in any case, his attention was moving to yet broader themes.

One was a grand survey of the changes in East Asia during the half-century between 1943 and 1993. This was an attempt to understand, as he himself put it, 'why the 1990s turned out to be so very, very different from both the world of the early 1940s and also from conflicting aspirations of those who "shaped destiny" in that far off age' and 'why even the aspirations of the early 1960s proved so wide of the mark, when measured against what actually came about by the 1980s and 1990s'. As a historian of the international relations of East Asia, Ralph regarded his subject as a region rather than as a collection of states, and he applied historical methods to its recent history which had so often been left to non-historians. This book would be the summation of his thinking over the previous thirty years and he provided a taste of what was to come in the Fourth Huang Hsing Foundation Distinguished Lecture in Asian Studies which he delivered at St Antony's College Oxford in November 1997. It was published the following year as 'Visions of the Future: East Asia in 1943 and 1993'. A second big theme which came to engross him was historiography but neither his writing on this nor his analysis of a half-century of change in East Asia had been completed before his untimely death on 20 December 2000.

When they examined Ralph's unfinished work, Beryl Williams (legal guardian of his papers) and the late Judith A. Stowe (former head of the Thai and Vietnamese sections of the BBC) were determined that it should be published. In addition to two articles on historiography and the book, *Changing Visions of East Asia, 1943–93* (edited by Chad J. Mitcham), a collection of essays on Indo-China was planned. Some of these had already appeared in diverse journals while others had remained unpublished. Such is their range and originality that the collection has grown to two volumes. The first starts with four essays on the pre-colonial period, including a pair which combines Ralph's interests in both Vietnam and England during the period 1300–1600. These are followed by five articles that discuss aspects of the Vietnamese response to French rule. Here local political developments are considered in relation to indigenous society and culture. The second volume focuses on the rise and victory of communism in Vietnam but also includes pieces on Cambodia and the impact of foreign intervention. The editors have adapted a discussion of the Tet Offensive, 'The Vietnam War from Both Sides: the Crisis of 1967–68', from a much longer paper which was delivered in Washington in March 1998. Meticulous respect for the evidence, fastidious care for chronology, together with bold handling of big themes are hallmarks of Ralph Smith's scholarship. So, too, is the clarity with which he interrogates the sources and develops his arguments.

As Lecturer, later Reader in the History of South East Asia and finally Professor of the International History of East Asia, Ralph Smith was an inspiring and caring teacher. For years his Special Subject on the Vietnam War, which he periodically revised in the light of new research, was one of the most popular in the undergraduate programme of the federal University of London. It was to his students that he dedicated his *International History*. Under his supervision graduate students from all over the world produced highly original doctoral dissertations, went on to distinguished careers and will for ever recall him with admiration and affection. Living within a few minutes' walk of the School of Oriental and African Studies, Ralph was unstinting with his hospitality and the time he bestowed on others. His high expectations and the warmth of his generosity were particularly in evidence at the research seminar on the Recent History of South East Asia which he convened during the 1980s and 1990s. This gathering was remarkable not only for the intellectual demands it made of its members but also for the sense of common endeavour and companionship that it fostered. In commemorating the life and work of Ralph Smith, this collection will ensure that his scholarship reaches a new audience, particularly among current students of Asia.

Anthony Stockwell
(Emeritus Professor of Modern History,
Royal Holloway, University of London)

1 Contrasting political, social and intellectual perspectives

A comparison of Vietnam and England in the fourteenth century

Source: Paper for Hamburg Symposium on Religious Diffusion and Cultural Exchange in South East Asia, 7–9 September 1998; corrected version March 1999.

I

The subject of historical difference between 'Asia' and 'Europe' has been of scholarly concern since at least the late 18th century, when J.G. von Herder posed the question: how and why did Europe emerge as the focal point of human history? The theme was important for many of the major philosopher–historian–sociologists of the period 1820–1940, and any serious historiographical treatment would need to take into account the works of Hegel and Comte, Marx and Weber – to mention only a few of the 'giants'. Their dominant concern was with European 'progress', which contrasted sharply with the apparently unchanging quality of Asian societies in the centuries since the emergence of classical Greek and Roman 'civilisation'. During the same period, however, Europe produced its own 'oriental' scholarship which, although assuming the same philosophical framework, also developed a high level of scholarly respect for the classical languages and texts of one or another of the Asian 'traditions'. Max Weber's comparative studies, especially, depended on that growing body of specialised research.

The influence of Weber's sociological approach remained strong in the 1950s and 1960s, especially in the United States. In the political aftermath of the European retreat from Asia and the rise of American hegemony, many Western social scientists and historians defined the 'task' of Asian 'modern-ization' in essentially socio-cultural terms. The 'quest for modernity' was seen as a product of the 'impact of the West' on Asian societies, during the 'age of imperialism' from 1800 to 1940.[1] Current and future problems of development were approached by way of essentially Western (and behaviourist) conceptual norms, centering above all on that of the nation-state and its theoretical sovereignty.

During the same period, Marxist theoreticians grappled with the issue of the 'so-called Asiatic mode of production', in terms which had grown out of a debate of the 1930s, when Stalin had insisted on eliminating Marx's own formulation of that concept and on the universality of 'feudalism' as a stage of Asian history. In 1957 Karl Wittfogel sought to rehabilitate Marx's concept, in terms which would also satisfy Weberian social scientists, by launching his controversial *Oriental Despotism*.

Much of the conceptual framework of Weberian sociology was incorporated into American social (especially political) science by the mid-20th century, and was also adopted by many historians. The trend was especially marked in the case of Asian studies which – in the United States more than in Europe – were avowedly inter-disciplinary in their focus on 'areas' defined according to the necessity of acquiring language expertise. It became most prevalent of all in the field of South-East Asian studies, whose financial viability depended on a small number of academic centres embracing expertise in several different countries of that region. The adoption of a common conceptual framework facilitated comparative discussion in seminars made up of specialists working on a range of different countries and languages.

Since the 1960s a somewhat different approach to 'pre-modern' Asia has developed, in an academic context shaped by Fernand Braudel's work on the expansion of long distance trade by Western capitalist enterprises; and by a debate on the European 'general crisis' of the 17th century, initiated by Eric Hobsbawm and H.R. Trevor Roper in the journal *Past and Present*. In relation to the social and economic development of Asia, the growing output of specialist research during the 1970s and 1980s contributed to a clearer understanding of the global significance of these themes. Long-distance trade was seen as having steadily transformed Asian society, at least in maritime regions, through a somewhat less one-sided process of interaction than earlier stereotypes had allowed. 'Traditional' Asian societies began to appear much less 'static' than had once been supposed, and much more lively in their response to external intrusions between the 16th and 18th centuries. In South-East Asia, Anthony Reid and others began to explore the repercussions of a seventeenth century 'crisis' whose scope and quality now appeared to be truly global, not just European. Nevertheless, the fact remained that it was Europeans who had expanded their operations into Asia – as traders and as missionaries – not the expanding economic activity of Asians which had taken them to Europe. As far as comparative history was concerned, the underlying question was still one of explaining European 'exceptionalism'.

It is not my intention in this paper to become deeply involved in these larger controversies. I am, however, tempted to take as a starting point some reflections on one important recent contribution to the continuing debate: namely Victor Lieberman's attempt to 'transcend East–West dichotomies' by developing a comparative analysis of societies in various parts of the 'rimland' of 'Eurasia' during the centuries from *c*.1450 to *c*.1830. It has direct relevance to my present theme since he gives special prominence to three countries of mainland South-East Asia (Burma, Siam and Vietnam), which he proceeds to compare with three more widely scattered 'rimland' countries: France, Russia and Japan. His main purpose is to demonstrate that – when seen 'from inside' rather than primarily in terms of their external contacts – all six of these societies exhibit a common trend towards greater political, social and cultural 'integration' during the period in question.[2]

I should say immediately that on one level I am entirely in sympathy with Lieberman's conclusion that these three South-East Asian countries (Burma, Siam and Vietnam) had already taken on what might be called their 'modern' political and social structure well before they experienced the 'impact of the West' in the first half of the 19th century. I am less convinced of the appropriateness of extending the (originally European) label of an 'early modern' to the history of Asian societies. But there is every reason to identify a period in that history during which significant political and cultural 'integration' took place, starting in the second half of the 16th century (possibly earlier) and ending by around 1800. I would go further and suggest that the developments of 1800–1940 can be seen as a postlude to that longer evolution: a period in which the region was 'internationalised' without being structurally transformed. In other words, I would argue that the transformation of the region which occurred in the period 1600–1800 was even more fundamental than that brought about by the 'impact of the West' in the colonial era.[3]

I do, however, wish to take issue with Professor Lieberman's methodological approach to his theme, and to the larger problem of comparative history in relation to Europe and Asia. Two possible criticisms seem to me worthy of closer attention.

First: It is impossible to attempt a comparative study of such widely distant and culturally different societies, each governed by its own language, without adopting a highly conceptualised approach: one which, for English-speaking scholars, is ultimately rooted in the 'Anglo-Saxon' political and philosophical tradition, and that of its 'classical' antecedents. Discourse originating in very different Asian languages is thus reduced to a common conceptual framework in order to allow the formulation of more general questions. But this carries with it the danger that some aspects of diversity will be neglected, while those common features most readily drawn into the conceptualised discourse receive disproportionate attention. When this approach is applied to comparisons between pre-19th century South-East Asia and other areas of 'Eurasia', the dangers become especially great.

On the one hand, considerably less research has been undertaken on the history of countries like Vietnam, Siam and Burma during Lieberman's period, than in the case of European societies or even Japan. Worse still, when we take into account of the actual volume of source materials available for the study of South-East Asian countries during the centuries before 1800 – especially the 'indigenous' sources – we find that European countries are vastly better off. Many types of detailed research that have been successfully attempted for European countries are inherently impossible for Burma, Siam or Vietnam in this period. The required sources, if they ever existed at all, simply have not survived. As a result, concepts originally formulated in relation to better-researched societies cannot always be effectively tested for their genuine applicability to less fully researched areas. The comparative historian may too easily fall into the 'trap' of allowing conceptualised generalisation – which ought in principle to be *based* on detailed research – to become instead a substitute for such research. In these circumstances, conceptual similarities and differences are liable to take shape 'in the eye of the beholder'.

Second: Lieberman's approach involves more than 'synchronic' comparisons between two or more societies as they existed at one particular moment in history. Influenced by the fashionable preference for studying the *longue duree* rather than events in a shorter time span, he seeks to compare European and Asian societies in terms of a dynamic process of change which he sees taking place over several centuries. He is thus measuring European and Asian societies against one another in terms of a 'shared' pattern of long-term political and cultural evolution. Such an exercise can begin by identifying an essentially European sequence of change, and then seek to impose it on the countries of mainland South-East Asia. Alternatively it can begin by identifying a number of apparent changes in the countries of the latter region, and then concentrate on highlighting those themes – at the expense of others – when looking at France or Russia. In either direction, the approach is liable to exclude from consideration those features which do not fit into the conceptual 'paradigm' and to produce a very superficial analysis of actual political, cultural and social change.

In relation to economic change during these centuries, Lieberman finds considerable difficulty in adducing hard information to sustain vague assertions about the pace and implications of 'economic growth' in his South-East Asian countries. He notes the increasing importance of monetary transactions as opposed to payments in kind, and also touches on modes of taxation from the point of view of the peasant; but these trends cannot be represented in statistical terms, even for particular localities. Nor does he get to grips with the problem of commercial capitalism – whether European or Asian – and the related question of government finance. Marxist critics would also emphasise his failure to explore the possible relevance of the issue of 'modes of production' to his general thesis. Clearly before we can attempt serious generalisations about long-term economic and social change it is necessary to attempt a great deal more research on material conditions and administrative regulations in particular localities at more precisely defined periods.

In the spirit of these criticisms, I would argue the need for a more tightly controlled approach to comparative history in the present state of studies: one limited in the first instance to bilateral exercises focusing on comparisons between only two countries, during relatively short time spans. The present paper will therefore seek to explore similarities and differences between the kingdoms of England and of Dai-Viet during the fourteenth century, with special reference to three sub-periods: the decades from 1320 to 1350; the crises of 1368–77; and the period 1385–1400. In a previous paper I have attempted a comparison of this kind with reference to the 15th and 16th centuries.[4] There are two reasons for extending that comparison to the 14th century. One is that it will take us back to a period before significant European commercial intrusion became a factor for change in South-East Asia. Another is that a preliminary study of the global perspective of the 14th century has convinced me of the wider significance of changes in Europe and in China at that time. It is especially interesting to compare two countries which were, relatively speaking, on the political and cultural periphery of those two larger regions.

II

In five respects England and Dai-Viet may be said to have been sufficiently similar in the 14th century to allow us to construct a framework of comparison. In the first place they are comparable in scale. The two countries were remarkably similar in size, and probably also in total population. The more precise measurements that are possible in the 20th century indicate that the surface area of what eventually became Vietnam, following its unification for the first time in 1802, is rather larger than that of the whole of the United Kingdom and the Republic of Ireland (the 'British Isles' in a geographical sense): around 332,000 sq. km. as compared with 300,000 sq. km. However, in the 14th century the kingdom of Dai-Viet was limited to the northern half of present-day Vietnam: essentially the area north of the Hai-Van pass. Further south lay the territory of the Cham kingdom. The kingdom of England had conquered the principality of Wales under Edward I (reg.1272–1307), although it was not administratively annexed until 1536; and only some areas of Ireland were under English dominion. Scotland was a completely separate country. Nevertheless, as the following figures show, Dai-Viet (slightly larger than the North Vietnam of 1955) was comparable in extent with England and Wales:

North Vietnam (1955–75): 158, 750 square kilometers
England and Wales: 150, 275 square kilometres

Comparisons of population are more difficult for a period as early as the 14th century – even in the case of England, where we can rely on surviving tax records of the period. The standard scholarly history of the period can do no more than report specialist estimates of the English population at the beginning of the 14th century, varying between 2.5 and 4 millions.[5] However, it is fairly certain that a substantial decline occurred in mid-century, as a result of the plague epidemic known as the 'black death'. (Its precise quantification is impossible and suggestions that as much as a third of the population died are probably an exaggeration.) In the case of Vietnam, even that kind of rough estimation is impossible in the Tran period. But Lieberman, citing research by Dr Li Tana, is able to give an estimate of 4.7 millions for the Vietnam of around 1600.[6] All that can be said with any confidence is that we are dealing with two countries whose population during our period was of roughly the same order.

A second basic similarity concerns the nature and level of material production. Both kingdoms were essentially agrarian societies, with a limited amount of small-scale industrial development – probably rather greater in England than in Dai-Viet. England, although it already had significant craft industries in such spheres as textiles, leather goods and cutlery, was still a long way from the 'industrial revolution' which would sharply differentiate its economy from those of South-East Asia by the end of the 18th century. The contrasts in this sphere relate mainly to the differences between an agriculture based on wheat, barley and oats (with a considerable emphasis on livestock) and one based on the cultivation of wet rice. Water control was a more important factor in Dai-Viet than in England, although its irrigation works and dikes did not need to be on the vast scale required by the larger rivers of China.

Thirdly, the two countries were both monarchies in the sense that an enthroned ruler (as king or as vua) stood at the focal point of a ruling elite, which recognised the royal court as the centre of government and power. Also, kingship was hereditary, or dynastic. In Dai-Viet the throne was occupied by the Tran dynasty from 1225 to 1400. In England it belonged to the house of Anjou, established by Henry II in 1154, which in 1399 became the house of Lancaster. (Chronicles of the 16th century refer to the whole period from 1154 to 1485 as the rule of the Plantagenets, but that surname was not adopted till around 1450.) In both countries membership of the ruling clan or family conferred aristocratic status on a number of individuals, who were thereby entitled to substantial resources in land and agrarian labour and had varying degrees of influence at court. The royal capital was connected with lower levels of administration by a hierarchy of non-royal officials, some of whom also controlled private resources of land and labour. In both cases, too, surviving historical works in the form of chronicles allow us to reconstruct an outline of court politics and intrigue, succession disputes, rebellions and external wars. As we shall see, these similarities were accompanied by significant differences of political and administrative structure and also of intellectual justification. But there were some striking resemblances – even including the seizure of power by an 'overmighty subject', and the foundation of a new house or dynasty, at almost precisely the same time in both countries in 1399–1400.

A fourth similarity was the fact that during the 14th century both countries were from time to time at war with their neighbours. In some respects the relationship between Dai-Viet and Champa was not unlike that between England and Scotland. England had attempted to dominate Scotland during the reign of Edward I. But his successor lost a major battle to the Scots at Bannockburn in 1314, allowing the northern kingdom to remain independent – although not free from English-inspired intrigues – during the following decades. Further fighting between them occurred in 1346 when the Scots tried to take advantage of England's involvement in a war with France but were defeated in battle at Neville's Cross. For its part, Dai-Viet appeared to be gaining the upper hand in its relations with Champa at the beginning of the century, when a marriage alliance between the two royal families included the transfer to Vietnamese control (in 1306) of two Cham provinces just north of the Hai-Van pass. But Cham reluctance to accept a dependent status in its relations with Dai-Viet led to new wars between them in 1318 and 1323, and again in 1352. Much more seriously, the balance of power between them was transformed by a major regional crisis from 1369–70: as a result the Cham king, Che Bong Nga, was strong enough to undertake a series of attacks on the Vietnamese capital at Thang Long between 1371 and 1383, and to defeat several campaigns sent against him during those years. In 1377 a Vietnamese king advanced as far as the Cham capital of Vijaya, only to fall into a trap and to be killed in battle. It is possible that the Chams at this period benefitted from having the approval of the

Chinese Ming emperor, whose disapproval of affairs in Dai-Viet was evident in the 1370s. However, a subsequent attempt by Che Bong Nga to attack Thang Long, in 1389–90, ended in his death. Thereafter the Chams ceased to present a threat to Dai-Viet, although Vijaya did not finally fall to the Vietnamese until 1470.[7]

A final similarity, although one which again involved important contrasts, was the geographical position of both Dai-Viet and England on the political and cultural periphery of a much larger – and collectively more powerful – region. Both countries had experienced several centuries under the control of those larger systems: Dai-Viet as a Chinese province under the Han and Tang dynasties, from the 1st to the 9th centuries; England, or rather Britain, under the rule of imperial Rome from the 1st to the early 5th centuries. Even in the 14th century, Dai-Viet cannot be understood without reference to China, ruled in this period by the Yuan and later by the Ming dynasty. England, too, must always be seen in relation to Europe, and to a pattern of temporal and spiritual authority whose roots lay in the Roman Empire.

The main contrast in this regard was that, following the collapse of the Tang dynasty around 900, China had been reunified under the Sung, Yuan and Ming dynasties. Thus Dai-Viet had had to resist Chinese attempts at re-conquest, notably in the 1070s and the 1280s, and continued to send periodic 'tribute' missions to the imperial court. Western Europe, on the other hand, had not been reunified after the fall of Rome to 'barbarian' invaders in 410. The efforts of the Carolingian 'dynasty' in the 8th–9th centuries, although they had significant consequences for the cultural unity of Europe, ended in political division. In the 14th century a 'Holy Roman Empire' survived in name, drawing together the leading princes of Germany and Bohemia, under a constitution defined by the 'Golden Bull' of 1356. For the rest, Europe was a region of monarchies whose rulers were gradually developing a sense of their own sovereignty; but none of which was powerful enough to dominate the whole region.

All that remained of the Roman tradition of unity was a widespread acceptance of the principles of Roman law in temporal matters, and an acknowledgement of the spiritual authority of the Papacy. But even the latter institution was losing the power it had claimed during the 12th and 13th centuries. From 1307 to 1378 the Pope was obliged by the king of France to live in Avignon rather than Rome; and the attempt to restore the authority of Rome in the latter year led to an actual schism, with two rival papacies continuing until 1417.

In these circumstances England was no longer faced with the challenge of 're-conquest' by a new Roman Empire. Spiritually its bishops participated in the Church of Western Europe, whose authority was challenged only in matters of papal taxation. Temporally, there was a relative equality between the English monarchy and those in other parts of Europe. A special relationship existed between the thrones of France and England, within a continuum of feudal interdependences which had been shaped by the Norman Conquest of 1066 and its aftermath. The house of Anjou thus had its own extensive possessions in a France not yet fully under the control of the Capetians. Intermarriage between the ruling families was also normal. Out of that situation grew Edward III's claim to the

French throne in 1337, followed by a long series of English military campaigns in France between 1340 and 1389. The initial successes of Edward III and his son (the 'Black Prince') at the battles of Crécy (1346) and Poitiers (1356) could not be sustained, however. By the 1380s most of the earlier territorial gains had been lost, and Richard II made peace in 1389.

This contrast of perspectives is of fundamental importance in exploring both political and intellectual differences between the Confucian world and the European world, at this and at later periods. The pattern of diplomacy which emerged under the Ming dynasty was based on an essential inequality between China and its neighbours, reflected in the practice of sending to China what Western scholarship finds it convenient to call 'tribute missions'. In 14th century Europe, by contrast, there was diplomatic equality between sovereign monarchies in the temporal sphere – even though it was transcended in the spiritual or ecclesiastical sphere by the continuance of papal authority.

III

Before moving on to consider a number of even more striking contrasts between England and Dai-Viet, we may pause at this point to remark upon one other aspect of similarity which, when pursued further, yet again reveals significant differences between the two intellectual traditions. In both countries the 14th century was a period when scholars were seeking to define, if not to assert, something like a 'national' identity *vis-à-vis* neighbouring kingdoms. They did so through the process of writing, or re-writing, historical and literary texts.

English historical writing had begun with the celebrated work of the Benedictine monk Bede, whose Ecclesiastical History of the English People was completed in 731. The Benedictine order had sustained a tradition of writing chronicles, producing works on English and Norman history between the mid-11th and 13th centuries. An important figure who continued that tradition in the late 14th century was Thomas Walsingham, whose writings became a major source for English political history in our period. Many chronicles whose main concern was with recording recent events, however, tended to preface their story with a 'universal' history going back to the Creation. In doing so, they often sought to identify the origins of the English, or British, people. But in that respect, competing traditions had begun to emerge.

Bede had begun his history with the Roman conquest of Britain and had gone on to recount the difficulties of the Britons after the Roman legions had left their island. He then introduced the Anglo-Saxon conquest, supposedly initiated by 'Hengist and Horsa'; but the central theme in his early chapters was the arrival of the Christian faith. However, a much more dramatic account of the origins of the British people, and of their valour in fighting both Romans and Anglo-Saxons, was given – one can probably say for the most part invented – by another Benedictine monk a few centuries later. Geoffrey of Monmouth's *History of the British Kings*, completed around the middle of the 12th century, attributed the foundation of the kingdom to Brutus: a great-grandson of Aeneas, who had participated in the siege of Troy and had arrived in Britain after his own long odyssey – several centuries before the coming of the Romans. Geoffrey's account follows the line of British kings from then until after the departure of the Romans, when the greatest hero of all emerged in the person of Arthur. Later historians would consign all of this to the status of 'legend' but it became increasingly popular during the following two centuries and more. It was taken over by an Anglo-French chronicle of the mid-14th century, appropriately known as the *Brut* chronicle, whose popularity is reflected in the known existence of as many as 160 manuscript copies written in either Latin, French or English.

Among those interested in the Arthurian legend in the mid-14th century was Edward III himself. In 1344 he held a tournament at Windsor, after which he is said to have taken an oath to create for his knights a 'round table' comparable with that of King Arthur's day. That appears to have been the origin of the Order of the Garter, inaugurated in 1348 after his victory at Crécy and the seizure of Calais. The king had every reason to use historical accounts for his own propaganda purpose of creating a chivalric basis for loyalty to England.[8] Perhaps in the same spirit, four years later he summoned to Westminster the most famous chronicler of the day: Ranulf Higden, another Benedictine living at the abbey of Chester, whose *Polychronicon* (or Universal History) had originally been compiled around 1327 and had been revised several times since. The outcome of Higden's audience with Edward III may, however, have been disappointing to both sides: for one thing, Higden seems to have been less than wholeheartedly convinced of the truth of the Arthurian legend. More generally, the contrast between the *Polychronicon* and the *Brut* suggests an important contrast, or at least ambiguity, in the intellectual parameters of the world of 14th century English 'literati'.[9]

Higden gave considerable space to an account of British and English history from the earliest times down to the 13th century, dutifully following Geoffrey of Monmouth for the exploits of the early Britons and showing considerable feeling for surviving British monuments, customs and institutions. But he also sought to place England into a wider historical and geographical perspective: one that embraced Asia and Africa as well as Europe. He had a smattering of knowledge of ancient Greece, and rather more of Alexander the Great; but his main interest was in the history of Rome. Thus he sought to illuminate the history and virtues of England, while entertaining no illusions about its place in the universe. His book also included a map on which the main areas represented were Asia (the upper half of the whole), Africa and Europe. ('Asia', however, did not extend to China at this period.) Britain was highlighted, in a different colour from the rest, but was placed at the lower edge in full recognition of its peripheral status.[10]

When we turn to Vietnam it is impossible to match either the quantity of historical scholarship in 14th century England or the authenticity of its surviving manuscript texts. This period nevertheless marked an important stage in the evolution of Vietnamese Confucian historiography, in that it saw the emergence of several new versions of the origins of the Vietnamese people. The *Viet Dien U Linh* was a collection of stories about the country and its past, relating to both kings and spirits, compiled around 1329 by a scholar named Ly Te Xuyen. It included the account of a 'hero king' (Hung Vuong) and a conflict between the spirits of the mountains and the waters arising from rivalry for the hand of his daughter. About the same time (perhaps in 1333) a Vietnamese living in exile in China wrote a formal history of his own country under the title *An Nam Chi Luoc*, which opened with the sending of a mission from 'Viet Thuong' to China in a year equivalent to 1115 BC. These two compositions already suggest a contrast between competing views of the early antecedents of Dai-Viet: one focusing on a purely Vietnamese – albeit legendary – perspective; the other emphasising from the outset its relationship with China.[11]

A slightly later work – the *Viet Su Luoc*, believed to have been compiled sometime between the 1340s and the 1370s – gives a somewhat fuller account of early Vietnamese history, tracing its origins back to the kingdom of Giao-Chi which lay completely outside the Chinese sphere and was much older than Viet-Thuong. The same work also introduced, for the first time, the ancient kingdom of Van Lang: founded by Hung Vuong (the 'hero king') and ruled by eighteen generations of his descendants before being conquered by another non-Chinese king in the 3rd century BC. Hung Vuong and Van Lang were also mentioned in a poem composed in the 1360s by a Tran dynasty official Pham Su Manh, which is believed by Professor Wolters to be the earliest datable reference to the hero and his kingdom. All of this was deemed to have occurred long before the foundation of the first 'Vietnamese' dynasty to be recognised by Chinese sources: that established by Trieu Da in 207 BC. The Han conquest of Giao-Chi, which initiated almost nine centuries of Chinese control, came later still.

Again, however, it is necessary to compare formal histories with a collection of popular legends. The *Linh Nam Chich Quai* of Tran The Phap, assigned by later bibliographers to the last third of the 14th century, provided a genealogy for the hero king (Hung Vuong) which made him a descendant of Kinh Duong Vuong: first ruler of the Viet people, and younger son of the Chinese sage ruler Shen Nong. Since the latter's elder son became the first ruler of China, the story established a mythological basis for near-equality between China and Vietnam. The question of relations with China was fundamental both to the current politics of Dai Viet and also to the writing of Vietnamese history in the second half of the 14th century. This became especially important after 1368, when the first Ming emperor sought to redefine the new dynasty's relations with neighbouring states as far away as Cambodia, Siam and Java – and expressed disapproval of the conduct of affairs in Dai-Viet after 1370.

Vietnamese insistence on their own separateness from China became even stronger in Dai-Viet during the 15th century, following the Ming conquest and occupation of 1407–27. One of the most famous of all among Vietnam's literary texts is the *Binh Ngo Dai Cao*, composed by the scholar Nguyen Trai and issued by the first emperor of the new Le dynasty in 1428. Proclaiming the defeat of the invaders (identified by the Chinese designation Wu: in Vietnamese, Ngo) he asserts the parallel validity of traditions and customs of 'the North' (China) and of 'the South' (Dai-Viet); the distinctiveness of their mountains and rivers; and the authenticity of their respective dynasties over many centuries.[12] The importance of this declaration should perhaps be related to the equally determined efforts of the Ming dynasty to absorb the spirits of the mountains and rivers of Dai-Viet into China's own system, making them merely an extension of the Chinese 'five sacred mountains and four sacred rivers'. In 1370 Ming Hongwu had sent a mission to Thang Long for that express purpose; he took back with him copies of classical Vietnamese texts.[13] Despite the independence asserted by Nguyen Trai's text, it was necessary to define the status of Dai-Viet in terms that were intelligible to the Chinese tradition.

These examples from both Vietnamese and English historical writing seem to reflect a parallel desire to assert the distinctive qualities, if not the 'national' identity, of each country. This apparently common trend, moreover, would fit in well with Lieberman's thesis regarding longer-term evolution. However, it is important also to recognise differences between the two cases. In the English chronicles (especially the *Polychronicon*) two perspectives are allowed to exist side by side: that of Britain (or England) and that of the World. There is a realistic appreciation of the interrelationship between them, and no pretence that England can be even the poetic equal of Rome or of Europe. Higden, for all the limitations of his actual knowledge, is genuinely seeking a better understanding of the large perspective. He is aware, too, that even before Rome there were Greeks and Persians; and that God first revealed His law to the Hebrews. Even the *Brut* chronicle is aware that greater status will be conferred on the British if it can be shown that their first king was a Greek who fought at Troy.

Dai-Viet, on the other hand, asserted not only its own distinctive identity but also a claim to equality between 'North' and 'South', in poetic terms that were essentially symbolic. That was the level of thought on which the difference really mattered. Dai-Viet could never have succeeded in asserting an actual geographical or material equality with China, of the kind that could be placed on a map drawn to any accuracy of scale. But we should be careful not to draw from this a conclusion that on other levels the Vietnamese were any less practical or pragmatic than English scholar–officials of the same period. What is different is that the Vietnamese 'national' perspective was not being defined in precise geographical terms. Poetry could express the profound ambiguity of the Vietnamese attitude to China, without seeking to establish a framework of reference within which Vietnam's 'place in the world' needed to be precisely and realistically defined.

A related feature of this period, again to be found in both countries, was the increasing use of the vernacular in literary texts – still, of course, alongside the continued use of the classical languages of Latin in England and Chinese in Dai-Viet. The emergence of 'middle English' poetry in the latter half of the 14th century is well known: William Langland's *Vision of Piers the Plowman* was probably first written around 1362 and revised fifteen years later; while Geoffrey Chaucer's *Canterbury Tales* was begun in 1373, to be followed by his numerous other poems in the 1380s. Higden's *Polychronicon* was translated into English by

John of Trevisa in 1387. There appears to have been a growing demand for such writings among an expanding literate 'public' more familiar with English than with Latin: a development which probably also explains a royal decision in 1362 to the effect that courts of law should conduct their business in English rather than in Latin.

Whether the same kind of 'public' was emerging in Dai-Viet is less certain. But it was during this same period that scholars began to write poetry in Vietnamese using the *nom* script: an elaboration of the Chinese method of composing new characters by inventing combinations of radical and phonetic elements. One of the strongest exponents of *nom* literature was the powerful official of the late 14th century, Le Quy Ly. In 1395 he ordered a translation into Vietnamese characters of a chapter of the 'Classic of History' praising the role of the Duke of Zhou as minister and teacher of a young ruler. The following year he himself composed a poem in *nom* to explain the meaning of the 'Classic of Poetry'.[14]

The growth of vernacular literature was one of the trends picked out by Lieberman, in relation to his longer period from the mid-15th to the early 19th centuries. In England and Vietnam, and equally in France and Italy, it was already under way by the mid-14th century. It did not in itself, however, guarantee – or reflect – any specific changes in the sphere of government and administration.

IV

From the point of view of present-day historians researching on the 14th century, one of the most striking differences between Dai-Viet and England relates to the quantity and nature of the available source materials. For both countries a basic narrative of events can be constructed from chronicles, compiled not too long afterwards, and therefore recounting relatively recent history. Even there, however, we find a much greater number of such sources relating to England than to Dai-Viet. In England it is often only by means of detailed comparative study of different versions of the same event, written independently, that we can arrive at a (probably) reliable account of 'what actually happened'. For Dai-Viet the range of formal histories is much narrower, and the opportunity for comparative analysis much smaller. We are dependent to a very large extent on the official history compiled by Confucian scholars of the Le dynasty in the 15th century: the *Dai-Viet Su-ky Toan-tho*. The Buddhist sects – by contrast with the Christian monkhood in England – contributed little to the Vietnamese record of 'lay' events during this period.

A very much more significant contrast arises with regard to the availability of authentic documents actually written during the 14th century: in England, the quantity of such archival materials is vast; in Vietnam they no longer survive at all for any period before 1800. Part of the explanation may be climatic: in tropical Vietnam only inscriptions carved on stone would have any chance of survival, whereas in temperate Europe parchment texts have survived for centuries. An equally important factor, however, was that the

Angevin monarchy – even by European standards – developed a remarkably effective and archive-conscious bureaucracy. As a result the British Public Record Office still has long series of rolls and patents originating in the 'courts' of Parliament, of the Exchequer, of Chancery, etc.; and surviving records of various forms of tax assessment and payment are remarkably complete. In addition a substantial number of ecclesiastical and baronial archives exist, including records of manorial and estate administration at the grass-roots level. In the case of Dai-Viet, all we have are chronicle references to the compilation of registers of the population and of land holdings, all the way down to the village level; and also the collection of administrative decrees from earlier dynasties compiled by the early 19th century scholar Phan Huy Chu. But we have none of the actual documents generated by such administrative activities.

Three examples will illustrate both the kind of sources available and therefore the kind of research that can be undertaken in relation to 14th century England. The first concerns the sphere of government finances. The military campaigns of Edward III in France between 1337 and 1360 required both manpower and material resources, which had to be paid for by raising royal revenues: principally through taxation. By this time a fairly well-developed system of public finance had begun to emerge, and its operations under both Edward I and Edward III can be analysed in great detail. But the system involved more than simply imposing and collecting taxes on trade (especially in wool) and on the valuables of the wealthier households in each town or village. It was already an established feature of English government that the king could raise such taxes only after consultation with a Parliament that included commoners as well as feudal magnates; and on the basis of respect for individual rights affirmed in the *Magna Carta* first issued by King John in 1215, and confirmed several times subsequently. In addition to taxation, royal revenues included income from Crown estates and also moneys raised – notably in the 1340s – by borrowing from foreign bankers. (The Florentine houses of Peruzzi and Bardi were bankrupted by Edward III's inability to repay their loans.) Another aspect of warfare was the opportunity to negotiate ransoms following the capture of important personages: English prisoners in the 1350s included, at different times, the kings of both Scotland and France. Thus the financial history of England in this period has to take into account a whole range of institutions and administrative devices; and the archives make it possible to do so.[15]

A second theme that can be pursued in some depth is the history of the 'peasant revolt' which broke out in south-eastern England in 1381, and which led to several assassinations and a good deal of plundering in the capital. The legal and other records compiled after the revolt, together with various chronicle accounts, allow us to identify its leaders and to reconstruct their motives and grievances in the light of the economic consequences of the plague years of the mid-century; particularly the resulting change in the balance between land and labour, which had led artisans and agricultural workers to demand higher wages and freedom from traditional service obligations. The records also provide clues to the probable emergence of grass roots literacy even at this early period.[16] We might note in passing that

Dai Viet also had peasant unrest in this period, and sometimes organised revolts such as that led by a Buddhist priest in Son-Tay in 1389, which coincided with the last major Cham offensive against the northern Delta. But our knowledge of Vietnamese rebellions is extremely limited and their roots in a changing rural society cannot be traced at all.

Thirdly, studies have been made of the substantial archival evidence concerning relations between the English crown and the merchant community, particularly of London. The city itself, and various other corporate institutions, were by this period seeking to defend (as rights) the privileges that had been granted in earlier centuries by royal charter. An important compilation of London legal records was made by one Andrew Horn, a fishmonger who rose to be chamberlain of the city from 1320 to 1328, and who also wrote a legally oriented history of the city during the reign of Edward II.[17] An array of government, urban and estate records also permits detailed study of the growing foreign trade of London, and of its impact on the agriculture of the surrounding area.[18]

All three of these illustrations take us, sooner or later, into questions about the economic history of 14th century England. There, too, the availability of archival sources has allowed historians to reconstruct a picture of the changing society and commerce of the period, using records of actual transactions as well as numerous statutory regulations. In the agricultural sector, although total population figures still present a problem, there is a good deal of material to indicate the effects of both population expansion down to the early 14th century, and of the contraction which followed the 'Black Death' of 1349. Changing patterns of trade can also be constructed and analysed. The export of wool was especially significant, as were the various royal decisions to limit that trade to one or more centres (known as 'staples') at which tax could be collected. Among imports, the trade in wine from Gascony was important, except that it was severely disrupted during the war between England and France. Small-scale industrial activity was expanding during the second half of the century, especially in certain rural areas: notably the production of woollen cloth (increasingly for export) and the mining of tin, lead, iron and coal.[19]

Attention has been given to the monetary history of the period, in terms both of coinage at the royal mints and of changes in the supply of bullion. The records of the mint suggest a growing shortage of silver bullion from around 1320, leading to an experiment with the debasement of smaller coins (in 1335) and the minting of gold coins in the 1340s. This trend has to be related to an increasingly global network of trade and bullion movements; and at least one scholar has sought to relate the English loss of bullion to factors as distant as the changing pattern of trade in the Eastern Mediterranean.[20] By placing the English economy and its finances into that wider perspective, moreover, we can recognise the peripheral status of London in relation to the much larger commercial centres of Italy and Germany. The emergence of double entry book-keeping in the latter areas gave their business enterprises considerable advantage in the growth of financial and commercial networks, while England was relatively late in adopting comparable accounting methods. The business activities of the city of London thus benefitted from the presence of the Italian banking houses, and of merchants of the Hanseatic League at the Steelyard.

By comparison, the administrative and economic history of Vietnam during this period cannot yet be studied in such detail. We must be careful, however, not to draw unwarranted conclusions from the extreme imbalance in the relative volume of archival records for England and Dai-Viet. It cannot be assumed, merely because no Vietnamese records of this kind have survived, that they never existed; nor that they were necessarily less extensive or less sophisticated than those of 14th century England. Such information as we have, from the chronicles and from Phan Huy Chu, suggests both some measure of economic change during this period, and also some attempt to increase government control over the population.

The mobilisation of economic resources during the war between Dai-Viet and Champa no doubt presented a significant challenge to the Tran system of administration; but we get only small glimpses of the measures which were taken to meet it. In 1378, the year following the second major defeat by the Chams, the Vietnamese official Do Tu Binh made a report on the taxation system which led to a series of reforms designed to increase the tax paid on land and to increase the number of soldiers recruited in the villages.[21] The extent to which such arrangements were based on monetary transactions was probably very much less than in the England of Edward III; disciplined organisation was required, nonetheless. The one clear difference was that in Dai-Viet no assembly of representative notables, comparable with the English Parliament, was required to give its assent: all was decided by the ruler and his top advisers. There are also hints in the chronicle record that the southern provinces of Thanh Hoa and Nghe An (the northern part of present-day Central Vietnam) were becoming economically more important during the second half of the century: orders were issued for a special census in the former area in 1361, and in the latter in 1370. Nor can we rule out the possibility that the Cham wars had an economic dimension, even though the hypothesis cannot be adequately tested. Both provinces were severely ravaged by the warfare of the 1370s and early 1380s.

Starting in 1396, a major overhaul of the system of government was carried through by Le Quy Ly, who was already by then in effective control of the Tran court.[22] He began with a decree regulating court dress, including the colour of the robes to be worn by officials of various ranks; and with another formalising the system of official examinations based on the Chinese classics. He then went on to establish greater centralised control over the administration of the 'inner' and 'outer' provinces, and to determine the records which must be regularly maintained in each province. Next came decrees (in 1397–8) ordering a register of private landholdings and restricting the amount of land that could be held by commoners, even officials, who did not belong to the Tran family. All lands were supposedly registered in the following five years. Also during these years Le Quy Ly decided to build a new capital in his native province of Thanh Hoa, to which he all but forcibly removed the young Tran ruler before bringing about his abdication in 1398. Further tightening of the administrative system and even more rigorous control of the population followed Le Quy Ly's actual seizure of the throne in 1400.

All the reforms of this period, however, were soon to be overtaken by the Ming conquest of Dai-Viet in 1407–8.

Two observations can be based on the limited information available. First, control over land was closely related to control over manpower, although the precise forms of that control cannot be gleaned from the available accounts. While only the Tran princes appear to have had extensive 'private' domains, the economic status of non-royal officials is unknown. There was probably considerable diversity from one locality to another; but there is nothing to suggest the existence of anything like the manorial system found in English villages. Nevertheless, some families were probably better off than others at the local level. Second, the main objective of Le Quy Ly's reforms was to increase government control over both land and labour at the expense of the princes, officials, and other better off commoners. Hence his decree in 1397 that ordinary families could own no more than 10 *mau* of private land; and his attempt to curb the enlargement of princely domains by the reclamation of land from the sea. In 1401 he sought to limit the actual number of retainers and labourers that could belong to individuals (or clans) outside the official administrative structure.

Whether the Tran 'system' can be characterised as 'feudal' or as an example of 'Asiatic despotism' is virtually impossible to answer. The latter designation was outlawed by Stalin in the 1930s, but Hanoi's Marxist historians during the decades after 1954 had to decide whether it was appropriate to regard the pre-14th century Tran system as still belonging to the 'slave-holding' mode of production, while designating the 15th century system that emerged following the Ming occupation (1407–28) as one of 'feudal landownership'. What seems clear is that economic and social changes taking place during the late 14th century were tending towards a more regulated society at the grass roots. Tensions between the court and the wealthier members of the provincial population are evident enough. But there was no opportunity in Dai-Viet for such tensions to become focused on issues of law, involving relations between king and parliament or between the royal courts and civic corporations, of the kind already evident in 14th century England.

The way in which the 'economy' of Dai-Viet worked, as a system of production, distribution and exchange, is even more difficult to reconstruct in any detail. We get only a few small clues with regard to the monetary system, which for most of the 14th century (as in earlier times) was based on the circulation of copper cash. It is highly probable that some of the coinage circulating in Dai-Viet was of Chinese origin; and it is by no means certain that every ruler of the Tran dynasty issued his own coins. There is a chronicle reference to the minting of zinc coins in 1323; and the reported issuing of new coins by the Tran ruler in 1360 may indicate a serious attempt at reform.[23] But since we have no statistical information about the volume of trade or the prices of commodities, it is impossible even to guess whether there was a bullion shortage here as in Europe.

In China itself, paper currency had been in use during the Sung and Yuan periods; there had also been increasing use of silver for larger transactions. But in the years after 1350, as law and order broke down, the last Yuan emperors issued vast quantities of unsecured paper notes and the system virtually collapsed.

Ming Hongwu attempted to restore it by issuing a new paper currency in 1374; and for several decades it proved acceptable.[24] That may have been the inspiration for Le Quy Ly's decree of 1396 introducing *hoi-sao* paper currency and banning private use of copper cash.[25] The measure may also have been a device to encourage (even to force) wealthy families, perhaps merchants, residing in Thang-Long to surrender their monetary assets to the state. But if so, the implication must be that such people had succeeded in amassing savings in that form; and that their wealth would otherwise have remained beyond government control.

Another sphere of activity about which we can do no more than guess is that of Dai-Viet's external trade in a region (the South China Sea) dominated by the commercial activities of China. The attempt of the new Ming dynasty, to force regional trade back into a more highly regulated 'tribute' system, centering on the single Chinese port of Guangzhou, has been remarked upon by Professor Wang Gungwu with reference to its impact on other parts of South-East Asia. He starts from the observation that in the decades before 1368 much of South China's foreign trade had been conducted through the Fujian port of Quanzhou. That was changed, however, by the regulations of 1374, which closed the ports other than Guangzhou; followed by a decree of 1381 insisting that Ming subjects must have passports in order to travel abroad. One result was to oblige Fujianese (Hokkien) business families to deploy their expertise in different directions within China itself, carrying on internal trade or moving into industrial production. Another consequence was that a significant number of them chose to migrate to, or to remain in, the South-East Asian cities where they had previously traded.[26]

Whether this brought more Chinese to Dai-Viet we can only guess; but there was probably room for a growing Chinese commercial presence in Thanh Hoa. One possibility, too, is that some of the 'sojourners' settled in Champa, in the port which later became Hoi-An. Conceivably an expansion of Chinese trade there was a factor both in Che Bong Nga's ability to maintain relatively good relations with the Ming in the 1370s and early 1380s, and in the resources he could deploy in his campaigns against Thang-Long. As in so many respects, speculative questions of this kind can only reinforce awareness of the historian's continuing ignorance about a great deal of Vietnam's social and economic life during this period.

V

At this point we must turn to the other obvious difference between England and Vietnam during this and other periods: that of religion, culture and intellectual activity. We are bound to ask what specific contrasts can be attributed to the fact that England belonged to the world of Roman Christianity, while the intellectual life of Dai-Viet was shaped by the three Chinese religions of Daoism, Buddhism and Confucianism. The question can be approached in at least three ways: by studying doctrines on the basis of religious texts; by looking at religious and educational institutions; and by comparing the intellectual careers of particular individuals.

The first approach lies beyond the scope of the present paper; let us concentrate on the other two.

Institutionally the Church of Rome was headed by the papacy, under which the bishops and dioceses of each area administered a single spiritual authority throughout Christendom. The separation of spiritual and temporal law meant that ecclesiastical courts were separate from royal courts. But the idea of law, and its content, was vital to all aspects of the Christian political and intellectual tradition. By the 14th century many different points of view were being expressed across Europe regarding the proper relationship between the powers of the papacy and those of monarchy: the idea of 'national' sovereignty was already competing with that of a 'universal' *imperium*. However diverse these opinions might become, all accepted a framework of divine law within which human affairs must be conducted.

Beyond the hierarchy of bishops and lower levels of pastoral authority, however, there was room for a wide range of distinct and often competing religious organisations, likewise cutting across the boundaries of temporal power. Particularly important were the religious orders, whose diversity embraced ways of life as different as those of the Benedictine monasteries (whose monks frequently wrote histories) and of the Franciscan friars (who were often prominent in the universities). The 'European' perspective was as important here as in the economic and financial spheres. Among educational institutions, it is relevant in our present context to recognise that the universities of Oxford and Cambridge (especially Oxford) had considerable stature during the 14th century, placing them on a par with the university of Paris if not with that of Bologna.

We can gain a brief insight into the intellectual achievements of 14th century England by looking at three individual scholars. One of the most active English theologians in the first half of the century was Thomas Bradwardine (*c*.1290–1349) who taught at Oxford in the 1320s and 1330s and also visited Paris – as well as the papal court at Avignon – during that period. In addition to being a controversial theologian, he was also one of the leading mathematicians of his day. Later on, in the 1340s, he was chaplain and confessor to Edward III, before becoming (very briefly) Archbishop of Canterbury – only to be struck down by the plague in 1349.[27]

One of Bradwardine's intellectual opponents was the even more celebrated William of Ockham (*c*.1285–?1347) who also studied and taught at Oxford. During the years 1318–22 he wrote his influential *Commentaries on the Sentences* (of Peter Abelard), which distinguished between faith and reason in terms which shaped the possibility of expanding scientific (not just mathematical) knowledge within the framework of Christian belief. He himself went on to produce several works on physics. But he later found himself having to defend his philosophical and theological views before the papal court at Avignon, where he lived from 1324 to 1328. That in turn led to his becoming involved in a dispute between the Franciscan order and Pope John XII, which forced him to flee to the court of Louis of Bavaria at Munich. In his later writings Ockham denounced Papal claims to absolute spiritual and temporal authority as an unwarranted innovation, even a heresy, and argued for the independence of temporal *vis-à-vis* spiritual power. He died sometime after 1347, possibly also of the plague.[28]

A more distinctively 'English' intellectual figure was John Wyclif (*c*.1320–1384), a native of Yorkshire, who likewise studied at Oxford and became a doctor of theology in 1372. During the last ten years of his life, when he was rector of the parish of Lutterworth, his ideas became increasingly controversial. He not only opposed the papacy on a number of 'political' issues – which gained him the patronage of John of Gaunt, Duke of Lancaster – but also began to preach that divine revelation was to be found in the Bible rather than depending solely on the teachings of the Church. He led a project to translate the Bible into English for the first time, which was completed by his followers after his death; and in 1380 he rejected the doctrine of 'transubstantiation', which was one of the theological foundations of priestly authority. He was also highly critical of the great wealth accumulated by the Church as an institutional landowner. The popular association of his ideas with the rebellion of 1381 – in which he himself had no part – made it possible for his enemies to attack him more effectively; with the result that the following year he and his followers were expelled from the university of Oxford.[29]

Once again the disparity between English and Vietnamese source materials hinders the task of comparison and makes the achievements and complexities of Vietnam appear less significant than they must have been. One theme, however, emerges quite clearly: the greater prominence of Buddhist activity in the early part of the century, and of Confucian scholarship by the end. Early Vietnamese Buddhism has been studied by Tran Van Giap, using sources which may have led to some over-emphasis on its Chinese characteristics but which nevertheless were compiled by Vietnamese in Vietnam. One of his principal sources, although it survives only in an edition dated 1715, appears to have been first composed sometime around 1337. It records the succession of teachers associated with three Buddhist 'sects' established in Annam during the Tang period, all of which had survived down to the early part of the 13th century.[30]

The principal Buddhist sect indicated by sources relating to the early 14th century is that known as the *Truc-Lam* ('Bamboo Forest') school, which had close connections with the Tran dynasty. Its first 'patriarch' was the former ruler Tran Nhan-Tong, who had become *thuong-hoang* following his abdication in 1293 and had lived on until 1308. The second and third patriarchs are also known: Phap-Loa who died in 1330, and Huyen-Quang who died in 1334. We know, too, that the ruler Tran Minh-Tong (king 1314–39; *thuong hoang*, 1329–57) was a patron of popular Buddhism. But a small number of poems constitute the only literary legacy of these leading figures.[31]

In the later years of the century Buddhists were sometimes associated with rural unrest and rebellion. Already in the years 1339–42 two surviving inscriptions record the more critical attitude to Buddhism of at least one scholar associated with the royal court, Truong Han Sieu (d. 1354).[32] His attack was directed not at the *thien* (*zen*) doctrines of the *Truc-Lam* school but against adepts of the *Lotus Sutra*, which has frequently been associated with a more politically subversive interpretation of

Buddhism – including the Buddhist revolt against the pro-American government in Saigon in the 1960s. The continuing importance of Buddhism in the 1380s is indicated by a report that in 1384 a Ming envoy to Dai-Viet praised the reputation of Vietnamese monks and requested that twenty of them be allowed to return with him to China.[33]

By that time, however, Confucian learning was becoming much more important in the context of Vietnamese government and scholarship. A leading figure in the middle decades of the century was Chu An (or Chu Van An) who around 1340 was appointed tutor to the future ruler Tran Du-Tong and deputy head of the court academy, the Quoc-Tu-Giam. Chu An appears to have enjoyed the patronage of Tran Minh-Tong (*thuong hoang*, 1329–57), but later he protested against the moral laxity of officials under Du-Tong's rule and retired to teach at his own school in the countryside. He was finally honoured shortly before his death in 1370, when Tran Nghe-Tong came to the throne and began the restoration of a more orderly administration. One index of the growing influence of Confucianism was the prominence given to examinations based on the Chinese classics. Examinations at the highest level were held in 1374 and 1384, and the system was formalised by Le Quy Ly in the 1390s. At this stage, however, the graduates of these examinations did not rise to the highest positions in government and did not acquire the high status that became normal in the later 15th century.

Confucianism itself by this time embraced a wide range of teachings, accumulated over many centuries, which were open to conflicting interpretations. In China during the 14th century there was growing respect for what Western writers usually call 'neo-Confucian' orthodoxy, embodied especially in the writings of the Sung scholar Zhu Xi (1130–1200). The latter was too controversial a figure to attain high office during his lifetime. In 1313, however, an imperial decree ordained that his commentaries on the 'five classics' and the 'four books' of the Confucian canon, together with those of another neo-Confucian Cheng Yi (1033–1107), should henceforth be central texts for the examination syllabus throughout the empire; an endorsement which was confirmed by the Ming dynasty in the 1370s.[34]

The interpretations of the classics by Zhu Xi were not, however, dominant in Vietnam until after the Ming conquest of 1407. During the second half of the 14th century, we find implicit criticism of Zhu Xi, and praise for the Tang scholar Han Yu (768–824). Le Quy Ly, as he became increasingly powerful in the 1380s and 1390s, placed most emphasis on the five classics of the ancient Chinese tradition, rather than on the 'four books' favoured by the neo-Confucians. In the account of the Duke of Zhou, given by the 'Classic of History' (*Shu-jing*), he found a model for his own role as senior guide to a young emperor (and virtual ruler of the country). This would suggest that the intellectual leaders of Dai-Viet were not simply imitating whatever 'Chinese model' was dominant in their own day. Chinese Confucian scholarship, in all its diversity, merely provided the intellectual context in which they could express the ideas and interpretations they deemed most appropriate to Vietnamese circumstances. As in other spheres, we cannot understand Vietnamese intellectual life without reference to China.

The disparity in size and strength between China and Dai-Viet made it unlikely that at any stage the Vietnamese would impose their own ways of thinking on the Chinese; on the contrary, Chinese cultural influence over Dai-Viet would for a time be strengthened by military conquest after 1407. But neither was intellectual activity in Dai-Viet merely an extension of that of China. Nor is there any reason to suppose that the most accomplished Vietnamese scholars were in any way inferior to the Chinese in their grasp of those ideas which they chose to take seriously.

VI

This paper has not been concerned primarily with the kind of historical perspective which generates 'grand narratives', intended to identify and explain structures of long-term change. Its purpose has been to apply the comparative approach in terms of a much shorter time perspective in order to identify contrasts which deserve to be taken into account before we attempt more hypothetical conclusions about the comparability of 'East' and 'West'. Three simple but important conclusions emerge:

(1) The striking difference between the respective quantities of source materials for the history of these two countries during the 14th century, and also between the volume of 'secondary' research so far undertaken, has to be seen against the background of their material comparability in terms of territorial extent, population, and political structure. By bringing to bear the very detailed knowledge we now have of England in this period, the comparison reveals how little we really know about Dai-Viet in the Tran period. That does not, however, justify a rush to substitute conceptual simplification for hard information. Twentieth century ignorance of the workings of Dai-Viet should not tempt us into supposing that its society in that period was either less complicated or less sophisticated than that of 14th century England. Nor should we suppose that existing research on Vietnam has entirely exhausted the range of questions which need to be asked of those source materials which are available. Above all, over-eager conceptualisation does not provide a basis for the premature integration of this simple comparative exercise into the even more ambitious structure of comparisons envisaged by Professor Lieberman.

(2) Nevertheless, one common feature does emerge very clearly: the need in both cases to relate the pattern of institutions, the course of political events, and the expression of ideas, to a wider regional framework: to see England in relation to the whole of Christian Europe, and Dai-Viet in relation to Yuan and Ming China. This is necessary for the study of at least three spheres of activity: war and diplomacy; money and trade; and intellectual thought. The attempt to treat the two 'national' polities as exclusive units of comparison or contrast does not work. (Nor, I would argue, does it work for any other period.) Ultimately the comparative study of Western Europe and Eastern Asia cannot avoid taking the Christian and Confucian 'worlds' as essential

units of analysis. What is also needed, on top of that kind of comparison, is a more comprehensive exploration of global networks of trade and monetary relations, as they operated at any given period in time; and an approach to those networks which makes no initial assumptions about the eventual superiority of 'Western' capitalism.

(3) Reviewing our rather cursory comparison between England and Vietnam in this light, one very important difference does begin to emerge. The Chinese, century after century, continued to recreate throughout their country a single, integrated system of institutions and orthodoxies; and to reduce their smaller neighbours to the status of cultural 'tributaries'. They were therefore able to equate their view of universality with the territorial extent of China's own empire – at least until the 18th century. The Vietnamese, for their part, could do no more than take over that way of thinking and apply it – symbolically – to their own much smaller realm. The Europeans, on the other hand, were never able to establish such a simple equation between intellectual and territorial perspectives. Even the Romans were conscious of having inherited part of their civilisation from the Greeks, and of having absorbed into their empire areas once occupied by even older (and even more distinctive) cultural and institutional traditions: Carthage, Egypt, Anatolia, Syria, Mesopotamia, even Persia. By the 14th century, even an Englishman with knowledge as rudimentary as that of Ranulf Higden was vaguely aware of the vastness of the Asian and African background to European culture, as well as of the Roman and European antecedents of the England of his own day.

After the collapse of the Roman empire, this sense of universal diversity was all the greater for the fact that Europe became divided along two 'fault-lines' simultaneously: authority was divided between the spiritual power of the popes and the temporal power of the kings; and temporal power was divided among increasingly sovereign monarchies. Already in the 14th century the centres of institutional life – and the possible refuges for intellectual dissidence – were sufficiently diverse to encourage individuality of thought and ambition, of a kind that was impossible in Ming China. In this context, the European conception of law was able to combine a sense of universality in principle with great diversity of theory and practice. It was possible, too, for sharp disagreements to be pursued, in relation both to jurisprudence and to the nature of physical world. In the economic sphere European urban communities were able to combine acceptance of their legal independence with the opportunity to accumulate capital. All these features were already evident, two centuries before the so-called beginnings of 'modernity' in the 16th and 17th centuries.

Notes

1 I should, however, own up to having myself pursued this 'paradigm' in *Vietnam and the West* (London, 1968; and Ithaca: Cornell University Press, 1971).
2 Victor Lieberman, 'Transcending East–West Dichotomies: State and Culture Formation in Six Ostensibly Disparate Areas', *Modern Asian Studies* 31(3) (Cambridge, 1997).

The same issue includes a series of more specialized papers relating to that central theme, originally discussed at a workshop on 'The Eurasian context of the early modern history of mainland South-East Asia, 1400–1800' held at the School of Oriental and African Studies (London) in June 1995, with an additional 'Introduction' by Professor Lieberman. He initiated exploration of this theme in an earlier paper: 'Local Integration and Eurasian Analogies: Structuring Southeast Asian History, c. 1350–c.1830', *Modern Asian Studies* 27(3) (Cambridge, 1993).

3 I have argued the case for a re-periodisation of South-East Asian history along these lines, in a paper given at the Bangkok meeting of the International Historians of Asia in May 1996: Ralph Smith, 'South-East Asian Polities in Global Perspective, 1590–1800'. I see this as being also a formative period in the emergence of 'modern' Indonesia and Malaysia, albeit for partly negative reasons; and in the 'integration' of the Philippines under Spanish rule.

4 R.B. Smith, 'England and Vietnam in the Fifteenth and Sixteenth Centuries: an essay in historical comparison', in C.D. Cowan and O.W. Wolters (eds), *Southeast Asian History and Historiography: Essays presented to D.G.E. Hall* (Cornell University Press, 1976).

5 May McKisack, *Oxford History of England: The Fourteenth Century* (Oxford, 1959), pp. 312–13.

6 *Modern Asian Studies* 31(3) (1997), p. 501.

7 These wars are recorded in the 15th century chronicle *Dai-Viet Su-ky Toan-tho;* for a brief account based mainly on that source, see John K. Whitmore, *Vietnam, Ho Quy Ly and the Ming (1371–1421)* (Yale Center for International and Area Studies: Lac Viet series, no 2: New Haven, 1985).

8 McKisack, *The Fourteenth Century* (1959), pp. 251–2.

9 For a study of Higden's work in the context of its time, see John Taylor, *The Universal Chronicle of Ranulf Higden* (Oxford 1966); also Peter Brown, 'Higden's Britain' in A.P Smyth (ed.), *Medieval Europeans: Studies in Ethnic Identity and National Perspectives in Medieval Europe* (London, 1998).

10 This was not, however, the earliest map of Britain to be found in an early chronicle: several were drawn by Matthew Paris for his *Chronica Majora*, compiled at St Albans abbey in the middle decades of the 13th century; see Taylor (as note 9) pp. 63ff.

11 For this and the following paragraph I have relied on O.W. Wolters, *Dai Viet in the Fourteenth Century* (Yale Center for International and Area Studies: Lac Viet series, no 9: New Haven, 1988), pp. 22–30; and E.S. Unger, 'From Myth to History: imagined polities in 14th century Vietnam' in D.G. Marr and A.C. Milner (eds), *Southeast Asia in the 9th to 14th Centuries* (Singapore and Canberra, 1986), pp. 177–86.

12 For a translation and commentary on this text, see S.D. O'Harrow, 'Nguyen Trai's *Binh Ngo Dai Cao* of 1428: the development of a Vietnamese national identity', *Journal of Southeast Asian Studies* 10(1) (Singapore, March 1979).

13 *Viet-Su Thong-giam Cuong-muc (Chinh Bien)*, Book 10: translated into modern Vietnamese (Hanoi, 1958), vol. vi, p. 60. The possible significance of this event is not noticed by either Whitmore or Wolters; nor is it clear how the mission was followed up. Relations between the Tran and the Minh courts were somewhat strained between 1371 and 1384.

14 J. Whitmore, *Vietnam, Ho Quy Ly and the Ming*, pp. 40–41.

15 For a modern study of the subject, in considerable detail, see G.L. Harriss, *King, Parliament, and Public Finance in Medieval England to 1369* (Oxford, 1975). The archival ground was broken much earlier, by scholars of the calibre of T.F. Tout.

16 For a 'conventional' study of the revolt see Charles Oman, *The Great Revolt of 1381* (Oxford, 1906); for a more radical 'postmodern' analysis: Steven Justice, *Writing and Rebellion: England in 1381* (Berkeley, 1994).

17 Jeremy Catto, 'Andrew Horn: Law and History in 14th century England', in R.H.C. Davies and J.M. Wallace-Hadrill (eds) , *The Writing of History in the Middle Ages* (Oxford, 1981).

18 A major project on the feeding of London in the period 1250–1400 was carried out in the 1990s at the Centre for Metropolitan History in University of London's Institute of Historical Research.

19 Some idea of these developments can be gleaned from M. McKisack, *The Fourteenth Century* (1959); the range of specialist historical literature on such topics is remarkable.

20 See the contribution of H.A. Miskimin, and also that of J. Munro, to J.F. Richards (ed.), *Precious Metals in the Later Medieval and Early Modern Worlds* (Durham, North Carolina, 1983). On 14th century English coinage, see C.E. Challis (ed.), *A New History of the Royal Mint* (Cambridge, 1992): chapter 2, by N.J. Mayhew.

21 R. Deloustal, 'Ressources financieres et economiques de l'Etat dans l'ancien Annam' (translated from Phan Huy Chu), *Revue Indochinoise*, vol. xii (1924), pp. 385–6.

22 Outlined by J. Whitmore, *Vietnam, Ho Quy Ly and the Ming*, pp. 43–50; see also items relating to this period translated from Phan Huy Chu's work, by R. Deloustal (as note 21), *Revue Indochinoise*, vols xlii–xliii (Hanoi, 1924–25).

23 See again R. Deloustal: *Revue Indochinoise*, vol. xliii (1925), p. 60.

24 Lien-sheng Yang, *Money and Credit in China, a Short History* (Harvard, 1952), pp. 65–7. However, from the 15th century silver and copper coins gradually reasserted their role and paper currency eventually disappeared in China until the 19th century.

25 R. Deloustal, as note 23. The measure is discussed by Whitmore in *Vietnam, Ho Quy Ly and the Ming*, pp. 43–4. Interestingly a similar issue of paper currency occurred in Korea in 1401.

26 Wang Gung-wu, 'Merchants without Empire: the Hokkien sojourning communities', in J.D. Tracy (ed.), *The Rise of Merchant Empires* (Cambridge, 1990).

27 His theological works are examined in depth, as well as his disputes with William of Ockham and others, in Gordon Leff, *Bradwardine and the Pelagians* (Cambridge, 1957). His importance as a mathematician is noted in Carl Boyer, *A History of Mathematics* (2nd edn, New York, 1991), pp. 262–3.

28 See Andre Goddu, *The Physics of William of Ockham* (Leiden, 1984); also, for his political ideas, George H. Sabine, *A History of Political Theory* (3rd edn, New York, 1963), pp. 304ff.

29 Again see McKisack, *The Fourteenth Century*, pp. 501–15. There is an extensive bibliography on Wyclif and the 'lollards'.

30 Tran Van Giap, 'Le Bouddhisme en Annam des Origines au XIIIe Siecle', *Bulletin de l'Ecole Francaise d'Extreme-Orient*, vol. xxxii (Hanoi, 1933), especially pp. 195–6.

31 See discussion in O.W. Wolters, *Dai-Viet in the Fourteenth Century*, pp. 72–75.

32 Wolters, *ibid*, pp. 17–18.

33 Whitmore, *Vietnam, Ho Quy Ly and the Ming*, p. 26.

34 For a short account of his importance, and that of the 11th century Sung scholars, see Wing-Tsit Chan's introduction to Chu Hsi and Lu Tsu-ch'ien, *Reflections on Things at Hand* (New York, 1967).

2   England and Vietnam in the fifteenth and sixteenth centuries

An essay in historical comparison

Source: C. D. Cowan and O. W. Wolters (eds), *Southeast Asian History and Historiography: Essays Presented to D. G. E. Hall* (Ithaca, NY: Cornell University Press, 1976), pp. 227–246.

Professor Hall has, at different periods in his life, taught both the history of Europe (including England) and that of Southeast Asia. To present in his honour an essay in historical comparison therefore may not be entirely inappropriate. The paper that follows had its beginnings in a lecture given under the auspices of the British Council in Saigon, when I found myself embarking upon a comparison between the histories of England and of Vietnam. At first sight one is bound to be overwhelmed by the immense contrasts between the two countries, situated as they are at opposite ends of the Eurasian landmass, but as I proceeded I became increasingly aware of certain remarkable similarities between their histories: similarities that make the contrasts themselves much more interesting and worthy of investigation.

I

To begin with, there is a similarity of scale. In population Britain is somewhat larger, but not so much so that comparison is impossible. The present-day population of Vietnam (both North and South) stands at approximately the level which was reached by Great Britain and Ireland together during the 1890s, and by England, Wales, and Scotland about 1908. In surface area Vietnam turns out to be rather larger than the whole of the British Isles (including Eire).[1]

The two countries are alike too in the chronological extent of their history. Both emerged into recorded history (into Chinese and Roman history respectively) during the second and first centuries BC, and both were firmly absorbed into neighbouring large empires during the first half of the first century AD. In broad outline, at least, their histories can be written continuously since that time.

In terms of material culture, too, Britain and Vietnam were comparable at least down to the eighteenth century. Before that time, they were both agrarian societies in which the vast majority of the population lived in the countryside and in which trade and rural industries developed at the edges of the economy.

Interestingly enough, by the seventeenth century both had flourishing textile industries in certain rural areas, and a small amount of mining, in addition to their agriculture. The fact that Britain belongs to the temperate zone and has always grown crops like wheat, barley, and oats, while Vietnam depends on wet-rice agriculture, does not affect this basic dependence on agriculture and the land over many centuries. True, after 1800 this similarity has disappeared, at least for the time being. Britain was by then beginning to experience its industrial revolution and the first stages of a complete social transformation. British colonial expansion had already reached North America, India, and Australasia, and during the next century it would produce an even vaster Empire, though most of it had become independent by the 1960s. Vietnam, on the other hand, was at the receiving end of Western imperialism, and during the nineteenth century its whole political and economic evolution was distorted by the French conquest. The country is still not finished with the consequences of colonial rule and of the struggle for national independence. A full-scale comparative study of the histories of Britain and Vietnam would need to take into account, perhaps even to try to explain, this great difference between them in the last two centuries. In the present paper, however, we shall confine our attention to a period before these differences became so marked.

In relation to the period before the nineteenth century, two other general similarities between English and Vietnamese history are worth noticing before we turn to the more detailed examination of a particular century. The first relates to their internal political development, and to the gradual inclusion of both countries, as they existed by 1800, within a single political framework which had not existed in, say, the tenth century. England itself was only effectively united during the tenth and eleventh centuries, and the process was not properly completed until the consolidation of unity by the Norman conquest. Wales was conquered in the thirteenth century by Edward I and finally absorbed into the English administrative system in 1536. Scotland, on the other hand, resisted the attacks of Edward I and his successors and remained a thorn in England's side until the two kingdoms were united by a peaceful dynastic succession in 1603. In the meantime, Ireland had been invaded by the Anglo-Norman kings in the twelfth century and was brought firmly under English control in the period between 1494 and 1540. But in the case of Ireland the process of conquest was never so complete that, despite further military campaigns in the sixteenth and seventeenth centuries and an act of union in 1801, it could not begin to be reversed in the twentieth century.

This gradual political expansion, from Athelstan to the Irish Union, can be paralleled to a remarkable extent in the history of Vietnam. The country which the Chinese lost about 900, and failed to reconquer in 937 and 980, was first unified as an independent kingdom by the Lý dynasty of the eleventh and twelfth centuries. But the Lý kingdom never extended beyond what is now North Vietnam, and its more southerly provinces were only conquered in 1069–1070. Central Vietnam was then, and for several centuries to come, occupied by the kingdom of Champa, while the whole Mekong delta was Khmer. The annexation of two Cham provinces by Đại-Việt in 1070 was followed by more than two centuries of border raids, without any significant territorial change. Then in 1306 the Vietnamese acquired two more provinces through a marriage treaty with the Cham king. There followed a long series of wars between the two kingdoms from 1371 to 1470, of which the eventual outcome was the Vietnamese conquest of all of Champa as far south as Bình-Định (including the former Cham captial of Vijaya). After another period of relative stability in the south, the Vietnamese resumed their expansion in the later seventeenth century, and by 1760 they had not only finally extinguished Champa but had also forced Cambodia to cede to them a large part of the Mekong delta. However, the Vietnamese kingdom itself became divided into two parts during the seventeenth century, and the present area of Vietnam was only finally united under a single ruler in 1802, the year after the union of Great Britain and Ireland. A further phase of expansion began in 1836–1840, when the Vietnamese tried to take over the remainder of Cambodia, but they had not succeeded in that aim by the time of the arrival of the French admirals in 1859.

The second of these general historical similarities concerns the external relationships of England and Vietnam: that is, their political and cultural relationships to Europe and China respectively. The Roman conquest of Britain, leading to nearly four centuries of government as a province of the Empire, has its parallel in the Han conquest of Chiao-chih, which made northern Vietnam a Chinese province from 111 BC to about AD 900. During these periods, England acquired a Roman culture without being completely Latinized, while Vietnam received a number of Chinese settlers and was deeply and permanently influenced by Chinese civilization. The Chinese failed to recover control of Vietnam despite invasions in 982, 1075–1077, and 1281–1288, and the Ming conquest of 1407 was reversed a mere twenty years later. Another Chinese invasion was repulsed in 1788–1789, and in 1884–1885 the Chinese were unable to prevent Vietnam from falling to the French. But, throughout the centuries from the fall of T'ang to the French conquest, Vietnam continued to look to China for cultural inspiration and often modelled its institutions on a Chinese pattern, while preserving its own language and insisting on its political independence (apart from tribute missions).

England might have had a similar experience in relation to Europe if the Roman empire had been reunified after the breakup of the fifth century. As it was, the cultural, spiritual, and, to some extent, political relationships between England and the Continent were reaffirmed by the conversion to Roman Christianity between 597 and 664, and then by the Norman conquest of 1066. In the latter year the victory of the Normans, coming immediately after the defeat of the Scandinavians, meant that England was embroiled in French-centred political conflicts down to the sixteenth century. Thereafter, with the final loss of its last French territory and the break with Rome which followed the Henrician Reformation, England went its own way and was strong enough to withstand attempts at invasion in 1588, 1805, and 1940. Like Vietnam, England preserved its own cultural and political identity, but within a cultural framework in which Latin played a role not unlike that of Chinese in Vietnam.

In this context, it seems not unreasonable to suggest a comparison between the two features which linked Vietnam to China between 982 and 1885 and England to Rome between 664 and 1534. In the former case it was a tribute system, in which all of China's close neighbours (including some not deeply influenced by Chinese culture) sent regular tribute missions, indicating their acceptance of the ultimate superiority of the Chinese Son of Heaven. Between England and Rome, the link grew out of the distinction between temporal and spiritual law; the Papacy was recognized as the supreme spiritual head of all Christendom, since the Pope had inherited the former imperial dignity *Pontifex Maximus*. But the relationship between spiritual and temporal authority was often very far from harmonious, and the tensions which it generated came to a head in the sixteenth century: hence the Reformation of the 1530s.

To suggest that the tribute system played a role for Vietnam comparable to papal authority over the Church in England, however, is to identify a fundamental difference between their cultures. For the position of the Pope depended on a concept of divine law, emanating from an omnipotent God, which had little meaning for the Chinese and Vietnamese. Likewise, the tributary relationship depended on a cosmological notion of kingship which lay at the core of the Chinese political tradition. We shall return in due course to the implications of this important contrast, reflected in the Confucianization of Vietnam and the English Reformation.

II

The period between 1460 and 1560, which I propose to examine in more detail, was an important one for the political development of both England and Vietnam: a century during which their institutions and patterns of political conflict took on the shape which was to characterize the period from then until the nineteenth century. It was also the last period before the beginning of the British economic and colonial expansion which was to make their modern histories so very different: Drake's circumnavigation of the world, the foundation of the first American colonies, and the first visit of an Englishman to Southeast Asia all came in the decade from 1577 to 1587. The century before 1560 therefore seems to offer an excellent opportunity for comparative study, an opportunity to increase our understanding of both countries by measuring them against one another.

It is a curious coincidence—it can hardly be more—that in both England and Vietnam the years 1459–1461 saw a serious political conflict, which brought to the throne a new young king; more curiously still, Edward IV and Lê Thánh Tôn were both born in the year 1442. Since neither was yet twenty years old, it is hardly surprising that at the outset of both their reigns power should lie with court magnates of an older generation: in England with the Neville Earls of Salisbury and Warwick and in Vietnam with Nguyễn Xí and the alliance of military leaders and scholar-officials who had brought about the *xuởng-nghĩa* coup of 1460.[2] But as the two kings grew older their power increased, and by 1471, despite the brief restoration of Henry VI in England, both were firmly in control of their respective courts and kingdoms. Their reigns marked important turning points in English and in Vietnamese history alike. Edward IV's policies began the trend towards the recovery of strength by the monarchy, which continued with only short interruptions between 1460 and 1560 and was thus a major theme of our period; Lê Thánh Tôn and his ministers were responsible for even more sweeping changes, which might well be summarized as the "Confucianization" of Vietnam, a phrase which will be explained in due course.

The stability which Edward IV brought to England was interrupted in 1483 when he died, leaving behind a child-king on the throne and an ambitious royal uncle. Two years of conflict followed, culminating in the seizure of power by Henry Tudor. But under the new dynasty which he established, the monarchy became even stronger: a fact reflected in the peaceful succession of his son in 1509. As the sixteenth century wore on, this new strength of the Crown was to be of the greatest significance in the face of growing religious and potentially political strife, which in France and Germany produced long periods of civil war. In England, by contrast, the monarch not only survived but was able to prevent any breakdown in the territorial unity of the kingdom.

Henry VIII's decision to seize full spiritual independence from Rome in 1532 began a period of religious and political change and of institutional reform, which was comparable in many respects to the "Confucianization" of Lê Thánh Tôn after 1460; a later section of this paper will attempt a comparative analysis of the two movements of reform. Such changes could not have succeeded without a strong monarchy. Opposition was inevitable, but, when the Pilgrimage of Grace finally erupted in 1536, it was joined by only a small group of diehards who were quickly defeated. When a new phase of reform began in 1548–1549 the Crown, despite the fact that Edward VI was a minor and power was exercised by two successive regents during his reign, was strong enough to impose its will on the people once again. Even more remarkable, when the young king died and was succeeded by two sisters in turn in 1553 and 1558, the mere changes of monarch were enough to carry England back and forth between the extremes of Edwardian Reformation, Marian Reaction, and finally Elizabeth's "Middle Way." The change of 1558, however, may have averted a catastrophe: Mary's policies were sure to have provoked more opposition had she lived. As it was, by 1560 England had a strong monarchy and had been "reformed" without a civil war.

In Vietnam there was a reverse trend from stability to instability during the early decades of the sixteenth century.[3] Throughout the reign of Lê Thánh Tôn (1460–1497), there was no serious political conflict which could not be contained by the court or any important challenge to the Confucian scholar-officials. Trouble began with the premature death of his son, Hiến Tôn in 1505. How he died remains a mystery, but the consequence was that a young prince was placed on the throne by a court faction which had not previously been very powerful: the relatives and associates of a former concubine of Hiến Tôn, whose son now became king. In the absence of a rule of primogeniture such as existed in England, there was often no single candidate with a universally acknowledged claim to the succession, and this led quite often to succession conflicts between

the candidates of different court factions. The faction which came to power in
1505, moreover, had its territorial roots in the region of Tongking immediately to
the north of Hanoi, Its rise meant a decline in influence for the leading clans
of the southerly province of Thanh-Hóa who had enjoyed royal favour and
great influence ever since their support of Lê Lợi had led to the foundation
of the Lê dynasty in 1427–1428. That these Thanh-Hóa clans would retaliate
was all but inevitable. In 1509 (the year of Henry VIII's peaceful accession
to the Crown of England) they supported a rebellion by a dissident prince, Lê
Oanh, and led an army from Thanh-Hóa to Hanoi to place him on the throne.
The Tongking clans who had held power since 1505 were thus driven out of
the capital.

The new king, Lê Tưởng Dực, reigned from 1510 to 1516, and the record of
those years indicates a serious attempt at further reform and a new revival of
Confucian scholarship. But these developments were brought to an end by the
revolt of Trăn Cảo in 1516; there had been sporadic disturbances throughout
the reign, but this new rising was of far more serious proportions. A native of
Hải-Dương province in eastern Tongking, Trăn Cảo claimed descent from the
Trăn dynasty (1225–1400) and used his position as some kind of priest in a
religious sect to become very influential in his own region. In 1516 he made a
bid for the throne, which briefly succeeded but failed in the end. More important
than his own fate, however, was the fact that his revolt showed very clearly the
extent to which the Lê dynasty depended for its survival on the power of the
Thanh-Hóa clans. The leaders of the two most prominent clans, Trịnh Duy Sản
and Nguyễn Hoăng Dụ, both had designs on the throne for themselves. During
the course of 1516, the Trịnh leader killed Lê Tùởng Dực and placed his own
nominee on the throne, a usual preliminary move before attempting to establish a
new dynasty, but he was prevented from getting his way by the intervention of the
Nguyễn. Another prince was made king, becoming Lê Chiêu Tôn (1516–1522).
But real power now lay with the clan generals, whose position was not unlike that
of the noblemen of fifteenth-century England whom Sir John Fortescue dubbed
"overmighty subjects." The years 1517–1519 saw virtual civil war between the
various court factions. The conflict between the two main Thanh-Hóa clans (Trịnh
and Nguyễn) eventually gave an opportunity for the re-emergence of the clans
of Tongking. The opportunity was seized by Mạc Đăng Dung, a native of the
Tongking delta, descendent of a former scholarly family, but himself a military
man. His intervention "saved" the Lê in 1519, and his opponents were forced to
withdraw to Thanh-Hóa. He went from strength to strength at the court of Lê Chiêu
Tôn, and he became so powerful that in 1522 the king fled from the capital in order
to encourage a new rising by the Thanh-Hóa men. The Mạc not only survived this
challenge but took control of Thanh-Hóa itself in 1525, and in 1527 they seized
the throne for themselves.

Unlike Henry VII, with whom he might interestingly be compared, Mạc Đăng
Dung was not able to restore the full might of the monarchy. His hold on Thanh-Hóa
was still tenuous. In 1533, Nguyễn Kim, who had fled to Ai-Lao (Luang Phrabang),
restored the Lê dynasty in exile in the person of Lê Trang Tôn (1533–1546); he then

appealed to China for recognition. The Mạc averted a new Chinese occupation in 1540 by submitting to a Ming army and accepting the status of governors of Annam, a move which guaranteed them the disfavour of subsequent chroniclers.[4] Even so, the Chinese did not intervene to prevent the Lê supports, in effect the Nguyễn and the Trịnh, from returning to control Thanh-Hóa and Nghệ-An in 1542–1543. Thereafter, for the next fifty years, Vietnam was divided into two hostile states: a situation which was only brought to an end by the Lê "restoration" of 1592, after Trịnh forces had recaptured Hanoi. In the meantime, the death of Nguyễn Kim in 1545 had been followed by a growing conflict between the Trịnh and Nguyễn themselves. The Nguyễn avoided almost certain elimination by securing the governorship of Thuận-Hóa (the Huê area) in 1558. There they laid the foundations for what became virtually a separate kingdom in the seventeenth and eighteenth centuries.

Thus the history of Vietnam in the sixteenth century was even more disturbed by internal political conflict than that of England had been during the so-called Wars of the Roses. By 1558, the year of Elizabeth's accession, Vietnam had entered a period of political division which would end only in 1802.

III

In the broad sweep of world history, it is easy to lump together countries such as England and Vietnam had become by 1500 under the general heading "traditional societies." But when it comes to making detailed comparisons, comparability of scale and economic similarities must be set against cultural differences as great as any that were to be found in the world of 1500. It is not enough to attach labels to societies, be they universal epithets such as "traditional" or cultural identities such as "Christian" and "Confucian." It is necessary to compare in detail actual situations and social and political arrangements.

Both these countries were monarchies and both have been described, in very different contexts, as "despotisms." The Vietnamese monarchy belonged to the type which K. A. Wittfogel has dubbed "oriental despotism."[5] The power of the king was quite arbitrary, untrammelled by such limitations as the need to obtain parliamentary approval for taxation and other impositions on his subjects, or by the need to borrow money from rich merchants and financiers who enjoyed sufficient independence to charge him high rates of interest. Nor were there any restraints or precedents which obliged him to respect the rule of law; nor any Church to insist that in certain spheres the king had no jurisdiction at all. Yet we have seen that during the sixteenth century the Vietnamese monarchy became weaker while the Tudor monarchy went from strength to strength. And even though the Crown was forced to give way to Parliament in the seventeenth century, the government still remained strong by comparison with that of Vietnam. There is a paradox in this contrast which calls for some explanation.

One respect in which the English monarchy was strengthened by its principles was in the matter of legitimacy and succession. Primogeniture was the rule, and in England (as opposed to some other European countries) a first-born woman could succeed in the absence of direct male heirs. The importance of legitimacy is shown by the fact that, even in fifteenth century England, no "overmighty subject" ever actually seized the throne without having some pretence to a legal claim: all those who actually became king were ultimately offspring of the Plantagenet line. Great power might reside with a Warwick or a Norfolk, but he never stood any chance of becoming a monarch in his own right. His peers would never have accepted it. In the sixteenth century, likewise, the principle of legitimacy made it possible for the three children of Henry VIII to take England in successively different directions in matters of religious doctrine and the jurisdiction of Rome.

The Vietnamese monarchy placed no such emphasis on legitimacy. Quite apart from the fact that women could never occupy the throne (though one woman had considerable power as a mother-regent in the 1450s), there was no rule of primogeniture. In a country where kings had several wives and many concubines, the number of royal princes was far greater than in England; and on the death of a king no one of them had an automatic right to succeed to the throne. The heir was usually nominated by the king before his death. But this left open the possibility that his choice might be influenced by a powerful court faction, possibly the blood relations of one of his queens, so that the selected heir owed his very accession to a group among his own subjects. It is not surprising that from time to time some "overmighty subject" secured so great a control over the king and the court that he was able to overthrow the dynasty and establish himself on the throne. Where this final step was impossible, a family like the Trịnh was nevertheless able to become virtual rulers of Vietnam and to confine the king to his palace and to his religious roles. Thus changes of dynasty meant the passage of royal authority from one clan to another, without any blood connection between them—except that the usurper might marry the wives or daughters of his predecessor. Such a change was, moreover, justified by reference to the Confucian doctrine of the "decree of fate" (or the "mandate of heaven").

The concept of legitimacy in England was rooted in an even more fundamental element of its political culture: the notion of law. Originating partly in the Hebrew, partly in the Roman tradition, the belief in law was fundamental to political thinking and institutional practice throughout the Europe of the fifteenth and sixteenth centuries. It was especially strong in England, where it had long since become bound up with the idea of the community. What an Englishman meant by law was first and foremost the common law, more deeply rooted in English tradition than either the civil or the ecclesiastical law of Rome. The king himself was expected to rule according to this law, and since the thirteenth century successive monarchs had admitted as much by their frequent confirmations of the Magna Carta.

The Vietnamese, like the Chinese, had a different conception of law; or, rather, it may be true to say that they distinguished between three concepts which are all somewhat different from the English idea of law. *Pháp* (Chinese *fa*) was the decree of the king or emperor, and it could not therefore bind the throne in the same way as a Magna Carta; nor could *hình* (*hsing*), the list of penalties to be imposed on those guilty of various offences, for no offence that a king could commit was covered by them. On the other hand, *lẽ* (*li*) was a principle of justice and universal harmony which touched the behaviour of all men, but it was not embodied in any precise formulation of law.[6] The king or emperor might be measured according to *lẽ*, but there was no means for any of his subjects to force him to rule according to it. Only the impersonal "decree of heaven" could affect the position of a king. The importance of *lẽ* was not that it laid down specific rules or procedures which the king or his officials must obey but rather that it provided a means of measuring the ethical quality of men. Where the Christian view of monarchy held that a king should govern according to good laws, the Confucian view was that he should govern through the appointment of good officials.

This contrast between the two conceptions of government and law can be well illustrated by comparing the "Confucianization" of Vietnam under Lê Thánh Tôn with the "Reformation" of England under Henry VIII. John K. Whitmore, whose study of the period 1428–1471 represents one of the most significant Western contributions to historical writing on Vietnam in recent years, has shown how the reforms of Lê Thánh Tôn represented the victory of a class of scholar-officials or *quân-tử* (the Chinese *chün-tzu*) over the great counsellors (*đại-thần, ta-chen*) who had dominated the Lê court since the beginning of the dynasty.[7] The latter, mainly originating from Thanh-Hóa province, were military figures; whereas the *quân*, more frequently natives of Tongking, were scholars whose claim to authority stemmed from success in the Confucian examinations.

The method of selecting officials by testing their proficiency in the Confucian classics and in literary composition, at formal state examinations, was already established in Vietnam by the thirteenth century. But in the Trần period (1225–1400) the scholars occupied a relatively unimportant place in the government systems, and the *đại-thần* were very often Trần princes. The scholars become a little more prominent towards the end of the fourteenth century, when the exmination system was reformed to permit a small number of candidates to reach a higher grade; and during the Ming occupation (1407–1427) Confucian scholarship in general received a great boost, especially in Tongking. But the end of Ming administration and the triumph of Lê Lợi meant a setback for the scholars, who were only very gradually able to reassert their influence during the fifteenth century. Although significant examinations were held in 1442 and in 1448, it was only in 1460 that the *quân-tử* achieved the kind of prominence, under the patronage of Thánh Tôn, which enabled them to reshape the government and regulate affairs of state according to Confucian principles. Inevitably they took steps to make the examination system a regular part of national life, and the pattern of triennial examinations in the capital established in 1463 was maintained (with only a slight break in 1517–1518) until the end of the Mạc dynasty. Candidates who passed the examinations and obtained the highest grade *(tiên-sĩ,* or *chin-shih)* became members of the Hàn-Lâm academy, from which the highest official positions were now filled. In this way, Lê Thánh Tôn ensured that the country would be run by men whose qualifications were well established in Confucian terms, with a less dominant role being played by military mandarins.

The latter, incidentally, were kept occupied by a policy of reforming the army from 1466 and then by the need to control the large area of territory annexed from Champa in 1471.

The rise to power of the scholar-officials was accompanied by an overhaul of the system of government more far-reaching than any attempted by earlier kings, and probably only comparable in later periods with the reforms of Minh Mạng (1820–1841). The general effect of the changes, whose details are much too complex to be covered by a short paper, was to bring into existence a more orderly pattern of government. In this situation a key role was played by the new "office of transmissions," which ensured communication between the throne and its numerous officials. Also important were the decrees for reforming provincial and local government and for regulating the communal lands, as well as the registration rolls, of the villages. The new system was enshrined in a number of officially inspired compilations of texts, notably the *Hoàng Triêu Quan Chê'* of 1471 and the *Thiên Nam Du' Hạ Tập* (a sort of administrative encyclopedia) of 1483. Another book of the period which reflects the new strength of the Confucian idea of government was the *Đại Việt Sử Ký Toàn Thu'*, a revised and extended version of the national chronicle, which Thánh Tôn ordered to be written in 1479.

In the reforms made by Henry VIII of England with the able assistance of Thomas Cromwell, there was also an emphasis on the good ordering of the state; but it was an order based upon law. The Reformation was, in some measure, a reaction against the policies of Cardinal Wolsey, who had been in power from 1515 to 1529. Wolsey had tended to favour arbitrary rule, tempered by a sense of equity, and his administration had been highly personal in character. This was resented by his opponents, and the 1530s saw instead a new emphasis on legality and the formal enactment of statute law. Wolsey had feared Parliament. Cromwell, on the other hand, welcomed the idea of using Parliament to bring about what amounted to a revolution by legislation. G. R. Elton observes that the role of Parliament as a legislative assembly was virtually established by the Reformation Parliament of 1529–1536.[8] At the same time, Cromwell also brought about changes in the practice of administration which amounted to the creation for the first time in England of a formalized bureaucracy, as opposed to government by means of the royal household, changes which Professor Elton has called the "Tudor revolution in government."[9] These aspects of the Reformation were of the greatest significance, and they amounted to a reaffirmation of the importance of the common law. At a time when England was almost bound to undergo some kind of political and institutional change in response to both the new intellectual mood in Europe and new developments in its own society, Cromwell's reforms ensured that for the next two generations the changes would be in the direction of Parliamentary sovereignty.

The element of law also entered into the other major aspect of the Henrician Reformation, the assertion of the power of the Crown in spiritual matters and the ending of papal jurisdiction in England. This meant a decline in the status and independence of the clergy, a change reflected in the suppression of the monastic orders which quickly followed. In this respect, the changes of the 1530s had almost the reverse effect of the reforms of Lê Thánh Tôn. They brought to an end the spiritual ties between England and Rome which had been forged in the early medieval period, and they reduced the power of the clergy in the nation's affairs. England would never again have a cardinal for Chancellor. In Vietnam, on the other hand, the effect of "Confucianization" was to strengthen ties with China and to increase the influence of the group most inclined to look towards the Middle Kingdom for inspiration. The changes of the 1460s and 1470s brought Vietnam closer than ever to the Chinese model of government established under Ming T'ai-tsu. The tributary relationship to China continued and was strengthened by the events of 1540–1541, when Mạc Đăng Dung, and then his successor Mạc Phúc Hải, accepted the status of *đô-thông-sứ'*, which made them virtually "governors of Annam."

The tributary relationship, however, had never been a form of jurisdiction, and it is important to insist on the difference between English and Vietnamese attitudes to religious law which underlies the contrast we are examining. The superiority of the Chinese emperor in the scheme of things might make it natural for a deposed Vietnamese dynasty to appeal for his intervention, as happened in 1405–1406 and in 1536–1537, but it did not give him any regular jurisdiction over the Vietnamese king or his subjects. In Christendom, such jurisdiction was a necessary consequence of belief in an omnipotent creator God and in an ultimate day of judgment for every human soul. That it was divided into the temporal and spiritual jurisdictions of king and bishops respectively is perhaps less fundamental than the fact that for every misdeed in his daily life any individual could be called to account before those charged with administering God's law. Absolutism such as this did not exist in traditional Vietnam, and it was quite alien to the Chinese religious tradition. For this reason it is necessary not to read into "Confucianization" the kind of religious changes that eventually followed upon the English Reformation.

Another contrast between the two countries relates to the question of religious tolerance. In 1462, a decree of Lê Thánh Tôn forbade the building of new Buddhist and other non-Confucian temples, and in the years 1468–1470 a series of decrees established new regulations for the maintenance of mourning rites and other Confucian ceremonies. Such concern for the Confucian proprieties stemmed naturally from the belief that the harmony of the kingdom and of the whole universe depends on propriety of conduct in the individual and on the correct performance of family rituals. On at least one occasion the King himself undertook a pious visit to the ancestral tombs of his own clan in Thanh-Hóa province. But these decrees did not involve a merciless persecution of Buddhist and other non-Confucian sects. Such sects lost royal patronage for a time, between 1460 and 1600, and so disappear from the royal records. But there is nothing to suggest that they ceased completely to exist or that Confucianization was accompanied by large-scale execution of heretics such as occurred under the Marian reaction. Confucianism was a religion that required a certain framework of order. But it did not impose a rigorous catechism of belief on all members of society and persecute those who refused to conform to it. In this respect, the Vietnamese tradition was far less absolutist than the European.

IV

An aspect of the growing strength of the monarchy in England after 1460 which has received a good deal of attention from historians in recent years was the question of the Crown's financial resources. Sir John Fortescue, writing in the reign of Edward IV, lamented the fact that when a king had smaller resources than his most powerful subjects the throne was bound to be weak and the realm unstable.[10] He was thinking in particular of Crown lands, which in the mid-fifteenth century were reduced to their smallest extent before the losses of the late sixteenth and seventeenth centuries. The period 1460–1540 saw a major recovery of land by the Crown, beginning with the union of the Duchies of Lancaster and York in 1461 and culminating in the seizure of the monastic lands in the years 1536–1539. By 1540 the Crown may well have owned as much as a fifth or a quarter of the productive land of England, though the proportion was soon to be reduced by the selling off of former monastic properties for ready cash. The growth of the royal domain was accompanied by a new concern for estate administration, and the process of reform which began under Edward IV was completed by Cromwell's transformation of government financial administration. Of course, the king was never able to live entirely "of his own" even during this period. Edward IV borrowed from Florentine merchants, and both the Yorkist and the Tudor kings depended for part of their revenues on Parliamentary grants of taxation in various forms. Henry VIII was reduced to debasing the coinage in an attempt to manipulate the whole monetary system in his own favour. But none of the monarchs in the century before 1560 was faced with the kind of financial desperation that compelled Charles I to summon a predictably recalcitrant Parliament in 1640, an event which culminated in a civil war of a kind quite unlike anything that occurred in either England or Vietnam during the period currently under review. Thus the fact that English law protected the rights of the king's subjects, including their property, and gave certain merchant communities a special independence under royal charter did not prevent the monarchy from building up its own wealth and so dominating the realm.

Unfortunately this aspect of monarchy is not so easy to study in the case of Vietnam. Not only has less research been done; there is also a dearth of relevant source materials, for there are no surviving archives recording the day-to-day activities of Vietnamese administration before the nineteenth century. We are therefore dependent entirely on chronicles and on the records of formal edicts and decrees from the throne. These tell us a certain amount about the obligations of the king's subjects and about the rewarding of his officials but very little about the private lands of subjects and officials or even about the "treasury lands" of the government itself. It is impossible to say whether the proportions of land in various categories of ownership increased or decreased during our period. All that we can be sure of is that the confiscation of land from the Vietnamese traitors who had supported the Ming meant that Lê Lợi and his successors had a reserve of land which they could use to reward their supporters and officials and that they probably used it to make official grants, for life or a term, rather than to create hereditary fiefs. In the absence of any records of private estates, it is impossible to test the argument of the Vietnamese Marxist historians that the rise of the scholar-officials under the Lê monarchy of the fifteenth century reflected an important economic change, in which resources passed from an aristocracy to a sort of gentry landowning class from which the *quan* were drawn. We know that there were private estates of some kind, known as *trang-trại*, and a decree of 1397 reflects government concern lest they grow too large and draw away too many labourers from the village. But we know nothing of their extent or organization at this period.

One contrast between England and Vietnam, however, can be drawn with some confidence: that between the manor and the *xã*. In fifteenth and sixteenth-century England, there was an element of territorial lordship of a kind never found in Vietnam: the existence of large estates in which whole villages were owned in perpetuity by hereditary lords. Even though the feudal lordship of noblemen over their free tenants was declining at just this period, the landed estates actually owned by nobility and gentry alike consisted of numbers of manors each comprising all or part of a village. The manorial court, which managed an important part of village affairs, was as much a possession of the lord as was his land.[11] In Vietnam, lordship in this sense did not exist; nor was there ever a strictly feudal system in which great lords enjoyed rights over lesser ones within their territorial fiefs. Instead, we find a pattern of society in which the whole country consisted of semiautonomous communities known as the *xã* (Chinese *she*),[12] They were all subject to direct regulation by the throne, without any intervening lord—except insofar as a prince or a high official was sometimes granted the usufruct of their obligations to the throne. Each *xã* had its small group of officials, members of the community appointed to office by the king, who were responsible for the fulfilment of its obligations. It also had its guardian spirit, formally appointed by royal decree though usually a local ancestor or other spirit. In economic terms, each village was responsible for registering its own population and for the performance of whatever services the government might demand. The *xã* also had, in addition to the private lands of its inhabitants, a section of land set aside as *công-diên* (common land) and regulated by the state. This was public land which was distributed regularly among the members of the village, according to rank, every so many years; it could not be alienated, and it was regularly taxed by the king. How strictly the regulations were maintained was perhaps a measure of the strength of the monarchy and government, and it may therefore be significant that such evidence as we have suggests a greater measure of control over the *xã* under Lê Thánh Tôn than at any other period of Vietnamese history.

But here, too, the absence of archival records makes it impossible to go beyond the formal regulations affecting the *xã* and its obligations in order to see how its resources were used in practice. Was there, for example, a regular relationship over many generations between certain villages and certain offices? Were the affairs of supposedly semiautonomous village communities in effect dominated by local magnates, despite the formal differences between the Vietnamese and English land systems? These are some of the many questions which at present seem almost impossible to answer.

V

Power is never completely and automatically a consequence of wealth and control over land: it also depends on control over institutions and over people. The ability to wage war against one's rivals, or against the throne itself, must be related to the ability to raise an army away from the capital. The ability to influence or dominate affairs at court depends on an individual's ability to manipulate the institutions of government to his own advantage.

In England this aspect of the nature of power was changing quite fundamentally during the century between 1460 and 1560. The territorial lordships which had been the most important form of lordship or patronage at the height of the "feudal system" (in the twelfth and thirteenth centuries) were by now declining in significance, though they were by no means finished in 1460.[13] More important by the sixteenth century were three other forms of patronage: the county community, the noble household (which could include men who had no territorial associations with its lord), and government appointments. At the local level the importance of the county grew as that of private lordship declined, from the reign of Edward I onwards but especially in the sixteenth century. It was an ancient English institution which had never been totally eclipsed by Norman feudalism, and it was now re-emerging into prominence as the focus of local justice and administration, and also of the militia. The power of the nobility tended to become weaker territorially and to depend increasingly on the maintenance of a large household and on the influence which a duke or an earl could exercise at court. Patronage, in the sense of ability to secure for one's followers appointment to an office in the expanding bureaucracy, was becoming increasingly significant by the middle of the sixteenth century. But down to 1560 the general effect of the changing nature of patronage was to strengthen the position of the Crown, for it meant the end of the age when a feudal nobility could use its power to raise private armies, at least in England south of the Trent.

Vietnam did not have a "feudal system" at any time, in the sense of a system of contractual tenure of large territorial fiefs from the throne and a hereditary nobility owing military contingents in return for land. We do not know a great deal about the internal structure of Vietnamese politics and government in the Lý and Trần periods, but there is nothing to indicate any arrangement of that kind. Royal grants of land may well have taken place, but they seem to have been made on a temporary basis as part of the rewards for office. That was certainly the case by the fifteenth century. Lordship over territory, in the strictly feudal sense, was probably not an element in Vietnamese patron-client relations.

What counted in Vietnamese political conflicts were offices in the bureaucracy and membership in a clan. Had office alone been the most important thing, with access to resources depending entirely on royal appointment, Vietnam might well have been a much more stable polity, as was the case in traditional Siam where kinship mattered much less. But in Vietnam the clan framework was at least as important as lordship in England. Kinship was the framework of the ancestral cult, which was the mainstay of Vietnamese religion and which was strengthened rather than weakened by the rise of Confucianism. A man was supposed to be in touch with all the descendants of his paternal ancestor of the fifth generation, and this was likely to be quite a large number of men. They were held together by a loyalty which might often conflict with their loyalty to the throne, and that loyalty was focused upon a regional centre, because every family was obliged to maintain its ancestral tombs. This helps to explain why the Trịnh and the Nguyễn, and indeed the Lê clan itself, had special sources of strength in the province of Thanh-Hóa. They may well have had important private lands there; but above all they had kinsmen. It is unfortunate indeed that we have no records that might tell us something of the internal organization of a powerful clan in Vietnam at this period.

Compared with the English lordship, and also with the newer forms of patronage that were emerging, the Vietnamese clan was somewhat inflexible as a political grouping. Lordship was a bond that could be created, or broken, at will; even territorial lordship could incorporate new followers through new granting of lands or manors by a powerful lord. A rising lord could always attract new supporters, and they would immediately become equal members of his patron group. But kinship depends on birth, and while blood may be thicker than water it cannot be the basis of a highly flexible community which any new follower can enter at will. It was necessary to be born into the clan in order to be a full member of it; anyone who was not born into this clan, moreover, was very likely to have existing loyalties to another. For clan loyalties could have a divisive effect as often as being the basis of combined political effort.

The Vietnamese monarchy, "oriental despotism" or not, was in practice based on the occupation of the throne by one clan in a land which had many. Herein lies the most essential reason for the weakness of the monarchy, in this period as in all others. The Trần clan in the thirteenth century had sought to preserve the throne by a twofold policy: regular abdication of the king while still in the prime of life, so that he could rule as *thượng-hoàng* while his heir secured the throne; and marriage of leading princes entirely within the royal clan. But despite these precautions, which the Mạc seem to have revived after 1527, the Trần dynasty was unable to survive forever. By the mid-fourteenth century it no longer had a *thượng-hoàng* because a king had died on the throne before abdicating and a clan from Thanh-Hóa had been permitted to supply two royal wives, whose nephew was subsequently to overthrow the dynasty. The long history of Vietnamese political conflict under the monarchy suggests that there was no way of preventing outside clans from weakening and threatening the throne or from seizing it outright. The supposedly highly centralized bureaucratic system could not prevent it from happening, since clan patronage and official position were always too closely intertwined.

If nothing else, this brief essay in comparison has shown that the differences between England and Vietnam were essentially cultural and institutional rather than material. And it has tended to undermine the crude notion that oriental monarchies were always despotisms while the Western political tradition placed greater emphasis on the limitation of monarchy. Monarchical arbitrariness was a less sure foundation for the strength of governments than an institutional system based on law, however it might appear to limit the power of the monarch; while kinship was a less flexible, and therefore less stable, basis of politics than lordship and simple patronage.

Notes

1 Figures from United Nations, *Statistical Yearbook 1970* (New York, 1971):

	Area (km²)	Population (1969 est.)
Vietnam	332,000	39,000,000
Great Britain	230,000	54,000,000
U.K. and Eire	300,000	58,000,000

2 On the political history of the two countries in the fifteenth century, for Vietnam see John K. Whitmore, "The Development of Le Government in Fifteenth-Century Vietnam (Ph.D. diss., Cornell University, 1968); for England, E.F. Jacob, *The Fifteenth Century* (Oxford, 1961).

3 The account of the period 1505–1527 in Vietnam is based on Phan Huy Lê, *Lịch sử' Chê đo' Phong kiên Việt-Nam* (History of the Feudal Regime of Vietnam), 11 (Hanoi, 1962), 222–243.

4 These events are very inadequately treated in most secondary works; see *Việt Sử' Thông giám Cương mục* (trans, into *quốc-ngữ*, Hanoi, 1959), XIV, 23ff.

5 K. A. Wittfogel, *Oriental Despotism: A Comparative Study of Total Power* (New Haven, 1957).

6 For a discussion of Chinese concepts of law, from which these Vietnamese concepts are derived, see J. Needham, *Science and Civilisation in China*, II (Cambridge, 1956), sec. 18.

7 Whitmore.

8 G. R. Elton, *The Tudor Constitution* (Cambridge, 1965), pp. 228ff.

9 G. R. Elton, *The Tudor Revolution in Government* (Cambridge, 1953).

10 Sir John Fortescue, *The Governance of England*, ed. C. Plummer (Oxford, 1885).

11 The English manorial framework was of course undergoing important changes during this period, as highly formalized arrangements of the twelfth and thirteenth centuries were breaking down; cf. R. H. Tawney, *The Agrarian Problem in the Sixteenth Century* (London, 1912).

12 On the *xã*, see Lê Văn Hào "Introduction à l'Ethnologie du Đinh," *BSEI*, n.s. 37 (1962); Nguyen Huu Khang, *La Commune Annamite* (Paris, 1946), etc. The latter argues that in certain respects the *xã* was more rigorously controlled from the capital in the fifteenth century than in the nineteenth.

13 On the question of territorial lordship in this period see R. B. Smith, *Land and Politics in the England of Henry VIII: The West Riding of Yorkshire, 1530–46* (Oxford, 1970).

3 Thailand and Viet-Nam

Some thoughts towards a comparative historical analysis

Source: *Journal of the Siam Society* 60 (1972): 1–21.

I

The contrast between Thai and Vietnamese history is readily apparent to all students of the history of South East Asia. In the twentieth century, it is possible to attribute some of the differences to the fact that Thailand was able to avoid complete domination and annexation by a European power, whereas Viet-Nam was conquered by the French. During the period when the Thai were pursuing the gradual modernisation of their political and economic institutions within a monarchical and bureaucratic framework, the Vietnamese were forced to devote much of their national energy towards the achievement of political and economic independence. But the contrast is equally marked in relation to earlier centuries, and there it cannot be so easily explained. Looking at the respective histories of the two countries between the fifteenth century and the nineteenth, one is struck by the remarkable stability which has characterised the political development of Thailand, and by the frequency of internal conflict and territorial division which have punctuated the history of Viet-Nam. By way of illustration, one need only site the events of the latter part of the eighteenth century. In 1767, Thailand was defeated by the Burmese and seemed on the verge of total disintegration; yet in less than a decade, by 1775, the kingdom had been united by Phya Taksin and was strong enough to resist all further Burmese invasions. In Viet-Nam, which was virtually divided into two states during most of the seventeenth and eighteenth centuries, the Tay-Son rebellion of 1771–5 set off a chain of inter-regional conflicts which ended in the final unification of the country only after thirty years of war.

Part of the explanation for this contrast lies no doubt in differences of geography. Both countries have seen a gradual process of political expansion over many centuries, and both the Thailand and the Viet-Nam of the mid-nineteenth century were much larger political entities than had existed under Thai or Vietnamese control in say the thirteenth or fourteenth century. But the geographical contexts of their expansion were very different. In Thailand, the Menam Chao Phraya and its tributaries provided a natural framework for political unity with easy river communications between north and south, which can be extended by land or by sea to include also the peninsula in the south. It was not difficult for a powerful state developing on the central plain of Thailand gradually to absorb first its near neighbours and later those that lay farther afield. Population growth could take place within a continuous lowland area which had plenty of uncleared land.

Viet-Nam on the other hand is geographically fragmented, with a series of river basins leading to the coast, often separated by hills and even by high mountains. The population of the Tongking delta region became sufficiently dense at an early period to force the Vietnamese to move beyond it: first into Thanh-Hoa and An-Tinh, which were already Vietnamese, and then into the smaller valleys of what is now Central Viet-Nam, which had previously been Cham, eventually they reached the lower Mekong delta, which they conquered from Cambodia during the late seventeenth and eighteenth centuries. In addition to migration, the Vietnamese also had recourse to double-cropping of rice in those parts of the northern and central provinces where it was feasible. Thus the geography of Viet-Nam gave rise to both land-scarcity and problems of communication between different regions: two important factors which go some way towards explaining the tendency to political instability and conflict

Geography alone however does not amount to a complete explanation of the contrast. it is necessary to consider the institutional frameworks of the two countries, and also the religious beliefs and cosmological notions which helped to shape them. It is easy enough to remark that Thailand was one of the 'Indian-influenced' countries of South East Asia, whilst Viet-Nam was more deeply influenced by China. But what this meant in practice can only be understood by comparing their institutions and beliefs in some detail. Recent writings on Vietnamese history have paid some attention to the question whether that country can truly be called 'Chinese', and how far it should be regarded as 'South East Asian'.[1] The contrast between Thailand and Viet-Nam leads one to raise the question whether there is any uniformly 'South East Asian' type of polity and culture at all.

II

During the period between the thirteenth and the fifteenth centuries, Viet-Nam came gradually to accept Chinese neo-Confucianism as its predominant political orthodoxy, whilst Thailand (that is, Sukhothai and early Ayuthya) became deeply imbued with the Sinhalese form of Theravada Buddhism. The institutional character of these two forms of orthodoxy must figure prominently in any search for an explanation of the contrast between the two countries.

Confucianism was always an elitist philosophy, or religion, in the sense that its adoption was limited to those few scholars who could study and master its classical texts. They were a sort of priesthood in relation to the Confucian cult; but also they were the guardians of moral orthodoxy and of social harmony, in administrative practice as well as in theory. Although their actual political power at court might vary from one period to another, from the fifteenth century onwards they always had a prominent part in government at least in Tongking.[2]

But this elite was not selected merely by the intervention in human affairs of some supernatural power, or by the working out of some cosmological moral force.

Its members had, in theory, to prove their individual right to enter the elite by passing through an elaborate process of examination, based on the Confucian classics. Indeed one might take the growth of the examination system, and subsequent fluctuations in its importance, as a measure of the relative strength and weakness of the Confucian scholars in Vietnamese political life at different periods. Although there are references to examinations to select scholars for royal favour as early as 1075 and 1086, the continuous history of the examination system as a regular feature of the Vietnamese administrative framework seems to begin in the Tran period. In 1232 the chronicle indicates the selection of five laureates by examination, without suggesting that the event was an innovation of that year. By the end of the Tran period (especially by the 1390s), the examination laureates had become quite prominent. In the 1460s they became the dominant element in government, and the period from 1463 to 1514 represents the first peak in Vietnamese 'Confucianisation' when as many as 816 laureates were chosen in the course of 18 successive triennial examinations.[3] The division of the kingdom between 1527 and 1592 led to a decline in the importance of examinations outside Tongking, and with the triumph of the Trinh clan in the 1590s that decline also affected the north itself. Although there was some reversal of this trend in the North in the century or so after 1660, and although the beginnings of an examination system are found in the Nguyen provinces of what is now Central Viet-Nam in the eighteenth century, it was necessary for the emperors of the Nguyen dynasty to undertake the process of 'Confucianisation' once again, after the unification of the country in 1802. Thus we find that the examination system and the strength of the scholar-officials reached its second peak, in the period 1820–60 on the eve of French colonisation.

Whilst the power of the scholars obviously had important effects on the nature of Vietnamese bureaucracy, and on the role of the monarch, the fact that they were selected in this way also had significance for the character of Vietnamese society and institutions outside the court and government. In the first place, it meant that the Confucian classics and the characters in which they were written became the basis of an educational system, within which young men prepared themselves for the examinations. It was both possible and necessary to acquire a knowledge of the sacred texts of the tradition before entering (indeed in order to enter) the select body of the elite. Many of those who prepared themselves for examination inevitably were rejected, so that there were always in Vietnamese society a substantial number of failed scholars who had acquired a greater or lesser degree of learning without achieving the position of status and power to which they had aspired. Although we know very little about such people, since they barely appear in the official chronicles and records and only occasionally became important literary figures, it is reasonable to assume that their presence in the country was a factor making for political instability. They may well have been active in village government, and in the formation of secret associations at the 'grass roots' level of society where, in certain circumstances, their influence might sometimes be greater than that of the court officials of their locality.

A second effect of the elitist nature of Confucianism was that the growth of the examination system left intact other kinds of elite, or other forms of priesthood. Confucianism was sometimes inimical towards Buddhism and Taoism (and later towards Christianity), and in the periods when it was strongest we find references to decrees intended to limit the numbers of Buddhist monks and other priests of various kinds. In the fourteenth century there were examinations to distinguish genuine Buddhist and Taoist priests from those who had merely entered temples and monasteries to escape the burden of taxation; and in the 1460s a decree explicitly forbade the building of new Buddhist temples.[4] But on the whole such measures were unusual. In any case, Confucianism was by its very nature not capable of absorbing the mass of the populace into its fold. Its tendency was to make it difficult for an aspiring young man to become a full member of the elite, whereas the tendency of other religions was to proselytise as widely as possible. The Confucian moral values which lay at the heart of such measures as the edict of 1662 for the 'reform of customs' were essentially an attempt by the elite to impose its own standards on society at large, rather than an attempt to force everyone to subscribe to a formal Confucian creed. Consequently, outside the Confucian hierarchy other religions continued to flourish. They were essentially sectarian, often related to the beliefs of a particular leader or patriarch, and often highly eclectic in their patterns of belief. To call them 'Buddhist' or 'Taoist' is not necessarily to define their beliefs in any rigorous way; orthodoxy of belief was maintained only within the sect, and not always even there. Outside Confucianism, therefore, one finds a great diversity of religious activity and belief in Vietnamese history: a diversity within which it was possible for Christianity to find a place from the seventeenth century onwards.

Decrees against sectarian activity should be related to the fact that the non-Confucian sects were not only quite often secret esoteric organisations, but also liable to become involved in politics. In 1516 we find the rebel leader Tran Cao, who claimed to be a descendent of the Tran dynasty, organising his followers under the cover of a religious sect in Hai-Duong province. In the Tay-Son rebellion which began in Qui-Nhon province in 1771, we find that one of the three brothers belonged to some kind of religious sect. Religious sects can thus be added to failed scholars as a factor making for instability in Viet-Nam. It is not impossible that the two were sometimes related, and that some people who played an active part in non-Confucian sects had originally been educated as candidates for the examinations. This relationship between politics and sectarian activity, and between sectarian leadership and education for the bureaucracy, can be seen even in the twentieth century in a movement like that of the Caodaists of southern Vietnam in the 1920s.[5]

When we turn to Thai history and the nature of the Thai religious tradition we find a very different pattern of beliefs and institutions. Theravada Buddhism, in the form which developed in Ceylon and Burma during the twelfth and thirteenth centuries, was already an important feature of the life of Sukhothai and Si Sachanalai, as it was reflected in the famous inscription of Ram Kamheng of 1292, During the fourteenth century it became even more important, both at Sukhothai and in the newly emerging kingdom of Ayuthya. Amongst the most important pieces of historical evidence relating to that period are inscriptions recording the foundation of Buddhist temples and the honouring of important *theras* by the kings of Sukhothai. Although Hindu elements also figure in the inscriptions and in some of the ceremonials of that and succeeding periods, it is clear that Theravada Buddhism was already the principal religion of the Thai at that early period. By the nineteenth century, it had become even more predominant.

Theravada Buddhism, like Confucianism, has its elite. But it is a spiritual elite, not an elite of scholar-administrators, and it is deemed to be selected by the impersonal process of the operation of *kamma*, not by anything so human and imperfect as a system of examinations. It is impossible within this tradition for a man to succeed in the spiritual discipline of the *sangha* unless his position is based on merit accumulated over many previous existences. Whilst it is normal for boys and young men to be educated at the wat, and to be admitted to the *sangha* for a brief period at the end of youth, those who become monks for a longer period do so for spiritual reasons rather than out of political ambition. Indeed on more than one occasion the *sangha* has been a safe retreat for princes anxious to avoid political conflict. Thus the Thai monks were (and are) very different as guardians of orthodoxy from the Confucian scholars of Viet-Nam. They have never been responsible for government and administration, outside the affairs of their own order. But they have played an important part in spreading their religion amongst the community at large. Theravada Buddhism, unlike Confucianism, was capable of becoming a 'popular' religion of the kind that would hold society together on all levels, from the royal court down to the ordinary village. By allowing for gradations of spiritual attainment, based on the principles of *kamma* and merit, it enabled every Thai to see himself as a Buddhist: It was possible for 'Thai' and 'Buddhist' to become synonymous terms, in a way that one could never regard being Vietnamese as being Confucian. Within this context it was possible for the king and his officials, though not a spiritual elite like the Vietnamese scholars, to justify their superior status by reference to their good *kamma* accumulated over many previous existences.

The universality of Buddhism for the Thai explains why there was little scope in Thailand for the development of non-Buddhist or unorthodox religious sects, of the kind that flourished in Viet-Nam. There was, too, little scope for intrusion by Christian missionaries: despite the willingness of the kings of Ayuthya and Bangkok to tolerate European missionaries, they had little success in converting the Thai to Christianity. This is a point of significant contrast between Thailand and Viet-Nam. With occasional exceptions, such as the revolt of the phumi-bun Khuang at the end of the seventeenth century, Thai history has not been disturbed by revolts arising from the ambitions of unorthodox sects or from the use of religious associations as a cover for political conspiracy.

The importance of orthodoxy can be seen in the history of the *sangha* itself. Whilst it lacks the Christian notions of spiritual law and obedience to God, that tradition places great emphasis on orthodoxy of ritual in such matters as ordination, the correct wearing of robes, and the performance of the ten precepts. In this respect,

Thai Buddhism differs greatly from the sectarian forms of Mahayana Buddhism in Viet-Nam. Theravada Buddhism offers no opportunity for eclecticism based on the inspired teachings of a new patriarch seeking to establish his own sect. On the contrary, the tendency in the Thai tradition is for the *sangha* to seek to purify its rules and rituals by eliminating any developments which on careful examination do not seem to have the sanction of the Buddha's own teaching. Thai Buddhism, although its monkhood was for long divided into the *Arannavasi* and the *Gamavasi* schools which had emerged by the fourteenth century, has known nothing of the kind of sectarianism characteristic of Buddhism and the other non-Confucian religions of Viet-Nam. It has not even experienced the kind of disputes over orthodoxy which sometimes characterised the development of Buddhism in Burma.[6]

This desire for a single orthodoxy throughout the religion, moreover, explains to some extent the relationship between Buddhism in Thailand and in Ceylon. In the fourteenth and fifteenth centuries parties of monks went from South East Asia to Ceylon on a number of occasions, and returned with a more orthodox form of ordination or more reliable versions of the scriptures. But they did not do so because Ceylon was in any sense the fountain-head of spiritual authority: it was merely the place where at that time the religion was held to exist in its purest form. In the mid-eighteenth century, it was the Sinhalese monks who came to Ayuthya to obtain orthodox texts.[7] Thus the relationship of Thailand to Ceylon was quite different from that of the countries of Europe to the medieval papacy, which claimed a spiritual authority that transcended the temporal authority of kings.

The relevance of Buddhism to government in Thailand was not that it laid down precise rules which kings and lay officials must obey, but that it provided an overall framework of ideals within which everything must be done. Where the Vietnamese scholars would produce a detailed code of behaviour and would work out a pattern of government, Thai Buddhism manifested itself in the *Dhammathat* which was essentially a set of general principles. And where the Confucian scholars were active in administration, as well as in formulating royal decrees, the Theravada monks left matters of that kind to lay officials appointed by the king. There was no question of those lay officials having to pass examinations, either in Buddhism or in any other kind of philosophical tradition. It was merely demanded of them that they live as good Buddhists. The king himself was expected to fulfil Buddhist ideals as well, by his patronage of monks, and sometimes by himself becoming learned in the *dhamma* and by occasionally withdrawing to the *sangha*. Among Thai kings who achieved great reputations as Buddhists may be mentioned Lu Tai Dhammajara of Sukhothai (1347?–*c*. 1370) and Boromakot of Ayuthya (1733–58).

There was however one feature of Thai political life which does not quite fit into the picture so far suggested: that is, the influence of Hindu beliefs and rituals, which were very important at certain periods, notably in the seventeenth century. They can be traced to Khmer influence from Angkor (coming especially by way of Lopburi), and they manifested themselves in certain royal rituals and in the presence at Ayuthya of a small number of brahmins. The significance of Hinduism in these respects should not be underestimated, but on the other hand its strength or weakness at any period would seem to have been essentially a matter of royal preference. There is nothing to suggest that the Thai court—and still less the country at large—was ever disturbed by conflicts between Buddhism and Hinduism.

To sum up the religious aspect of the contrast between Thailand and Viet-Nam, we might say that it involved three principal differences. First, Vietnamese Confucianism was the religion and philosophy of an educated elite, and could not be anything else, whereas Theravada Buddhism was to a far greater extent a 'popular' religion. Second, Confucianism was the orthodoxy of an elite who had administrative functions as well as a religious role, whereas the Thai *sangha* stood completely outside government and court politics. Finally, whereas Theravada Buddhism embraced virtually the whole population, leaving little scope or need for other religions, Viet-Nam always had room for a number of non-Confucian sectarian religions and consequently presents a picture of great religious diversity. Although the various sects were on the whole tolerant towards one another, and certainly did not involve themselves in religious wars of a European kind, none of them was able to embrace more than a minority of the Vietnamese population.

These differences between Confucianism and Buddhism represent an important dimension in any explanation of the contrast between the two countries. They do not however amount to a complete explanation in themselves. Equally significant are the differences to be found when one looks at some of the fundamental institutions of the two societies at the 'grass-roots' level, that of the family and the village.

III

It is impossible to understand the Vietnamese tradition without reference to the central role played in it by the cult of ancestral spirits, in 'popular' and in 'court' religion alike. Confucianism, with its emphasis on filial piety, gave support to that cult; but it was not ultimately dependent on Confucian orthodoxy, and certainly was unaffected by the relative strength or weakness of the scholar elite at different periods. At the lower levels of society, in fact, one finds a significant Buddhist element in the ancestor cult and in funeral rites.[8]

The cult of ancestors in many ways corresponds more closely than Confucianism to the role of popular Buddhism in the Thai tradition. But whereas we find that Buddhism tends to draw the Thai together into a national community, dominated by a single monarchy and a single *sangha*,[9] the effect of the ancestor cult in Viet-Nam is quite the opposite. A man can choose to be Buddhist, and can accept a place in a Buddhist community of almost any size; he cannot choose his own ancestors or join anyone else's family at will. Consequently the kinship group or clan, which is the only possible religious community in the cult of ancestors, is bound to be exclusive and inward-looking. For the Vietnamese the clan is perhaps the most fundamental element of the social framework; anyone who belongs to his own kin-group is somehow on a different level from the rest of the community at large. This is undoubtedly a factor tending towards the fragmentation of Vietnamese society. There is of course no necessary conflict between loyalty to the clan and other loyalties or aspirations, and Confucian texts emphasise the need for harmony between all levels of piety. But in practice conflicts of loyalty were bound to arise in the context of political rivalry, and the clan usually counted for more than loyalty to the king. The importance of the clan is reflected also in the tendency for religious sects and secret associations to imitate kinship structures in their own hierarchies and patterns of mutual obligation. A Vietnamese Buddhist patriarch filled a role not entirely different from an ancestor in a clan, and a secret society was a sworn brotherhood in which the leader and followers had mutual obligations comparable to those between father and son.

A further aspect of the ancestral cult is significant in the present argument. It included the practice of inhumation (as against cremation), and attached great importance to the tomb as a family shrine. Whilst an ancestral tablet was in some circumstances movable from one place to another, the tomb could not be moved once established on a satisfactory site. Consequently every Vietnamese had (and has) an attachment to the home village and province where the tombs of his ancestors lay. This is perhaps the most important factor in what is usually referred to as 'regionalism' in Viet-Nam.

It would be wrong to suppose that a sense of ancestry does not figure at all in the Thai tradition, in the Sukhothai period at least there are references to royal ancestors, including a remarkable inscription of 1393 in which the ancestors of Sukhothai and Nan are named and called upon to witness a treaty between the two states.[10] But the cult of ancestors is not a regular part of Thai religious belief and practice, and the kin-group is not so important a social institution in Thailand. The practice of cremation, moreover, means that neither tomb nor attachment to an ancestral locality play a part in the pattern of Thai society. Only in relation to major centres which were once distant dependencies of Ayuthya or Bangkok—such as Chieng Mai or Nakorn Si Thammarat—does regional attachment count for a great deal amongst the Thai. Here too, the tendency is towards the evolution of a national community in which men's attentions are focussed upon national institutions.

In relation to the village too, the Vietnamese tendency is towards local separateness rather than towards national identity. One of the most important non-Chinese (and therefore 'South East Asian') features of traditional society in Viet-Nam is the cult of the local protective spirit, enshrined in the village temple or *dinh*. The belief that every locality has its own spirits and that each community has a special association with a certain spirit is common to both Thailand and Viet-Nam. Ram Kamheng's inscription refers to the great spirit Phra Khaphung, dwelling in the hill to the south and protecting the city if properly reverenced.[11] All the major Thai cities have, or had, *lak muang* shrines in honour of the local spirit of the town, and many villages have their *chao ban* and other spirit shrines. But in Viet-Nam this belief has become institutionalised and occupies a dominant place in the village structure.

The problem of the origins and significance of the *dinh* has exercised the minds of a number of historians and anthropologists, without anyone so far reaching a definitive conclusion about it.[12] The character and identity of the spirit who was (and is) honoured there might vary a great deal from one village to another. He was often a local hero, sometimes an ancestor and founder of the village; but the fact that the village community is known as the *xa* (Chinese *she*) suggests that he might also have originally embraced a local spirit of the soil. What is quite clear is that the cult of the village spirit lies completely outside the framework of either Confucian orthodoxy or the non-Confucian sects, as well as outside the cult of ancestors. It tends to bind the villagers together into a community that is religious as well as functional, and to separate them from their neighbours. In this respect, the *dinh*, rather than any local Buddhist or Taoist temple, serves as the same kind of focus for local community life as the Buddhist *wat* in Thailand. But whereas Thai Buddhism is united by a single spiritual focus, each Vietnamese village has its own cult. The insistence of Vietnamese kings that village spirits must be formally appointed, by royal edict, reflected a desire to bring all villages within a national framework. It has something in common with the policy of the Mon king Dhammaceti, in fifteenth century Pegu, who used the cult of the *dewatau sotapan* as a means of drawing together the provinces and localities of his kingdom.[13] But in the end the Vietnamese *xa* retained a great deal of independence from the king and his officials: one more feature making for the strength of local loyalties as against loyalty to king and country.

The religious aspect of the Vietnamese village can be related to its position within the system of government. Each village had its own council, its own taxation register and its own communal land. These features all derived ultimately from the fact that it was the village, rather than the individual or a personal patron, who was responsible for the fulfilment of the ordinary people's obligations to the state. The obligations were partly personal, in that each family had to provide an appropriate number of able-bodied men for royal service when required, and partly in the form of taxation of land. Before the eighteenth century, the only land which contributed produce or taxes to the king was the *cong-dien*, or communal riceland. This was supposed to exist in each village, and was held in common by the community as a whole. Successive kings laid down regulations about its inalienability and about its regular repartition amongst the inhabitants of the *xa*, although in practice probably each locality had its own customs. The need for this material property of the village to be managed by a council of notables made the Vietnamese *xa* a far more elaborately formal community than was the Thai *ban*.

In the traditional Thai system of government, responsibility for the performance of services lay with the *nai*, whose role was that of a patron of men rather than a territorial lord. The village community was clearly very important indeed, although the relationship between the hierarchy of patrons (*nai*) and the *phu-yai-ban* has not yet been fully explained. But there was no Thai equivalent to either the *dinh* or the *cong-dien*, and the Thai village has probably never had quite the same sense of corporate independence as one finds in Viet-Nam.

IV

In the light of these various differences between the social institutions and cultures of Thailand and Viet-Nam in the centuries before about 1850, it is possible to make some attempt to answer the question about political stability and instability with which we began. Actual political events in both countries must be examined in terms of the nature of court conflict and of the relationship between the court and bureaucracy and the country at large. Both countries experienced conflicts within ruling circles, in almost every generation; but in Viet-Nam these conflicts showed a regular tendency to become territorialised, whereas in Thailand they were usually kept within the confines of the capital.

Two situations from the history of Viet-Nam will serve to illustrate the ways in which this territorialisation of conflict could take place. Perhaps the first occasion on which we can observe the development of a court conflict in that direction occurred in 1369.[14] During the Tran period, down to 1357, the kings had made a habit of abdicating in the prime of life in order to ensure that by the time they died their sons would be securely established on the throne; the abdicated king was known as the *thoung-hoang* and in that capacity was usually able to continue to direct the affairs of the realm. But in 1357 the *thoung-hoang* died whilst his son, the king, was still not yet powerful enough to abdicate in his turn. In 1369, still having failed to abdicate, that king (Tran Du-Tong) died; moreover, he left no son of his own, and a succession conflict was almost inevitable. Shortly before his death he nominated as his successor the illegitimate son of a Tran prince, known as Nhat-Le; he was illegitimate because his mother, Duong Khuong, was a court actress. This nomination meant that two other princes were passed over: Trac and Phu, who were the sons of the former king Tran Minh-Tong by his marriage to a woman of the Le clan of Thanh-Hoa province. Nhat-Le, on taking the throne, gave these two princes high positions, but inevitably they plotted against him. One of them was killed as a result of a plot in 1370. Thereupon prince Phu and his sister withdrew to Thanh-Hoa province, raised an army, and marched on the capital. Nhat-Le was deposed, and Phu became king as Tran Nghe-Tong.

The most interesting feature of this conflict is that it involved rivalry between the sons of two mothers who came from outside the imperial clan. The Tran had earlier managed to keep the succession within their own clan, by allowing only Tran princesses to take positions as consorts of kings and high-ranking princes. But now the pattern of court conflict included the relatives and factions of outsider-clans: the Le of Thanh-Hoa and the followers of Duong Khuong. One of these clans had territorial links—understandable in view of what has been said above— and used them in order to force its will upon the capital. But although Tran Phu gained the throne, he had to allow some of the former Tran power to pass to the Le clan. His mother's nephew, Le Quy Ly, became head of the *khu-mat-vien* in 1371: the first step in a slow rise to power which culminated in 1400 in his seizure of the throne. His emergence was complicated, perhaps facilitated, by the sequel to the events of 1369–71. The mother of Nhat-Le, the actress Duong Khuong, fled to the court of the Cham king Che Bong Nga under whom Champa was stronger than at any time in the previous century. The result was that Cham forces attacked the Vietnamese kingdom, and sacked its capital on three occasions between 1371 and 1383. It was in the conflict with Champa that Le Quy Ly was able to prove his superiority over any possible rival for power, and by the 1390s he was master of the kingdom.

The events of the second half of the fourteenth century had the effect of giving Viet-Nam two political centres of gravity in place of one. Thanh-Hao was a region to be reckoned with in all subsequent periods, and indeed it was a native of that province (Le Loi) who drove out the Chinese army of occupation from Tongking in 1427 and founded the Le dynasty. Professor Whitmore has shown how the subsequent conflict between the clansmen of Thanh-Hoa and the scholars of Tongking dominated the politics of the Le dynasty until it was settled by Le Thanh-Tong—largely in favour of the scholars—after 1460, But a second period of political turmoil came in the first half of the sixteenth century, beginning with the death of Le Hien-Tong in 1504.[15] The reign of his effective successor Le Uy-Muc (1505–9) was dominated by two clans from Tongking who had married into the royal family, and had forced out the Thanh-Hoa faction. In 1509–10 they, together with Uy-Muc, were overthrown by the prince Le Oanh after he had raised an army in Thanh-Hoa. The parallell with events in 1370 is striking. Here too, the effect was to permit the rise to power of two Thanh-Hoa clans outside the Le family: those of the Nguyen and the Trinh. But on this occasion the Thanh-Hoa men were not able to prevent further opposition in Tongking. A rebellion in Tongking led by the priest-pretender Tran Cao developed into a serious threat to the capital in 1516. The Trinh and the Nguyen, after successive (and abortive) attempts to place their own Le nominees on the throne, had to unite in the face of the rebellion. Tran Cao briefly seized Hanoi and made himself king, but was soon driven out by his opponents. The situation during the next few years was one of growing chaos, in which no single faction was powerful enough to dominate the capital or the country. Eventually, as in the 1370s, one strong man emerged: the Tongkingese general Mac Dang Dung, and in 1527 he followed the example of Le Quy Ly by seizing the throne for himself. But where Le Quy Ly failed to reckon with the Chinese, Mac Dang Dung found himself insufficiently powerful to deal with the Thanh-Hoa clans. During the 1530s the latter were able to 'restore' the Le dynasty in Thanh-Hoa province; and in 1541 the Chinese—to whom they had appealed—virtually permitted the division of the kingdom into two parts. That division continued until the complete 'restoration' of the Le in 1592, only to be followed almost immediately by the division of North and Centre between the Trinh and the Nguyen *chua*.

It is unfortunate that we lack the kind of historical evidence that would make it possible to explore the social roots of these various conflicts. We cannot reconstruct the actual process by which prince Phu and his followers in 1370, or prince Le Oanh and the Trinh-Nguyen in 1509, were able to raise armies to march on Hanoi. But it is clear that the king in his capital was helpless to prevent such events from happening, and in general terms it is reasonable to suggest that part of the explanation lies in the factors making for local independence which were discussed earlier on.

What is very noticeable is that between the Tran period and the seventeenth century there occurred a remarkable decline in the effective power and political importance of the monarchy in Viet-Nam. By keeping royal marriages within the clan, and by adopting the *thuong-hoang* policy of regular abdication, the Tran had been able to ensure that power rested with themselves They encouraged some development of Confucianism, but were more deeply imbued with Buddhism, and indeed one *thuong-hoang* retired to a monastery and became a patriarch of the sect known as the Truc-Lam ('Bamboo Forest'). Above all, they kept control over the country, although probably more loosely than in the kind of control achieved for a while under Le Thanh-tong. With the decline of the Tran, beginning in 1369, monarchical supremacy also began to decline. From the fifteenth century onwards, kings of the stature of a Le Thanh-Tong or a Minh-Mang were rare: that is, strong kings who had inherited rather than merely seized the throne. Power lay more often than not with military leaders and their clans, or sometimes with scholar-officials. In either case, the power of those who dominated the court rested on something other than the mystique of monarchy. From 1592 until 1789, the Le monarchy had hardly any political role at all: like the emperor of Japan before 1868, he did no more than perform the ritual acts upon which the cosmological stability of the kingdom was deemed to depend.

Events in Viet-Nam during the first half of the sixteenth century might significantly be compared with those in Thailand between 1546 and and 1569. There too a succession conflict occurred in which the court was divided, following the death of king Phrachai in 1546. His son, Keo Fa, was a child at his accession, and effective power lay with his widow Si Suda Chan. A crisis developed in 1548 when her new husband, known as Worawongse, deposed Keo Fa and seized the throne for himself. This kind of usurpation of the throne by a commoner was to occur again in the history of Ayuthya, and was quickly successful in 1630 and 1688. But on this occasion it did not succeed. The new king was himself deposed by a court revolt in 1549, and replaced by prince Thienraja (king Mahachakrapat), the younger brother of Phrachai. But that was not all. A key role in the restoration of 1549 was played by a young prince of the house of Sukhothai (Khun Phiren), who married the daughter of Mahachakrapat. The eventual effect of this marriage was to unite the ruling houses of Sukhothai and Ayuthya, and to place a Sukhothai prince on the throne of Ayuthya. But this did not happen without the intervention of an external force. In the conflict which developed between Pegu and Sukhothai during the 1560s, Khun Phiren took the side of Bayinnaung whilst the sons of Mahachakraphat were strongly opposed to Pegu. It was the Burmese forces which eventually made Khun Phiren king at Ayuthya in 1569, where he revived the Sukhothai title of Mahadhammaraja. However, the Burmese domination of the country was less important in the long term than this unification of two kingdoms which had previously been less closely integrated, and had once been completely separate entities. Thus where the events of 1505–41 in Viet-Nam led to a political division of the country, those of 1546–69 in Thailand resulted in a greater degree of unity, which was used to recover full independence from Pegu by 1592.

The unification of Ayuthya and Sukhothai in the sixteenth century was the culmination of events that had begun in the 1370s, about the same time as the first major intervention of Thanh-Hoa clans in the politics of Dai-Viet. If one looks back to that period of Thai history, one can see a pattern of political relationships which can be regarded as a protype for Thai evolution in much the same way as the conflict of 1369–70 was a prototype for subsequent developments in Viet-Nam. Fourteenth century Thailand—that is, the area which is now Central and northern Thailand— was a land of small kingdoms in perpetual conflict and alliance with one another, within an institutional framework which owed something at least to the influence of the Khmer. Each had the ambition to dominate its neighbours, but not necessarily to absorb them into its own centralised administrative system. The pattern that emerged was one in which a small number of states established positions of supremacy and made their neighbours into dependencies, rather than into directly administered provinces. Thus the tendency was for previously independent entities to be gradually coalesced into larger systems, but without too great an insistence upon centralised control. The irony is that whereas in Viet-Nam unity tended to precede fragmentation as a result of territorialised conflict, in Thailand it was the other way round: a fragmented political pattern gradually became the basis for stable unity and growing centralisation. In this respect, one might well regard the so-called 'modernisation' of the Thai state undertaken since about 1890 as no more than the logical next stage in an evolution which stretches back to the fourteenth century and perhaps farther.

At all periods, it is noticeable that Thai cities have tended to dominate the countryside; allowing for changes in scale over the centuries, this is just as true of Sukhothai and early Ayuthya as of later Ayuthya and Bangkok. When the Burmese attacked Ayuthya in 1563–4, in 1569, and in the 1760s, they were able to concentrate on taking the cities, knowing that the country would then be theirs. Conversely, it was only necessary for Phya Taksin to establish an effective new capital at Dhonburi, and the country was soon willing to accept his power and control. In Viet-Nam, almost the exact opposite has been the case. To hold a city alone in Vietnamese history has not given anyone control of the country. Time and again, in 1285, in the early fifteenth century, and in 1788, Hanoi fell to the Chinese: but they were quite unable to follow up that success by establishing permanent and effective control over the whole country. In the war of 1946–54, the French learned that the same is true in the twentieth century. Viet-Nam is a country where what matters politically is the countryside. Men have tended always to be attached to the clans and to their villages. Only the Confucian scholar-elite ever looked primarily to the court and to the towns, and as we have seen they were the dominant element in Vietnamese history only during certain limited periods. Their power, and the influence of their orthodoxy, was always bounded by a society in which the ancestors and the land mattered more than theories of harmony and virtue.

In the twentieth century, quite apart from the effects of the 'impact of the West' on the countries of South East Asia, there are fundamental changes taking place in both Thai and Vietnamese society. Much that is traditional has been swept away, and more will go yet. New styles of government, new patterns of economic life, are gaining ground. Even so, it may well be the case that in the longer perspective of history, the social and political contrasts which have been briefly touched upon in this paper will turn out to have a continuing importance and to make for new contrasts in the future.

Notes

1 A notable example is A.B. Woodside: *Vietnam and the Chinese Model, a Comparative Study of Nguyen and Ch'ing Civil Government in the first half of the nineteenth century* (Harvard, 1971).

2 The process by which Confucianism attained this position of predominance in the Vietnamese system of government during the fifteenth century has been analysed by J.K. Whitmore: *The Development of Le Government in Fifteenth Century Viet-Nam* (Ph.D. thesis, Cornell University, 1968).

3 *Dai-Viet Lich-Trieu Dang Khoa Luc* (Saigon, 1963), passim; cf. R.B. Smith: 'The Cycle of Confucianisation in Viet-Nam', to be published by the University of Hawaii.

4 See Tran Van Giap: 'Le Bouddhisme en Annam des Origines au XIIIe Siecle', *BEFEO*, xxxii (1932), pp. 264–66.

5 Cf. R.B. Smith: 'Introduction to Caodaism', *Bulletin of the School of Oriental and African Studies*, xxxiii (1970).

6 Cf. N,R, Ray: *Introduction to Theravada Buddhism in Burma* (Calcutta, 1946).

7 S. Paranavitana: 'Religious Intercourse between Ceylon and Siam in the thirteenth to fifteenth centuries', *Journal of Ceylon Branch, Royal Asiatic Society*, xxxii.

8 This is indicated by G. Dumontier: *Le Rituel Funeraire des Annamites* (Hanoi, 1904).

9 This generalisation is not seriously affected by the growth of a second order within the monkhood, the Dhammayutikanikaya, during the nineteenth century.

10 A.B. Griswold and Prasoet na Nagara: 'The Pact between Sukhodaya and Nan: Epigraphical and Historical Studies, no. 3', *JSS*, lvii, pt. 1 (January, 1969), pp. 80 ff.

11 G. Coedes: *Recueil des Inscriptions du Siam: i, Inscriptions de Sukhodaya* (Bangkok, 1924).

12 E.g. Nguyen Van Khoan: *Essai sur le Dinh et le Culte du Genie*, Tutelaire des Villages au Tonkin', *BEFEO*, xxx (1930); Le Van Hao: 'Introduction a l'Ethnologie du Dinh', *Bulletin de la Soc. des Etudes Indochinoises*, n.s., xxxvii (1962).

13 H.L. Shorto: 'The *dewatan sotapan*, a Mon Prototype of the 37 Nats', *Bulletin of the School of Oriental and African Studies*, xxx (1967).

14 The account of the events which follow is based on *Dai-Viet Su Ky Toan Thu*, vol ii (Hanoi, 1967).

15 This account is based on Phan Huy Le: *Lich Su Che Do Phong Kien Viet-Nam*, ii (Hanoi, 1962).

4 The cycle of Confucianization in Vietnam

Source: Walter P. Vella (ed.), *Aspects of Vietnamese History* (Honolulu: The University Press of Hawaii, 1973), pp. 1–29.

Part I

Vietnam has, more than once, been called a crossroads of civilization. Quite apart from its encounter with the civilization of the West, which began in the seventeenth century, it lay between two very different cultural worlds – on the one hand, that of China, to whose emperor Vietnamese rulers paid regular tribute for centuries until 1883; and, on the other hand, that of Southeast Asia, with which it is increasingly associated by Western scholars. The relationship to Southeast Asia is more than artificial. Linguistically, Vietnamese is related to Khmer and Thai at least as closely as to Chinese, and some of Vietnam's institutions, notably the village *đình*, have close affinities with those of the hill peoples of the "Annamite Chain," whom ethnographers regard as Indonesian. Moreover, the southern part of the country was only drawn into the Sino-Vietnamese cultural sphere in the seventeenth century – that is, just as recently as the period in which Vietnam first came into contact with the West. Nevertheless, in terms of literate civilization, the Vietnamese belong to the area in which Chinese was the dominant classical language, and even their vernacular language was first written in characters based on Chinese principles. This was because the northern part of the country was a province of China from the second century BC till the tenth century AD and for the next thousand years was occupied by a state which maintained political independence of China (apart from the payment of tribute), but which continued to draw its cultural inspiration from the Middle Kingdom.

It is with one aspect of this cultural inspiration that the present paper is concerned. But at the outset it must be remarked that *Chinese inspiration* and *Confucianism* are not necessarily synonymous terms which can always be substituted for one another. For one thing, Vietnam also acquired Buddhism from China, although at an early stage in the eastward spread of that religion, Vietnam probably played its own part in the development of Chinese Buddhism. It should also be remembered that in China, itself, Confucianism developed over the centuries and was not always so dominant as it was under the dynasties of Ming and Ch'ing. It would be a serious error for the historian of Vietnam, while being conscious of Chinese influence, to take China too much for granted or to assume that China itself was an unchanging model for Vietnam to imitate.

Chinese historiography has by now completely escaped from the notion of the "cycle of Cathay," and Vietnamese historiography must take that into account. When one comes to speak of "Confucianization" in Vietnam, one must remember that it was a process which China also went through, and not necessarily at a very much earlier period.

But what is meant if one says that Vietnam by the mid-nineteenth century, at the latest, was a Confucian state or, perhaps more correctly, a Neo-Confucian state? The answer to this question must, of course, lie partly in the definition of Confucianism (or Neo-Confucianism). There is not space in the present paper to attempt such a definition, nor is it necessary, since one can refer to several works in English which deal with the subject at length.[1] In brief, it can be stated that Confucianism was an aspiration to have order obtain at all levels of society; to ensure that the individual, the family, and the state were in harmony with Heaven and Earth and the Five Agents of the universe. Without going into detail, one can observe, therefore, that a Confucian state was one in which the government sought, by edicts and decrees, to ensure that everyone observed the requirements of propriety (*li*). We have here, thus, one practical measure or indicator of the Confucian state: when Vietnamese rulers were insisting on propriety, Confucianism was probably strong; when Confucianism was weak, propriety would have mattered less. Another indicator, given the nature of Chinese historical writing, might be the occasions on which Vietnamese rulers ordered the compilation of historical records; for historical writing was very often another way in which attention was drawn to the virtues and failings of mankind, judged by Confucian standards.

These indicators alone, however, are not enough as a guide to the Confucianization of Vietnam. Whether a state followed Confucian principles or not depended not only on the content of Confucianism itself, but also on the character of its rulers. It would be quite wrong to see the Confucian state as one in which every single individual had been converted to Confucianism in the way that medieval Western states were converted to Christianity and might then be called Christian states. The Confucian state, rather, was one in which life was regulated and political decisions made by an elite of scholars, recruited through examinations based on the Confucian classics. And it is the presence or absence, and the relative power, of Confucian scholars that must be taken as the principal indicator of Confucianization. It is because there were some periods when such scholars were powerful, and other periods when they were not, that it is possible to speak of a cycle of Confucianization in Vietnam. Nor should one think of monarchy as being specifically Confucian, although it was only through the monarch that scholars could control the country. There were elements of Taoism in the religious function of monarchy, which Confucians may have disapproved of, but which they were unable to remove. Monarchy was the keystone of traditional government both in China and in South-east Asia; what the Confucian scholars had to do, if they were to ensure that the country was ruled according to their principles, was to capture the throne. The alternative was that it would be captured by some other kind of elite. Thus, Confucianization must be seen also in terms of political struggle between the scholars and other political groups, such as the army or the adepts of some religious sect. Having said all this in general terms, let us now consider the history of Confucianization in Vietnam between the eleventh and nineteenth centuries.

Part II

The key to the development of an elite of scholar-officials was the examination system. In China, the first origins of this institution may be found under the Former Han dynasty, but its continuous history began under the Sui dynasty, around AD 600 By the later Sung period (say, the eleventh and twelfth centuries), when Đại-Việt first became established as an independent state, the examination system was an essential part of the Chinese governmental framework, with the *chin-shih* degree being the highest qualification for official status. But it was not until the early Ming period that the examinations finally superseded all other roads to bureaucratic appointment and the expansion of education made the Confucian classics the basis of an all-embracing orthodoxy.[2]

In Vietnam, the first reference to an examination occurs in the *Đại-Việt Sử-Ký Toàn-Thư* under the year 1075; a second reference occurs under 1086. But, while these references do seem to indicate the practice of choosing scholars by examination in the capital and the existence of a Hàn-Lâm-Viện (Han Lin Academy) by the latter date, they cannot be taken as evidence of a regular triennial examination system. The third reference comes about a century later, in 1185, when we learn from the same source that thirty men were chosen by examination to be allowed to study in the capital.[3] After that, we have to wait until 1232, when the chronicle mentions the names of five laureates, in an examination which is not in any way stated to be an innovation of that year.[4] This was the first of seven examinations in the first half of the Trần period, given between the years 1232 and 1304, in which an increasing number of laureates (including the five mentioned above) appear.[5] Thus, one can say that, by the Trần period (corresponding to the later years of the Southern Sung in China), an examination system was established in Vietnam. It is clear, too, that some of the laureates later rose to high positions in the state, although we have no means of knowing what their social origins were, and therefore how much they owed to education and how much to birth. But there can be no doubt that during the thirteenth and fourteenth centuries the dominant position in Vietnamese society and government belonged to the imperial clan and its relatives, and not to any group of people chosen by examination.

Under the Trần dynasty, until at least 1320, the imperial clan succeeded in guaranteeing peaceful successions by a system of abdication of emperors, which meant that power usually lay with the emperor's father, as *thượng-hoàng* ('the emperor above'); and there is no example from that period of an emperor's allowing a female member of any other clan to gain power for her relatives by becoming queen. In the thirteenth century, the dominant positions belonged quite clearly to the Trần princes bearing noble titles such as *đại-vương* and *vương*, with descent in rank at each generation. In this period, laureates from examinations would have little chance to become powerful figures, and, so far as one can see, none did. Đại-Việt was much more monarchical (and also Buddhist) than Confucian. Even in the fourteenth century, the way in which the Trần monopoly of power broke down was through the rise of another clan (the Lê of Thanh-Hóa, forerunners of Lê Quý Ly), which at last succeeded in placing a female member on the queen's throne and so was able eventually to claim blood relationship to the emperor. In 1369 Đại-Việt experienced its first succession crisis, in which two princes vied for the throne with the support of conflicting court factions. The previous emperor's nominee was overthrown by an army from the province of Thanh-Hóa which was led by Trần princes, but which relied on the support of the Lê clan. Thereupon, the mother of the defeated candidate fled to Champa and was able to secure a Cham attack on Hanoi in 1374.[6] During the war with Champa that followed, the leader who emerged in Đại-Việt was Lê Quý Ly, who was powerful enough by the end of the century to seize the throne for his own family, inaugurating the short-lived Hồ dynasty. In the Trần period Đại-Việt was thus in no sense a Confucian state: Buddhism still flourished, and, although it was Chinese (Mahayana) Buddhism, the Vietnamese monarchy was not at this period fundamentally different from, say, the Buddhist monarchy of the Mon-Thai state, of which Ayutthaya became the capital in 1350. Indeed, the latter experienced a succession crisis of its own in 1369 which was remarkably similar to that of Đại-Việt's in the same year. It was with the growth of Theravada Buddhism in Siam and Confucianization in Vietnam (only just beginning in the fourteenth century) that the sharp cultural contrast between the two areas in modern times began to take shape.

To return to the examinations, in 1374 (five years after the triumph of the Ming in China) we find reference to a Vietnamese examination in which it is stated that the custom was for thirty laureates to be chosen every seven years, though only three are named.[7] We have no means of knowing whether this represents an actual innovation, but certainly there were further examinations in 1384, 1393, 1400, and 1405 – not precisely at seven-year intervals, but, nevertheless, the largest number of examinations so far within a thirty-year period.[8] It is probably from this time that we can date the continuous history of the Vietnamese examination system. But, as we shall see, that history was by no means smooth throughout the centuries which followed.

It was in the fifteenth century that Confucian scholarship began to dominate the Vietnamese polity. Probably the Ming occupation of the greater part of the country between 1407 and 1427 played some part in this. For those twenty years, Vietnam was again a Chinese province, and during that time it sent 161 "tribute students" to the Chinese capital to study for the examinations.[9] To judge from the location of the schools founded by the Ming administration, probably most of the students were from Tongking. In that area, but not farther south, the Ming period saw a deepening of Confucian culture.

But it was not the Confucian-educated scholars who drove the Chinese out of Đại-Việt; it was the growing body of followers of Lê Lợi, whose leaders eventually emerged as a military elite with its roots in the province of Thanh-Hóa. The success of Lê Lợi meant an interruption of the rise of the scholar-officials: the politics of Đại-Việt in the period between 1428 and 1460 revolved around a conflict between "counselors" (*đại-thần*), who were mainly military men from Thanh-Hóa, and "scholar – officials" (*quan*). This conflict has been studied in great detail by Dr. J. K. Whitmore and therefore need not be described in detail here.[10] What is important in the present context is that later, during the first decade of his reign, Lê Thánh-Tông (1460–97) was able to achieve a new political stability in his kingdom, within which, for the first time, political and administrative power came into the hands of the scholar-officials. It is probably a mistake to see this as the work of the emperor, alone; rather, it was the result of a situation in which an emperor who had been educated by Confucian scholars was placed on the throne by an alliance between a military court faction and the leading scholars. Such, at least, would appear to have been the nature of the *xuống-nghĩa* coup of 1460. By 1470 the scholars were firmly in the saddle. They reformed the structure of government in such a way as to give primacy to the "six boards" and to the Hàn-Lâm Academy, from which they were staffed. They insisted on a more serious observation of customary rites, including proper mourning periods and sacrifices to the cult of Confucius; and they limited the number of Buddhist temples. Above all, in 1463 they introduced regular triennial examinations, in which *tiên-sĩ* (*chin-shih*) laureates were selected to fill the growing number of administrative positions made necessary by other reforms. Between 1463 and 1514 there was no break in the triennial pattern, and in those eighteen examinations as many as eight hundred sixteen laureates were selected.

The spirit of that court is reflected also in the literary history of the country. The emperor established a literary group at court, the Tao-Đàn, whose poetry still survives in both Vietnamese and Chinese, and the Hồng-Đức reign (1470–97) is regarded as the Golden Age of Confucian scholarship in Vietnam. Among its products may be mentioned the encyclopedic collection finished in 1483, the *Thiên-Nam Dư' Hạ Tập*, and the *Đại-Việt Sử-Ký Toàn-Thư'*, a history of Vietnam by Ngô Sĩ Liên, which was commissioned in 1479. The latter, significantly, includes commentaries by Ngô Sĩ Liên on chronicles of earlier periods which reveal a strong Confucian concern that things were not done properly under the Ly and Trần dynasties.

All this, however, cannot be presented as the final establishment of Confucianism as the unifying orthodoxy of Vietnam. Had that been the case, the title of the present paper would be meaningless. In fact, the Confucianization of the fifteenth century was all but undone by the end of the sixteenth. Two factors combined to produce this result – the tendency toward clan conflict which was inherent in the Vietnamese tradition and the gradual expansion of Vietnamese settlement, which meant that there was always a frontier area where Confucian scholarship was not firmly established. Dr. Whitmore's analysis of the conflicts of the period between 1428 and 1460 has shown that it was the military men of Thanh-Hóa who were most unwilling to see power fall into the hands of the scholar-officials of the Tongking Delta. Thanh-Hóa was a province which had relatively recently come under extensive Vietnamese settlement; when the scholars finally had their way, in the 1460s, it is significant that in the first examination (in 1463) only five of forty-four laureates came from Thanh-Hóa, the rest being from the four provinces of the Tongking.[11] Presumably, during the course of the reign of Lê Thánh-Tông, Confucianism became stronger in the South, but it is unlikely that the contrast between the two areas was completely eliminated.

The tendency toward clan conflict came to the fore in the early sixteenth century. By the year 1509, there were two parties contending for power at Hanoi, one with its roots in Tongking, and the other associated with Thanh-Hóa; each had female members who were imperial wives or widows. In 1509 the throne was seized by a Lê prince whose support lay in Thanh-Hóa, and the Tongking party was driven from power. But, then, in 1516 there was a major rebellion in Tongking, when the throne was briefly seized by Trần Cao (who claimed descent from the Trần emperors). He was driven out in a matter of days, but in the conflicts which followed, a number of clans emerged as centers of power, including the Trịnh and the Nguyễn, with their roots in Thanh-Hóa, and the Mạc, whose power-base was in Tongking.[12] Yet, despite the fact that none of these clans was involved in scholarship, the examination system did not completely break down. The examination due to have been held in 1517 was postponed till the following year; but a further one was held in 1518, and thereafter the triennial pattern was resumed. Nor did the system break down in 1527, when the Mạc finally seized the throne and deposed the Lê ruler. The triennial examinations continued in Tongking throughout the Mạc period (1527–92), with the sole exception of the year 1559, when there was an attack on the capital from the South. The number of laureates was smaller, and quite probably they held less power than in the Hồng-Đức period; but they were by no means eliminated.

However, the Mạc did not succeed in controlling the whole of Đại-Việt. In 1534 the Lê emperor was restored in Thanh-Hóa by the two powerful clans of that area, the Nguyễn and the Trịnh, and from then till 1592 there were two rival monarchs in Đại-Việt. The one in the South was much less Confucian. The Lê court did, in fact, hold eight examinations between 1554 and 1592, but they received, at the most, only sixty-five laureates throughout that period, compared with the two hundred twenty who succeeded in the twelve examinations held by the Mạc during that time. It is not surprising that when the Mạc were finally driven from Hanoi by the armies of the Lê-Trịnh-Nguyễn party in 1592, the examination system ceased to be an important element in the system of Vietnamese government for a time. But it did not, even then, go out of existence altogether. Triennial examinations were held at Hanoi through most of the seventeenth century, but in the forty years from 1595 to 1634 there were only ninety-three laureates – fewer than seven per examination, compared with an average of forty-five per examination between 1463 and 1514. The pattern is indicated more clearly in Table 1.

The declining importance of the examinations in the first half of the seventeenth century coincides with other indicators of the relative unimportance of Confucianism. For one thing, it was a remarkably thin period in literary history. Hardly any important authors were writing at that time, either in Vietnamese (*chữ nôm*) or in Chinese. Secondly, it was a period of renewed Buddhist activity, which may

Table 1 Examination laureates (*Tiến-Sĩ*), 1463–1691

	Number of examinations	Number of laureates	Average number of laureates per examination
1463–1514	18	816	45
1518–53	13	330	25
1556–92 (Mạc only)	12	220	18–19
1595–1634	13	93	7
1637–91	19	270	14

Source: Đại-Việt Lịch-Triều Đăng-Khoa-Lục (Saïgon, 1963).

or may not be coincidental. Clearly, Buddhism had not completely died out in Vietnam as a result of the decree of 1461 which had sought to limit its expansion. But it seems to have received very little encouragement from the court during the succeeding century and a half. When the writer Trần Văn Giáp searched the *Cương-Mục* chronicle for references to Buddhism, he found only one between 1465 and the early seventeenth century, and that related to the repair of a pagoda in 1498.[13] But in the early decades of the seventeenth century we once again find references to new sects and to the arrival of Buddhist monks from China. Trịnh Tráng, virtual ruler of northern Vietnam between 1623 and 1657, seems to have been a patron of Buddhism, and the empress of Lê Thần-Tông (1619–43) was converted to that religion by a Chinese monk in the 1630s. The same trend is noticeable in the southern part of the country (what is now Central Vietnam), where the Nguyễn clan established virtually an independent state after 1600. The Nguyễn ruler Hiền-Vương, who reigned from 1648 to 1687, was a notable Buddhist, and gave protection to a number of monks who fled from China after the fall of the Ming.[14] In both areas, the importance of Buddhism continued into the eighteenth century.

The figures in Table 1 suggest a slight recovery of Confucianism during the latter part of the seventeenth century, at least in the northern half of the country. The reason for this is by no means clear, for, as yet, the politics of the seventeenth century have not been studied in the detail with which Dr. Whitmore has explored those of the fifteenth. There was a marked revival from 1659, and in the examinations between then and 1691 there were only three occasions when the total did not reach ten or more – in 1670, it reached 31. This revival, moreover, coincided with other events during the rule of Trịnh Tạc (1657–82). In 1662 he published "Instructions for the Reform of Customs," a severely Confucian proclamation which was critical of both Buddhism and Christianity and which was followed by an active persecution of Christians.[15] The following year, Phạm Công Trứ and other scholars were commissioned to revise and extend the *Đại-Việt Sử-Ký Toàn-Thư* (which was finished by 1665, though not published till 1697). And in 1664 the same official came forward with proposals for the reform of taxation. One has the impression of a new spirit in government and scholarship, though not of the same vigor as that seen under Lê Thánh-Tông.

With the eighteenth century, we come to a period for which no examination figures are readily available, but in which there is other evidence of periodic conflict between Confucian scholars and their non-Confucian enemies. During the 1720s there are indications of a new, more rigorous approach to the country's growing financial problems, in which the lead would seem to have been taken by a *Tongkingese* official. It is even possible that the officials were able to gain in power at the expense of the Trịnh clan. But in 1731 and 1732 a new Trịnh ruler, Trịnh Giang (1729–40), reasserted his family's power by having the Lê emperor put to death, and the attempted reforms were abandoned.[16] What is remarkable is that after his coup there was a period in which Buddhism flourished and Confucianism did not: In 1734, Trịnh Giang forbade the importation of Confucian texts from China, but shortly afterwards sent a mission to obtain Buddhist texts. Three years later he forced the court to make donations for a large image of Buddha for an important pagoda. Although the examinations probably went on, it was at this period that offices were first sold for cash in Vietnam. It is hardly surprising that in 1738 there was a revolt in Tongking aimed at a Lê restoration, which led to a prolonged period of rebellion in certain areas. It is to be hoped that in due course these events will become the subject of detailed study, for the period presents a fascinating opportunity to look at traditional Vietnamese politics in action. Far less information is available concerning the internal development of what is now Central Vietnam during the seventeenth and eighteenth centuries, when it was under the rule of the Nguyễn clan and virtually independent of Hanoi. We know that reorganizations of the country occurred in 1702 and 1744, but their precise character is obscure. However, it seems very unlikely that Confucianism was dominant in the Nguyễn provinces at that time.

One fact about the eighteenth century is very clear, however: whatever degree of Confucianization had been achieved by about 1770, either in the North or in the South, was totally disrupted by the events which followed the Tây-Sơn rebellion of 1774. By 1790, none of the three centers of government in Vietnam was strongly Confucian: Hanoi, under the Tây-Sơn emperor Quang-Trung (who also built a new capital in Nghệ-An province); Qui-Nhơn, under his brother, who was ruling as Thái-Đức; or Saigon, where the last survivor of the Nguyễn clan had just reestablished himself. Quang-Trung is noted for his decision to make *chữ nôm* (Vietnamese) the language of administration instead of Chinese – which does not suggest any strong attachment to the Confucian classics – while Nguyễn Ánh depended a great deal on the support of a group of French mercenaries raised for him by the Catholic missionary Pigneau de Behaine. It was Nguyễn Ánh who unified Vietnam in 1802 and ruled over it until 1820 with the reign-title Gia-Long. Even with the return of peace, therefore, and in spite of a revival of local and provincial examinations in 1807, there was no sudden return to Confucian orthodoxy.

This came with the death of Gia-Long and the accession of his son Minh-Mạng, who, like Lê Thánh-Tông, had been educated by Confucian scholars. Dr. A. B. Woodside has drawn attention to the completely different characters of Minh-Mạng's reign and that of his predecessor.[17] Indeed, the years from 1820 to 1847 (under Minh-Mạng and Thiệu-Trị) saw a pattern of Confucianization not at all unlike that of the period from 1460 to 1497. The examination system was revived (see Table 2), and the number of laureates increased from decade to decade. The machinery of government was overhauled, with a key role being played by the Nội-Các (Grand Secretariat), closely linked to the Hàn-Lâm Academy.[18] A new historical office was established, which produced the Veritable Records (*thực-lục*) of the dynasty and later the *Khâm-Định Việt-Sử Thông-Giám Cưởng-Mục*, which summarized Vietnamese history down to 1789. Moreover, as time went on, it is clear from the records of examination successes that by the middle of the century Confucian education was establishing itself in the provinces of Central Vietnam, and even beginning to count for something in the Far South.

Two other indications of the growth of Confucian orthodoxy under Minh-Mạng and his successors may be cited. The first is reflected in a series of measures taken with regard to the land system of Bình Định province in 1839.[19] Their purpose was to try to increase the amount of communal land possessed by each village and reduce the extent of privately owned land. The insistence that each village should have its communal land, which until 1724 was the only kind of land subject to land tax, was a peculiarly Vietnamese feature of the social system. Its origins are still somewhat obscure, but it does not appear to have derived from any Chinese example. Nevertheless, it fitted in well with the Confucian view of an ordered society, and it is therefore not surprising to find it being reinforced by imperial edict (albeit in relation to only one province) in the latter part of the reign of Minh-Mạng, The fundamental issues in Vietnamese Confucianization were whether and how society should be ordered and regulated from above. Insistence on communal property, which was regularly redivided among the inhabitants of a village, was an important element in that regulation.

Table 2 Examination laureates, 1822–80

	A. By period		B. By region of brith	
	Number of examinations	Number of laureates	Area	Total number of laureates, 1822–80
Minh-Mạng (1822–41)	6	66	Tongking	150
Thiệu-Trị (1841–47)	5	79	Thanh-Hóa	16
			Nghệ-Tĩnh	75
Tự-Đức			Central Annam	115
(1848–56)	5	93	Lục-Tĩnh	
(1862–80)	9	112	(Far South)	4
TOTAL 58 years	25	360	TOTAL	360

Source: Quốc-Triều Đăng-Khoa-Lục (Saïgon, 1962), passim.

The second manifestation of orthodoxy in this period was the growth of persecution of Christianity from 1825. Under Gia-Long Christianity had been tolerated throughout Vietnam, and in the South it was tolerated by Lê Văn Duyệt until his death in 1832. But in 1825 we find an edict against Christian missionaries and churches, which marks the beginning of a trend that was to culminate in 1833 in a decree completely proscribing the Christian religion.[20] This policy was maintained officially (though the rigor of its application may have fluctuated) from then until 1862, and it was one of the principal reasons for French intervention in Vietnam.

Part III

It might be asked whether this theme of Confucianization in Vietnamese history has any relevance for the study of more recent times. I think that it may. Clearly, Confucianism itself, as a principle of government, ceased to appeal to the Vietnamese about the same time as it declined in China, although one might well apply to Vietnam some of the thoughts on Chinese intellectual continuity developed by the late Professor J. R. Levenson.[21] But what has been said in the present paper about the fluctuating fortunes of the Confucian scholars as a political group may well reflect something deeper than just the intellectual content of Confucian philosophy. Confucianism is but one example of the human tendencies to desire order in society and to seek to discipline the individual according to principles whose first appeal is to the intellect, rather than the heart. Is not communism equally an example of the same tendency? If it is admitted to be such, then perhaps communism has a similar appeal to the Vietnamese mind and to a similar sort of Vietnamese person.

Since 1954 in North Vietnam there has, in fact, been a developing conflict between two tendencies which have sometimes been identified with specific personalities in the leadership. The conflict is best reflected in the contrast (and, it would seem, the mutual hostility) between Trường Chinh (Đặng Xuân Khu) and Lê Duân. The former was secretary of the Lao-Động party from 1951 until 1956 and, as such, responsible for the policy of land reform carried out during those years; Lê Duân has filled virtually the same post since 1960, Hồ Chí Minh having held it in the interval. The details of Hanoi politics are beyond the reach of the Western scholar, but observers seem agreed that, in general terms, Trường Chinh stands for a more doctrinaire approach to policy, and Lê Duân for a greater degree of pragmatism. These are surely the same opposing tendencies to be found in Vietnamese politics in the fifteenth and, again, in the early nineteenth centuries.

Indeed, one might suggest that in many respects the whole situation in North Vietnam between 1954 and, say, 1965 was comparable to that which had existed in the first decade after the defeat of the Chinese in 1427. Lê Lợi had driven out the Ming; Hồ Chí Minh had led a successful campaign to drive out the French. And, just as Lê Lợi was surrounded by a following of men who had proved themselves militarily rather than through scholarship, so Hồ Chí Minh was supported by a group of men whose military daring and organizational skill were probably more important than their commitment to communism or any other political philosophy. Nevertheless, there were in the same movement men like Trường Chinh (dare one compare him to Nguyễn Trãi, the only Tongkingese scholar in Lê Lợi's close entourage?), for whom Marxism as a philosophy mattered just as much as Confucianism did to the fifteenth-century scholars. The principal difference would be that in the fifteenth century the Confucians had the disadvantage of being more closely associated with the Ming than with Lê Lợi and were therefore deliberately kept out of positions of influence for a generation, whereas under Hồ Chí Minh military figures like Võ Nguyễn Giáp were united with the more doctrinaire Communists in a single movement. Even so, after 1954 one finds the same kind of rivalry between doctrine and pragmatism as after 1427. Might one anticipate the same kind of result? In the fifteenth century, when the generation of military leaders who had actually fought the Chinese died away, their successors could not prevent the reemergence – stronger than ever – of Confucian scholars. Is it possible that as time goes on (assuming an eventual return to peace) a new generation of doctrinaire Communists will take over?

Notes

1 For example, see W. de Bary, Ed., *Sources of Chinese Tradition* (New York: Columbia University Press, 1960), and Wing-tsit Chan, *A Source Book in Chinese Philosophy* (Princeton: Princeton University Press, 1963).

2 Compare W. Franke, *The Reform and Abolition of the Traditional Chinese Examination System* (Cambridge, Mass.: Harvard University Press, 1960), and Ho Ping-ti, *The Ladder of Success in Imperial China* (New York: Columbia University Press, 1962).

3 *Đại-Việt Sử-Ký Toàn-Thư* (Vietnamese translation, Hanoi, 1967), 1:236, 240, 295.

4 Ibid., 2:12.

5 *Đại-Việt Lịch-Triều Đăng-Khoa-Lục* (Vietnamese translation, Saigon, 1963), pp. 13–17.

6 *Toàn-Thư*, 2:153 ff.

7 ibid., p. 165.

8 *Lịch-Triều Đang-Khoa-Lục*. pp. 18 ff.

9 A. B. Woodside, "Early Ming Expansionism: China's Abortive Conquest of Vietnam," *Papers on China* (Cambridge, Mass.: Harvard University, 1963), 17:1–37.

10 J. K. Whitmore, "The Development of Le Government in Fifteenth Century Viet-Nam" (PhD dissertation, Cornell University, 1968).

11 Ibid. , p. 129.

12 The complexities of the period between 1505 and 1527 are analyzed in Phan Huy Le, *Lịch-Sử Chế-Độ Phong-Kiến Việt-Nam* (Hanoi, 1962), 2:222–44.

13 Trần Văn Giáp, "Le Bouddhisme en Annam," *BEFEO*, vol. 32 (1932):191–268.

14 E. Gaspardone, "Bonzes des Ming refugies en Annam," *Sinologiaa* 2 (1950): 12–30.

15 Translation by R. Deloustal, *BEFEO* 10 (1910): 23–33.

16 For details of the decrees of this period, see R. Deloustal, "Ressources Financières et Economiques de l'Etat dans l'Ancien Annam," *Revue Indochinoise*, n.s. vol. 42–43 (1924).

17 A. B. Woodside, "Some Features of the Vietnamese Bureaucracy Under the Early Nguyễn Dynasty," *Papers on China*, vol. 19 (Cambridge, Mass.: Harvard University, 1965).

18 See the detailed study of the memorial system in Chen Ching-ho, "The Imperial Archives of the Nguyễn Dynasty," *JSEAH* 3(2) (September 1962): 111–28.

19 Nguyễn Thiệu Lâu, "La Reforme Agraire de 1839 dans le Bình-Định," *BEFEO* 45 (1951).

20 G. Taboulet, *La Geste Française en Indochine* (Paris, 1955), 1:322, 327–29.

21 J. R. Levenson, *Confucian China and Its Modem Fate*, 3 vols (London, 1958–65).

5   South-East Asian polities in global perspective, 1590–1800

Source: *Paper for the* 14th *IAHA Conference, Bangkok,* 20–24 *May* 1996.

I

The period from the early 1950s to the early 1970s can now be recognised as a distinct phase in the historiography of South-East Asia, especially with regard to 'Western' historical writing on the region. It was characterised, on the one hand, by the later stages of what is nowadays dubbed 'Orientalism': the study of chronicles and inscriptions, laws and religions, on the basis of classical texts and a thorough knowledge of philology and linguistics. On the other hand, it saw the rise of 'area studies' (especially in North America) in which historians were given a place alongside political scientists and anthropologists in the study of predominantly national or ethnological topics and themes. This second trend led historians to focus much of their effort on the study of South-East Asian nationalism as a 'response to the West', and on the contrast between 'tradition' and 'modernity'. It also fitted in with an underlying concern for the question why South-East Asia – indeed Asia as a whole – failed to 'develop', in a sense recognisable to 'modern' Westerners, during the centuries from 1400 to 1800. That supposed failure was the main reason why traditional Asian societies had to bow down before the 'forces of change' represented by Western colonial expansion. The result was a strong emphasis on the period between about 1840 and 1940, as the century which saw the unfolding of both the 'impact of modernity' and the 'nationalist response' – sometimes culminating in a debate about the similarities and contrasts between 'nationalist' and 'communist' revolutions after 1945.[1]

It is the purpose of the present paper to challenge that 'modernist' approach to South-East Asian history, and to suggest a much greater degree of continuity embracing a period lasting from the late 16th century to the mid-20th century. One of the implications of focusing on 1840–1940 was that the period between the sixteenth and the early nineteenth centuries was too often regarded as essentially transitional in character: definable in 'maritime' South-East Asia as the preliminary stage of Western colonialism; and on much of the 'mainland' as a period of consolidation in which new Buddhist kingdoms emerged from the fragmentation left behind by collapse of the 'ancient empires' of Angkor and Pagan. (Vietnam was seen as something of an oddity: its Confucianism, reflecting 'Chinese influence over many centuries', led to its being treated sometimes as part of East Asia and sometimes in South-East Asia.) In practice, few Western scholars before 1975 got to grips with Asian-language source materials relating to the internal administrative and political history of the principal South East Asian monarchies in the eighteenth and early nineteenth centuries. Such erudition was for the most part reserved for periods before the fifteenth century.

During the past two decades, some progress has been made towards more detailed study of these 'traditional' polities. There has also been important new research on early 'European activities' in the region, which has often taken as its point of departure the global perspective inspired by the work of Fernand Braudel. Nevertheless, there remains even now a tendency for the assumptions of the 1960s and early 1970s to shape the overall framework of reference of South-East Asian history.

The approach which I shall suggest here would require historians to focus much more on the events and transformations of the late 16th and early 17th centuries, as the starting point of developments which by around 1800 established the broad pattern of political and economic relations that existed before the nineteenth century 'impact of the West' began. Many features of that pattern of relations persisted, moreover, until the middle decades of the 20th century. It is only since then, with the 1930s and 1940s as a kind of prelude, that truly comprehensive changes have occurred: changes which transcend the single region of South-East Asia, but which must be explored in terms of the coherence of global change rather than of the supposed cultural superiority of 'the West'. Such an approach would require us to abandon any tendency to regard 'traditional' South-East Asia as a continuous whole, stretching all the way back from the early 19th century to the centuries of 'Indianisation'. It might be best, in the end, to abandon the terms 'tradition' and 'modernity' altogether; but if that proves impossible, then we should probably regard 'modern' South-East Asia as the product of the period 1590–1800 rather than of the 19th and early 20th centuries. As in Europe itself, whatever qualities may have justified the application of the term 'modern history' to a period that began in the 16th or 17th centuries must by now be regarded as belonging – irrevocably – to 'a world we have lost'. In that perspective, however, the 'modernity' of South-East Asia must be seen as having its own characteristics and its own roots, rather than being merely the product of a 'response to the West'.

II

The 1590s were a particularly eventful decade throughout East and South-East Asia: that is, the Asian 'half' of what we now call the Asia-Pacific region. The historian whose perspective remains essentially Euro-centric might be tempted to start by observing that that was the decade when Dutch rivalry with Spain– Portugal first became a factor in the region, signalled by the trading expedition of Cornelis de Houtman (1595–7). But the full significance of that intrusion did not become apparent for another two decades. We should concentrate first on the more immediately consequential events of the 1590s, which were certainly influenced by the continuing presence of Spanish and Portuguese traders – but only as one element in a complex pattern of trends, ambitions, and conflicts arising in the region itself.

Although we are not principally concerned here with East Asia, it might be useful from a comparative point of view to begin with events in Japan, Korea and Manchuria. By 1590 the military campaigns of Oda Nobunaga and Toyotomi Hideyoshi had succeeded in unifying Japan. They developed a new type of fortified 'castle', capable of withstanding heavy artillery, and also the technique of using volley-fire by massed ranks of foot soldiers armed with European-style muskets – twenty years before it was 'invented' by the Dutch. By these means, they were able to dominate the feudal *daimyo* once and for all and to establish foundations for the centralised government of the Tokugawa shogunate. But when Hideyoshi decided in 1591–2 to apply the same techniques to dominate Korea, perhaps as a preliminary to invading Ming China, he ran into the problem that an island state can expand only with an effective navy. Successful in land warfare, the Japanese were defeated at sea by the Korean 'turtle-ships' of Yi Yin-sun; a defeat which would prove decisive in 1597.[2]

The result of this Japanese defeat was to leave the field open for the Manchu to exert pressure on the north-eastern borders of the Ming empire. The Ming dynasty itself, under the Wan Li reign (1573–1620), is generally seen as having already entered a period of corruption and decline by the 1590s. By contrast, the same decade was an important period in the rise of the Manchu ruler Nurhachi (reg. 1586–1626), who established a base for the military and administrative power that would eventually allow his successors to gain control of Beijing and establish the Qing dynasty in 1644. At this stage the Ming still had a decisive military advantage along the Great Wall, where by this time they were using units of musketeers and light artillery; but already in 1595 they recognised Nurhachi as commanding the allegiance of many lesser Manchu chieftains and bestowed on him the title of 'dragon-tiger general'. At the end of the decade he ordered the use of a modified Mongolian script for the Manchu language, enabling his officials to read the Confucian classics in translation.

The interrelatedness of events in Eastern Asia is well illustrated by the letter, received by the Wan Li emperor in 1592, in which King Naresuan of Ayutthaya offered to help the Chinese to defend the middle kingdom against any attack by the Japanese forces then advancing through Korea. The offer was rejected, but it serves as a reminder of the continuing Chinese influence in mainland South-East Asia. Although the number of 'tribute' missions was smaller in this period than had been normal in the early 15th century, the nature of formal relations with the Chinese court 'had not changed; and there were significant communities of Chinese merchants at the principal port cities of South-East Asia. The 1590s also saw an increasing Japanese presence in the region, associated principally with the growth of trade. In 1592 Hideyoshi is known to have issued 'red seals' (*shuin jo*) authorising Japanese ships to trade with Tonkin, Quang Nam, Champa, Cambodia, Siam, Ligor, Patani and Manila; and Japanese communities already existed at several of those places.[3] The effect of the newly established stability in Japan was to increase demand for products from both China and South-East Asia: a demand which continued to be met by Chinese and European merchants even after the 'closure' of Japan itself in 1636.

Continuing our survey we find that the 1590s were equally eventful in Vietnam, where several decades of civil war – between the Mac dynasty in Hanoi and the Trinh-Nguyen clans of Thanh Hoa and farther south – came to an end in 1592 with the defeat of the Mac. The Trinh and the Nguyen joined in restoring the Le dynasty to the throne of Dai Viet, forcing the Mac to retreat to the Chinese border area where they were able to survive as rulers of Cao-Bang (and its silver mines) by securing Ming protection. In 1599, however, a power struggle in Hanoi between Trinh Tong and Nguyen Hoang forced the latter to withdraw to the separate power-base which he had established since 1558 in Central Vietnam. It was in Nguyen Hoang's territory that the successful port of Hoi An (or Faifo) had grown up, generating revenues which helped him and his successors to maintain their, independence from the Trinh for over a century and a half – as well as to expand into what was at that time lower Cambodia. The Chinese, however, continued to recognise only the Le dynasty as entitled to send tribute to Beijing. There was thus a curious analogy between the status of the Trinh and Nguyen 'lords' on the one hand, and that of the Tokugawa Shoguns who succeeded Hideyoshi in Japan in 1598. But the continuing influence of Chinese-style Confucianism, with its examination system for scholar-officials, meant that both parts of Vietnam remained (like Korea) much closer than Japan to the 'Chinese model'.

The rest of mainland South-East Asia was by this time dominated by Theravada Buddhist monarchies which recognised the spiritual power of the *sangha.* There too, the last decade of the 16th century saw important events which would shape the eventual territorial relations between Burma, Thailand and Cambodia. That region had previously been dominated by the temple-building centres of Angkor and Pagan: very different in their architectures and in their conceptions of power, but both capable in their prime of controlling vast resources of manpower and territory. The building of large temples had ended by the end of the 13th century, and both places had eventually become too weak to avoid capture by invaders from the periphery: Pagan by the Shans and the Mongols in the late 13th century; Angkor by the Thai of Ayutthya (probably twice, in 1358 and 1420[4]). Nevertheless, their symbolic power may have survived at least into the middle decades of the 16th century, even though the rulers of both countries had by then established capitals nearer to the sea. In the case of Pagan we know that King Tabin shwehti of Pegu chose to be crowned there in a special ceremony of 1544. The site probably still had some significance under his successor Bayinnaung (1551–81), who reunified Burma by recovering Ava from the Shans and who made Pegu one of the most remarkable Buddhist cities of its day. In the case of Angkor, there is evidence from Portuguese and Japanese sources of its continued occupation in the 1560s and 1570s – during the reigns of Ang Chan (1516–67?), the founder of Lovek, and his son Satha (1567?–94).

In the meantime the declining power of Pagan and Angkor had permitted the rise of new kingdoms in the Menam Basin, notably at Sukhothai and Ayutthaya. In the 1560s and 1570s, however, Pegu and Lovek were still sufficiently powerful to encroach upon the territories of the latter: both Sukhothai and Ayutthya had to submit to Bayinnaung's forces in 1563–4 and again in 1569. The main significance of the 1590s for this part of the region lies in the recovery of Siam and its emergence as a more unified kingdom than before, effectively combining the resources of Sukhothai and Ayutthaya. King Naresuan (1590–1605) refused to acknowledge the continuing claim of Pegu to suzerainty and drove off the last of a series of Burmese campaigns against him in 1593. He then proceeded to lead an army into Cambodia, where he captured and sacked Lovek in 1594. Five years later he led his forces into Burma, but reached Pegu only to find it had already been devastated by the Arakanese. His main achievement in that direction was to secure Thai control over the Indian Ocean province of Tenasserim, which continued until the mid-18th century.

The fate of Bayinnaung's Pegu, and particularly his inability to control the basin of the Menam Chao Phraya as well as that of the Irrawaddy, had lasting significance for the evolution of the political geography of mainland South-East Asia. His power had been based on three things:, the trade of Pegu as an Indian Ocean port; the availability of Portuguese mercenaries and their firearms, whose services had first been acquired by Tabinshwehti; and his use of that fire-power to defeat the Shans of upper Burma (and also Chiang Mai), which gave him the substantial reserves of manpower he needed in order to establish a temporary advantage over Ayutthya in the 1560s.[5] But manpower proved a declining asset as the wars continued: his son Nandabayin (1581–99) could not indefinitely repeat Bayinnaung's battlefield successes. The contrast with Japan is significant. The geography of mainland South-East Asia was too complex for it to be easily dominated from any one centre, with or without firearms. After 1600, Naresuan and his successors did not attempt to impose permanent domination on areas beyond the reach of their military technology and resources of manpower. They benefited from events in Burma and Cambodia to secure control over their own territory; in the long term that was enough.

The destruction of Lovek and of Pegu in the 1590s marked a critical (though not yet final) stage in the eventual eclipse of both lower Cambodia and lower Burma as focal points for long-term political and economic development, at least until the mid-19th century. The more immediate aftermath, however, was especially significant in defining limits to the power of the Europeans when they sought to take advantage of the chaos arising from the collapse of those two cities. In lower Burma the Portuguese adventurer Felipe de Brito, originally a mercenary in the service of Arakan, was allowed to take possession of the port of Syriam in 1599. He subsequently tried to make it a Portuguese possession under the Viceroy of Goa: an attempt which was to fail by 1613, at least in part because the Portuguese lacked adequate resources to hold out indefinitely against a revival of Burmese power.

In Cambodia the main protagonists in the attempt to extend European power were the Spaniard Bias Ruiz de Hernan Gonzales and the Portuguese Diogo Veloso, both of whom had been present at Lovek before its capture by the Thai. The following year (1595) they signed a formal treaty in Manila on behalf of

Satha (who had survived but was then at Srei Santhor) and in 1596 a small
Spanish expedition set sail to restore him to the throne. Following their restoration
of Satha's son. Bias Ruiz and Veloso imposed a virtual Spanish protectorate over
the new king. It all ended badly, however, when their royal patron was deposed
by rebels in 1599 and the Europeans were massacred at Phnom Penh. The Spanish
presence was by then well established on the other side of the South China Sea:
Manila had been founded in 1572 and was able to survive various threats to its own
existence in the 1580s and 1590s. But intervention on the mainland of South-East
Asia was beyond Spanish capabilities, then or later.

There was already a noticeable contrast between the impact of the Spanish
and Portuguese on their respective areas of penetration in South-East Asia. The
Philippines, although its pre-Hispanic culture was more considerable than was
once believed, had not yet begun to develop towards a unified political system
when the Spaniards arrived in the 1560s. By the end of the century the creation
of half a dozen European-style 'cities' governed ultimately by a single authority
had created the basis for what would eventually become a distinct national polity.
The Portuguese, on the other hand, were unable to make Melaka into the 'capital'
of 'Malaya': the surrounding Malay polities refused to acknowledge Portuguese
suzerainty and were too powerful to be coerced. The Malay world at that time was
characterised by rivalries among relatively small states, most of them by this time
converted to Islam, which depended on trade and shipping rather than on ricefields
and large armies. Among those whose power was increasing in the 1590s was
Aceh, in northern Sumatra, under the rule of Ala'uddin Riyat Syah (1589–1604).
But it was unable to inflict decisive defeat on its principal rival Johor, and neither
of them could effectively challenge the Portuguese at Melaka. It can be argued,
nevertheless, that European control over the wealth generated by an expanding
spice trade rendered it impossible for Johor, Aceh, or any other Malay state, to
bring about Malay unity. There were, of course, other factors making it difficult
for any one of the riverine trading states of the Malay Peninsula or Sumatra to
dominate the rest; but the negative consequences Portuguese control of Melaka
were already evident by the 1590s.[6]

Java had also been largely converted to Islam by this time. There, too, a number
of relatively small states – some with significant ricelands, others concerned mainly
with trade – were competing for control of different parts of the island. Banten in
the West and Surabaya in the East were among the most important polities along the
northern coast; while in Central Java the new state of Mataram expanded its power
by conquering Demak, Madiun and Kediri between 1588 and 1591. The logic of
political and commercial rivalry was that at some point one of these kingdoms –
perhaps Mataram – would eventually succeed in combining control over ricelands
in the interior with profits from the trade of the northern ports, in order to unify the
whole island. But the Dutch arrived before that could happen. In that respect the
presence of the Dutch at Batavia after 1619 was more comparable with Portuguese
control of Melaka than with Spanish rule at Manila.

For both Melaka and Batavia, the day of reckoning would come in 1629. In that
year the sultan of Aceh gathered a large force of ships and men to lay siege

yet again to Melaka, only to be defeated once more by the Portuguese – while Johor and other states remained uninvolved. Also in 1628–29, Sunan Agung of Mataram (having reduced the East Javanese state of Surabaya three years before) set out to capture Batavia and drive out the Dutch once and for all; after which he would hope to absorb Banten. But despite the death of the Dutch governor-general during the siege, the Javanese were driven off and Batavia too remained securely in European hands. Thus the two most important 'Western' cities of the archipelago not only survived; their survival made it impossible for any Asian ruler to unite either the Malay Peninsula or the whole island of Java. Such unification became even less likely after the Dutch themselves captured Melaka in 1641. It can be argued that the longer term consequence of these events is still reflected in the present-day territorial structure of Indonesia. It is futile to speculate on possible futures of the region if Java, in the absence of Dutch power, had been unified by Sultan Agung (or one of his descendants) sometime before the end of the seventeenth century. But by making Batavia into a port capable of dominating the trade of the archipelago as a whole, and at the same time preventing the political unification of Java, the Dutch presence certainly contributed to the gradual emergence of an Indonesian unity which did not depend on more localised ethnicities or loyalties.

Returning briefly to the 1590s, it would be idle to suggest that the geography of political and economic relations across the region was completely reshaped in a single decade. This was, nevertheless, a period in which certain limits were established: especially the limits of European penetration, before the 19th century, but also those of Burmese and Cambodian power on the mainland. It was within those limits that a further stage of political and commercial evolution would unfold during the first half of the seventeenth century.

III

The most immediately obvious aspect of the European presence in the region, following the arrival of the Dutch, was the extension to Asia of a war that had begun in Europe with the revolt of the Netherlands against Spain; a war which, under the 'union of the crowns' from 1580 to 1640, involved conflict with Portugal too. The Dutch came to South-East Asia determined not only to make commercial profits for themselves but also to deny that opportunity to their enemies; and they were the first Europeans to develop a long distance naval fleet of highly manoeuvrable and well-armed warships. As a result the first half of the seventeenth century was a period of endemic warfare between the Dutch East India Company and the settlements and business enterprises of Portugal and Spain. By the end of the war in Europe (1648) it was clear that the Dutch had established dominance over the archipelago spice trade, controlling major centres at Batavia and Melaka and a series of forts in the spice islands. It was equally clear that they had failed to expel the Spaniards from the Philippines: their last and most serious attempt to do so ended in defeat in a battle in Manila Bay in 1647. Also important was the fact that, following the prohibition against Japanese navigation overseas and then the expulsion of the Portuguese (1636–39) the Dutch had the unique privilege of being the only Europeans allowed to trade at Deshima, near Nagasaki. This enabled them to make considerable profits from participation in Sino-Japanese trade and from trade between Japan and various parts of South-East Asia.

The 1630s and 1640s also saw a further stage in the evolution of the pattern of territorial control and diplomatic relations among the South-East Asian polities themselves, in which the Dutch sometimes became entangled without playing a decisive role. A succession crisis at Ayutthaya in 1628–29 led to the emergence of another 'strong' ruler there, known later as Prasat Thong (1630–56).[7] The first few years of his reign were spent in gaining effective control of the kingdom. One casualty of that process was the group of Japanese mercenaries who had served his predecessor well, but who were sent by the new king to Nâkorn Sri Thammarat (Ligor) and subsequently expelled altogether to Cambodia. Although Japanese traders eventually returned, relations with Japan remained cool during the following decade and more. To the South, Prasat Thong was eager to expand his power in the Malay peninsula; but he failed to subdue a 'rebellion' by Patani (whose queen had good relations with Johor and Melaka) and had to settle for a token submission of tribute in 1635. Ten years later he reasserted suzerainty over Kedah, which remained the effective limit of Thai authority in that direction down to the 19th century. In relation to Cambodia, too, Prasat Thong had to accept that the resources of Ayuthya were insufficient to allow a repetition of Naresuen's successful expedition of 1593–4: although he began to prepare an army for the task, plans for an attack were abandoned in 1636. Meanwhile in the North he had led an expedition against Chiang Mai soon after his accession; but he withdrew without launching an attack, leaving that city to remain under Burmese domination for another century.

The Burmese likewise made a realistic assessment of their resources and priorities in the reign of Thalun (1629–48), who decided to move his capital 'back' to Ava in 1635.[8] That had been the base from which his elder brother and predecessor Anaukhpetlun had reunified the country (including the Shan states as far south as Chiang Mai) between 1610 and 1615; but he had then chosen to rule it from Pegu. As in the time of Bayinnaung, royal power continued to depend on a combination of revenues from trade and control over ricelands. Pegu and Syriam remained significant ports even after 1635, but by now the rice areas were probably the more important element, especially those situated in upper Burma. (The agricultural techniques which made lower Burma a major rice granary in the late 19th and early 20th centuries had not yet been developed.) It was no doubt easier, too, for Burmese control of the Shans to be sustained from Ava than from Pegu. The move to Ava highlights a contrast between Siam and Burma which was to remain significant throughout the following two centuries and more. Siam had both its principal port and the centre of its strategic rice granary in the same area; it could therefore control both its mercantile community and its administrative system from a single capital at Ayutthaya, and later from Bangkok. In Burma, however, the two functions were geographically separated by a considerable distance, and there was always the danger of revolt or insubordination in the trading centres of the South.

That was not a problem for Thalun himself, but it became serious in the 1740s; and again – with even more disastrous results – in the mid-19th century.

The 1630s were equally important in the history of Vietnam. Following the withdrawal of Nguyen Hoang from Thang Long (Hanoi) in 1600, he and his successors had built up their own province in the South to become something like a separate kingdom. Part of their strength derived from the continuing expansion of trade at Hoi An (Faifo), which at this period had a thriving Japanese community as well as being visited by Chinese and Portuguese merchants. There was perhaps a certain irony in the fact that the Ming (and later also the Qing) refused to recognise the Nguyen as entitled to send tribute missions to China. That remained the prerogative of the Le emperor, by now virtually a prisoner of the Trinh but still nominally on the throne, which meant that only the Trinh could participate in the official trade with China associated with those missions. On the other hand, the unofficial trade of Hoi An probably brought greater actual revenues to the Nguyen.[9] When the Trinh decided in 1627 to reassert control over the supposedly 'rebel' provinces, the task proved more difficult than they anticipated. Their first campaign failed, and in the early 1630s the Nguyen strengthened their military defences by building the celebrated 'wall of Dong Hoi' in Quang-Binh province. A second campaign by the Trinh was also defeated, with Portuguese help, in 1634. Three years later the Dutch established a factory in Tonkin, and eventually the Trinh sought their help against the Nguyen. But even that assistance failed to give the northerners an advantage in 1642–3, when yet another campaign had to be abandoned after a number of Dutch ships were sunk or driven off. The Nguyen continued to survive further campaigns over the next thirty years, before the Trinh finally abandoned their efforts.

The Nguyen were not yet strong enough, however, to expand farther south towards the Mekong Delta. We have also seen that in 1636 Prasat Thong decided not to send another Thai expedition against Cambodia. For the next few years the effective ruler at Oudong – Prince Outey, acting as regent without actually occupying the throne – enjoyed complete independence from external pressures. At this stage, the long term future of lower Cambodia still remained remarkably fluid: an area which, as in the 1590s, could still be seen as potentially belonging to 'maritime' South-East Asia rather than necessarily closed off from the trading patterns of the South China Sea. Cambodia, like Siam, was already an important rice-producer which in some years had enough to export to other parts of South-East Asia; as well as a source of forest products from the hinterland. Phnom Penh was therefore still a significant port. After 1636, moreover, Outey was willing to trade with the Dutch, as well as with the Chinese and other foreigners. Then, in 1642, he and his son were overthrown by another branch of the royal family which enjoyed Malay and Cham support. The new king, Ram Thupdey Chan (1642–58) also known as Ibrahim, quarrelled with the VOC in 1642–3 and was strong enough to resist Dutch attempts to impose their own terms during the next few years. Having married a Malay, he became a Muslim: a move which should be seen in relation to the conversion to Islam, at about the same time, of some of the Chams of what is now Central Vietnam. Cambodia might, just possibly, have become another Islamic country during the second half of the century. It was not the Dutch who prevented such an outcome, but the growing strength of the Nguyen: following the death of Ibrahim in 1659, and another succession struggle, the Vietnamese finally did begin to intervene in Cambodian court politics.

IV

It is hardly possible to trace in detail the evolution of each of the South-East Asian polities in turn throughout the period from the middle of the seventeenth century to the beginning of the nineteenth. The purpose of the present paper will be served by looking at a more limited range of further developments which contributed to the emerging 'modern' pattern of political and economic relations across the region. The period of the 1680s and 1690s seems especially worthy of attention; also that of the 1780s and 1790s.

1680s–90s: The main changes of this period arose from events in southern China which affected particularly those countries bordering the South China Sea. The collapse of the 'revolt of the three feudatories' in Guangdong and Fujian, followed by the defeat of the Zheng clan on Taiwan in 1683, allowed the Qing finally to secure control over the coastline of southern China. One result was the arrival of new groups of 'Ming' refugees in lower Cambodia. The new situation also permitted the Qing to adopt a more relaxed policy towards private overseas trade on the part of Chinese merchants.

Three groups of Chinese refugees arrived in the region of lower Cambodia around 1680. One group, led by Mac Cuu, was allowed by the Cambodian court at Oudong to establish itself at Ha Tien, which during the 18th century became a fairly significant commercial centre – presumably taking some trade away from Phnom Penh. The other two groups turned up at the Nguyen court at Phu Xuan (Hue), whose ruler had recently intervened in a fresh conflict in Cambodia and had enabled his own nominee to set up a second Cambodian court at Saigon. The Chinese refugees were encouraged to settle in the latter's territory, at Bien Hoa and My Tho, and to provide support for a further (still unsuccessful) bid to capture Oudong in 1682. Apart from that political involvement, however, the Chinese settlers played their part in developing the area around Saigon independently of the main Cambodian capital. A decade later, in 1693, the Nguyen absorbed the territory of the last of the coastal Cham states, to create the province of Binh Thuan. In 1698–99 further intervention by the Nguyen in Cambodia's internal affairs was accompanied by the virtual annexation of Saigon and creation of the two Vietnamese provinces of Bien Hoa and Gia Dinh. Thus began the course of events which by around 1760 would lead to almost complete Vietnamese control of the Mekong Delta. For Cambodia the outcome was a truncated kingdom, virtually excluded from major participation in the trade of the South China Sea and unable to avoid being continually squeezed by Thai–Vietnamese rivalry for domination over Oudong and Phnom Penh.

The ending of formal restrictions on Chinese commercial navigation from the ports of Guangdong and Fujian – the *hai-jin* regulations, which had never been totally enforced but which were not rescinded until 1684 – was to have even more important consequences for the region as a whole. It permitted a further expansion of the Chinese junk trade with Manila, Hoi An, Ayutthaya, Batavia and Melaka, and consolidation of the emerging Chinese commercial network in South East Asia. This occurred, moreover, at a time when the Dutch were beginning to reassess their own policy towards direct trade with China. In earlier decades, in addition to the spice trade with Europe, the VOC had made substantial profits from a pattern of intra-Asian trade which embraced Japan and the various ports of China and South-East Asia. By the 1680s, however, the latter was no longer so profitable, and competition in the Indian Ocean was also becoming more severe. In 1687 Batavia sent an embassy to Beijing to try to negotiate a more stable trading relationship with China. When that mission failed to secure an agreement, it was decided (1690) that in future Dutch ships would cease trading directly with Chinese ports. The VOC would rely instead on Chinese junks to bring to Batavia those products for which there was a market in India or in Europe.[10] The Chinese also gained, after 1688, from the defeat of French attempts to establish themselves at Ayutthaya which came to grief on the death of King Narai. That episode marked a further stage in the delimitation of European power in the region, but it did not damage Siam's external trade.[11]

If we are looking for reasons why South-East Asia was different from Western Europe, at this period and later, part of the answer lies in the contrast between the commercial practices of this Chinese network and the techniques and procedures on which European commerce and accountancy had come to be based by the end of the 17th century. The Chinese had long been familiar with skills of accountancy based on the abacus, with the need for commercial credit, and with the handling of substantial quantities of specie. They already had their own highly complex – although not well documented – procedures, which were probably far more sophisticated than was once imagined by J.C. Van Leur. (Similar arguments can be adduced in relation to the Indian commercial networks to be found on the Western seaboards of South-East Asia.) A vital element in the Chinese role was reliance on personal relationships (*guanxi*) to sustain their trading network; and the consequent difficulty of separating transactions and obligations from the individuals most directly involved. Such personal *guanxi* also included relations between merchants and officials in the various port cities of the region. The smooth flow of trade depended on the making of 'presents', which was often the only way – apart from taxation – of transferring to the monarchical bureaucracies income generated by commercial activity.

What was different in Europe was the development of very specific, largely impersonal, procedures for settling commercial payments; and the creation of transferable paper obligations which could be handled by banks and other financial institutions. There may have been a certain irony in the fact that such instruments as the all-important bill of exchange were probably rendered necessary by the fact that so much silver, arriving in Europe from the Americas, was almost immediately transported to Asian markets in the 16th and 17th centuries – leaving Italian, Dutch, and later British, merchants and bankers to devise new forms of transaction and obligation as a basis for the expansion of European trade.[12]

It was a logical consequence of the nature of the Chinese mercantile network that it could not generate the same kind of public or state finance as had grown up in Europe since the 15th century. There was no South-East Asian equivalent, for example, of the Bank of England – formed in 1694 to allow William III to finance his war against France by borrowing large sums, at interest, from the merchants of the city of London. If that type of relationship is the historians' main criterion for using the word 'modernity', then it must be admitted that South-East Asia was not yet 'modern'. But might it not be equally reasonable to suggest that the latter region had a different form of 'modernity', in the sense that its own political institutions and economic relations were by the 18th century considerably more 'advanced' than those of any period before the 16th century? In particular the capacity of monarchical administrative structures to combine their control of ricelands and military service with the exploitation of trade revenues was greater than ever before. We might have had a much clearer understanding of how those structures worked if the actual archives of Ava, of Ayutthaya or of Dai Viet, had survived from the seventeenth and eighteenth centuries (as was the case with European governmental and commercial archives of that period).

1780s–90s: Looking at the situation a century or so further on in time, we find that the region was entering upon yet another new phase of its political and commercial evolution, but still along lines already set. On the mainland, the kingdoms of Burma and Siam had both undergone severe crises in the middle decades of the eighteenth century, but had emerged stronger than ever by 1782: the year in which Bodawpaya founded a new capital at Amarapura and Rama I began to reign in Bangkok. Wars between them continued until the second decade of the 19th century, but that did not prevent measures to improve still further their capacity to administer and control their respective territories. As in the 17th century, the situation was more complex in Vietnam, where the relatively stable division of the country between the Trinh and the Nguyen was brought to an end by the Tay-Son rebellion of the 1770s, and its aftermath in the 1780s. A Chinese attempt to reconquer Tonkin in 1788–9 was defeated by the Tay-Son leader Quang Trung, who then began to lay the foundations of a new dynasty in the North while one of his brothers established a new southern capital at Qui-Nhon. But the Tay-Son rulers were unable to prevent the recovery of Saigon in 1789 by the last surviving Nguyen prince – known later as the emperor Gia Long – who finally reunified the whole of present-day Vietnam for the first time in 1802. He too founded a new city at Hue which took its place alongside Bangkok and Amarapura as the capital af a more centralised kingdom ruled by an increasingly efficient Confucian bureaucracy. Only Cambodia and the Lao principalities along the Mekong remained as 'two-headed birds': not yet completely subject to either Vietnam or Siam but unable to resist the ambitions of one or the other at any particular time.

In the Philippines, Spanish domination was no longer seriously challenged, except for the brief occupation of Manila by a British naval force in 1762–4 (at the end of the Seven Years' War) which was followed by an important but short-lived rebellion in Luzon. In Java the Dutch had consolidated their position in relation to both the northern ports and the kingdom of Mataram. After several Dutch interventions in the latter's wars of succession, it was partitioned by the Dutch-sponsored treaty of Giyanti in 1755. The Dutch had also strengthened their ties to the spice islands and to the ports of southern Sumatra, and they retained Melaka till 1795. The most important new factor in the situation was the growth of serious British interest in the region, following the East India Company's expansion into Bengal in the 1750s. Britain's acquisition of rights in Penang in 1786 marked the beginning of a phase which became more pronounced after the French annexation of Holland in 1795 and the consequent British seizure of Sri Lanka, Melaka and other Dutch possessions. Further developments during the second part of the Anglo-French war, including Raffles' temporary control of Java from 1811 to 1816, led eventually to the treaty of 1824 under which Britain and the Netherlands established their respective 'spheres' of power in 'maritime' South-East Asia.

We find continuity, too, in the role of the Chinese commercial network which remained strong in the late eighteenth century. There was, however, an important change in the policy of the Chinese government during the 1780s. The increasing number of official 'tribute' missions from the mainland kingdoms, observable at that point, probably reflected a new desire on the part of the Qing to bring more of the region's trade into formal channels. The following figures are based on lists drawn up by Fairbank and Deng in their classic account of the 'tribute system' in this period:

Numbers of missions from: Siam + Dai Viet	Total Laos + Burma
1771–80:	22	4
1781–90:	94	13
1791–1800:	104	14
1801–10:	61	7

J.K. Fairbank and S.Y. Teng, 'On the Ch'ing Tributary System', in *Harvard Journal of Asian Studies*, vi, (1941).

This increase coincided with the attempt by the Qing to recover direct control over Tonkin in 1788, which the Vietnamese roundly defeated in battle. More ominously, it also coincided with the increase in Britain's power in India and its desire to expand trade with South-East Asia and with China. British trade at Canton, especially the purchase of tea, had expanded considerably during the 18th century. In 1792–3 Lord Macartney undertook his famous diplomatic mission to Beijing, both to obtain more information about the 'middle kingdom' and to negotiate a Western-style commercial treaty opening up additional ports to British trade. His failure to achieve the second aim left unchecked a situation in which the East India

Company, and also private British traders, still sought to expand their exports from India to China (including opium, which the Chinese tried to ban in 1800); while on their side the Chinese sought to expand their own trade in South-East Asia, within a system which the Europeans found ultimately unacceptable. The British eventually got their way, as far as treaty ports, opium, and the terms of trade were concerned. In South-East Asia that merely created a new environment, to which the Chinese commercial network had to adjust in order to go on playing its long-established (and vital) role in the region.

In conclusion, therefore, I would suggest that the changes of the period from the 1590s to the 1640s represent the true starting-point for any study of the evolution of 'modern' South-East Asia. This is not to suggest that the intensification of European influence, including a new phase of colonial expansion in the mid-nineteenth century, did not have important consequences for the region. But the resulting changes, at least down to the end of the European War of 1914–18, took place within an already established pattern of political and economic relations. The underlying continuity of South-East Asian history was broken not by the new stage of European imperialism which was marked by extensive territorial annexations; nor by the first emergence of 'nationalist' – but essentially 'Westernising' – elites in the early twentieth century. The real break came with the revolutionary aspirations and changes which began to take shape in the 1940s (or possibly the 1930s) and which have gathered pace during the past two decades.

Notes

1   Lest what follows seems to treat the writings of the 1960s and early 1970s too harshly, let me immediately own up to have adopted precisely this kind of approach in my own *Viet Nam and the West* (London 1968; Cornell 1971). The present paper should perhaps be read as a self-criticism, in the light of my own more recent thoughts and a great deal of recent research by others.

2   For the military aspect of these conflicts see Geoffrey Parker, The *Military Revolution* (Cambridge 1988), pp. 140–2; 108–10.

3   Noel Peri, 'Essai sur les relations du Japon et de l'Indochine au XVIe et XVIIe siecles,' *Bull, de l'Ecole Française d'Extrême-Orient,* xxiii (1923); more such authorisations were issued by his successors in the period after 1604. See also Anthony Reid, *Southeast Asia in the Age of Commerce 1450*–1680,vol. ii (New Haven, 1993) pp.16–18.

4   These dates are based on an acceptance of the *Phan Chanthanumat* version of the Thai chronicles, which can most easily be reconciled with the Chinese sources. I am aware that such an interpretation requires to be more fully substantiated before most historians will feel able to reject the dates offered by the *Luang Prasoet Phongsawadan.*

5   For an analysis of the rise and fall of Pegu, and the role of Portuguese mercenaries, see Victor B. Liebermann, 'Europeans, Trade and the Unification of Burma, c.1540–1620' in *Oriens Extremus,* xxvii (no.2), 1980.

6   For an examination of the Portuguese (and later Dutch) impact on the surrounding Malay states, see J. Kathirithamby-Wells, 'Forces of Regional and State Integration in the Western Archipelago, c.1500–1700' in *Journal of Southeast Asian Studies* 17(1) (1987).

7   For a detailed account of his reign, see Dhiravat na Pombejra, A *Political History of Siam under the Prasatthong Dynasty, 1629–1688* (Unpublished PhD thesis. University of London, 1984).

8 This interpretation is explored by V.B. Liebermann in his article 'The Transfer of the Burmese Capital from Pegu to Ava', in *Journal of the Royal Asiatic Society* (London, 1980), pp. 64–83.

9 See John K. Whitmore, 'Vietnam and the Monetary Flow of Eastern Asia, 13th to 18th centuries' in J.F. Richards (ed.), *Precious Metals in the Later Medieval and Early Modern Worlds* (Durham, N. Carolina, 1983), pp 377ff; also Li Tana, *'The Inner Region': a Social and Economic History of Nguyen Vietnam in the Seventeenth and Eighteenth* Centuries. (Unpublished PhD thesis, Australian National University, 1992.)

10 The logic of this decision is analysed by L. Blusse, 'No Boats to China: The Dutch East India Company and the changing pattern of the China Sea trade, 1635–1690', in *Modern Asian Studies* 30 (1996). One reason for Dutch confidence in making this move was their virtual annexation of Banten in 1682.

11 For a discussion of the significance of the rescinding of the *hai-jin* for the expansion of Chinese trade with Siam after 1684, see Sarasin Viraphol, *Tribute and Profit: Sino-Siamese Trade 1652–1853* (Cambridge: Harvard, 1977), chapter iii.

12 For a brief but useful account of these developments, see Ralph Davis, *The Rise of the Atlantic Economies* (London, 1973), pp. 242ff.; also, on British bills of exchange in this period, Eric Kerridge, *Trade and Banking in Early Modern England* (Manchester, 1988).

6 The development of opposition to French rule in Southern Vietnam 1880–1940

Source: *Past and Present* 54 (February 1972).

I Introduction

'I THINK WE MAY CONSIDER AS CLOSED THE FIGHTING PERIOD OF OUR occupation [of Cochinchina]. For four summers, no attempt at revolt has occurred...'. So wrote the Governor of French Cochinchina, Le Myre de Vilers, to the Minister of Colonies in Paris on 19 June 1882.[1] His very appointment as governor indeed, three years previously, was a reflection of French confidence that their control over the southernmost part of Vietnam was established; for he was the first civilian governor, and his task had been to bring more regular civilian rule to the colony in place of that of the Admiral-Governors who had held the post since 1860. For the next sixty years or so, French rule in Cochinchina continued uninterrupted. But it was not unopposed. The purpose of the present article is to analyse the development of Vietnamese opposition to the French, which by 1940 had reached a peak of intensity, even though it was only after the Japanese intrusion, and subsequent Japanese defeat, that it became strong enough seriously to challenge the power of the colonial government. It would be a mistake to suppose that Vietnamese nationalism — or at least, national consciousness — was the *creation* of European rule or influence. The Vietnamese had a long history of wars against China, whose spirit we should now call nationalistic, and for that reason if for no other an awareness of being Vietnamese was an essential part of their tradition. But with the arrival of the French they found themselves faced with a new kind of domination, whose overthrow demanded new kinds of political action. Consequently their national awareness had to find new forms of expression, and that search is one of the principal themes of the period 1880–1940.

A definitive study of the growth of modern Vietnamese nationalism would, of course, have to embrace the whole country and not just one of its three regions. But in the present state of knowledge, concentration on a narrower area may be justified on two counts. First, while there have been several studies of the leading nationalist figures of Vietnam[2] — both their ideas and their often very exciting clandestine careers — much less attention has so far been paid to the grass roots of opposition to French rule in the countryside. The French found it very difficult to prevent local opposition movements from springing up in this or that province, but they were strong enough to hinder coordination between different localities. As a result there were a good many localized movements which, though having tenuous links with nationalist leadership elsewhere, were able to build up strength in only one of the regions. Moreover, Vietnam is a country where a regional approach is especially necessary, because its society is far more village-centred than capital-centred. Some countries in Asia are so dependent on their capital that a change of control at the latter is immediately effective in the countryside. Not so with Vietnam: throughout its history, control of the countryside has been more important than control of the towns, as for example when the Chinese occupied Hanoi in 1285, and again in the years after 1407, only to be driven out by Vietnamese armies which could still operate and gather strength in the countryside.

A further reason for limiting our attention to one region is that Vietnam is a very diverse country. The South, which was conquered by the Vietnamese only after 1600, has its own special characteristics. It was (and still is) less densely populated than other areas; it was never so deeply imbued with Confucian tradition as the Centre and North; and also its society was quite strongly influenced by direct Chinese immigration thither, from the seventeenth century onwards. Finally, being conquered by the French in the 1860s (whereas French rule in the Centre and North dates only from 1884), it was open to a deeper penetration of French cultural influence than the rest of the country. Consequently we can expect to find that opposition to the French in this area had some features not shared by the rest of the country.

In order to explore the progress of Vietnamese opposition to French rule — as it manifested itself in the South — I propose to take in turn four periods of a few years each, in which anti-French activity came to a head. They are the periods 1882–5, when the French were advancing into Tongking; 1905–8, when the influence of Japan (and of Chinese reformers and revolutionaries) began to be felt; 1912–16, when the French faced their most serious challenge since the 1870s; and lastly 1926–31, when — partly under the influence of Communism — a new generation resorted to new ideas and new methods in the hope of achieving a social revolution as well as independence.

II 1882–5

Even before the end of the year in which Le Myre de Vilers wrote his confident report, there were signs of new trouble. In December of that year, three arrests were made in the provinces of Chau-Doc, My-Tho and Bien-Hoa respectively.[3] The first was that of a man who was believed to be the son of the famous Nguyen Trung Truc, whose attack on a French post at Rach-Gia in 1868 was to become a legend among Vietnamese nationalists. In 1882, the son had been preparing flags, bamboo spears, and brevets of appointment in a rebel army. The second, at Phuoc-Thuan (My-Tho province) was the arrest of a 'sorcerer' who had announced to his followers that an army of spirits was about to descend from the Seven Mountains region of Chau-Doc province, and would behead all people who did not have one of his amulets; in addition to the 'sorcerer' himself, forty villagers were arrested for being in possession of the amulets. Third, on 19th December, the French arrested one Lam Van Gieng (in Bien-Hoa province), who confessed to having been a 'sorcerer' since 1873 and to having been in contact with a man from Tongking who had given him an appointment as 'general' in a rebel army, and had promised him deliveries of arms. It was rumoured, about the same period, that there were bands of Chinese 'Black Flag' soldiers in the upland areas of Bien-Hoa province, ready to advance into the lowlands on a signal from Tongking. Whether this was true or not, the hard evidence certainly suggests that plans were afoot to make positive moves against the French. For the time being they came to nothing, perhaps because the French themselves had already taken the initiative by attacking Hanoi and forcing the Vietnamese on to the defensive, but it was hardly true that all militant opposition was dead.

During the following year, as the French advanced further into Tongking and became determined on a protectorate over Vietnam as a whole, there was still no serious action against them in the South. Nevertheless, two incidents are worthy of mention. In March 1883, an anti-French plot was revealed in Soc-Trang province, when a group of Cambodians and Vietnamese belonging to a secret sect (known to the French as *Dao-Lanh*) assembled at a temple or 'pagoda' and killed two Vietnamese notables.[4] They had just conducted a ceremony at which their leader, a monk called Luc-Hien from Phnom-Penh, had proclaimed himself *vua*, or 'king'. Four leaders of the group were arrested, and Luc-Hien himself fled to the woods of Rach-Gia province; nothing further is known of his activities. Second, in the following June the Governor acted to expel from Saigon the Vietnamese consul and vice-consul, representatives of the still independent court of Hue, for having had relations with secret societies, and trying to raise money for the support of the Vietnamese goverment.[5] Mere ripples on the surface, but signs that trouble was possible at any time.

It was not until the beginning of 1885 that serious trouble occurred in the South. By then — in June 1884, in fact — the French had imposed a protectorate on the government at Hue, and in the same month had forced a new treaty on the king of Cambodia which gave them greater financial and administrative control over his kingdom. On this occasion it is impossible to demonstrate any connection between events in Cochinchina and anti-French groups in other parts of Vietnam; but there was very probably some connection between Cochinchina and events in Cambodia. On the 8th January 1885, an attack by Cambodian insurgents on a post manned by pro-French Vietnamese soldiers at Sambor marked the beginning of the rising of Prince Si Vattha, a half-brother of the Cambodian king Norodom. Eleven days later French reinforcements were able to prevent the fall of Kompong Cham, but not to suppress the rebellion completely; an attack on Si Vattha's camp on the 21st January failed to lead to his capture, and he withdrew to prepare further operations. Meanwhile plans for action had already been laid by Vietnamese resistance-leaders in Cochinchina, and on the 22nd January the six hundred Vietnamese prisoners in Saigon prison set fire to the premises at a time when the garrison there had been reduced to a minimum — only two hundred European troops. The latter were able to control the situation however, and the fire was extinguished without any of the prisoners escaping; next day they were moved elsewhere. The object of this incendiary attack appears to have been to force the French troops to concentrate on the prison while other insurgents infiltrated the city and massacred their compatriots. It proved impossible to implement the plan smoothly, but on the 8th February, before the French had recovered their balance, the insurgents of the area north and west of Saigon were ready for action. About six hundred of them gathered in the vicinity of Hoc-Mon (Gia-Dinh province) and attacked a post defended by one of the leading Vietnamese *collaborateurs*, Tran Tu Ca; the latter was killed, and the post burned, before the rebels began a march on Saigon. Two other groups gathered in the province of Cho-Lon, to the west of the city, and one of them advanced as far as Tan-Son-Nhut. But before any of the groups reached Saigon, they learnt of the arrest by the French of their leader, a butcher named Nguyen Van Buong, and soon afterwards they began to disperse.[6] The proximity of the rising to the capital, if nothing else, meant that it was a narrow escape for the French. But Saigon, throughout its history, has proved curiously resistant to attack and infiltration, however carefully planned; the most recent attempt was that of 1968.

Before the end of January 1885, a new area had risen against the French: on the 29th a group of Cambodians attacked a Christian village in Svai-Rieng province, near the Vietnamese–Cambodian border, making the commander at Saigon fear for the safety of his post at Tay-Ninh and forcing him to reduce further the strength of his garrison at Saigon. But the attack was not followed up for the time being. It was late April before the Cambodian rebels returned to the attack, leading to a threat to Phnom Penh in early May; but they were held in check. In December 1885 and January 1886 the French were strong enough to take the initiative, and the 'pacification' of the country that continued throughout 1886 proved relatively effective.[7] These later stages of Si Vattha's rising did not have any parallel in Cochinchina, however. That area remained immune from serious political disturbances for another ten years; and then, after a minor abortive plot in 1895, for another ten years more.

The evidence for Vietnamese opposition to the French in this first period is far from complete, and does not enable the historian to attempt a thorough analysis of the situation. Probably the secrets of those who organized this resistance are lost for ever. Nevertheless, it is possible to discern a number of significant features of opposition which were to recur in one form or another in later years. First, we have at least one occasion on which opposition in Cochinchina was related to Vietnamese resistance activity elsewhere: in this case in Tongking, the main focus of Franco-Vietnamese conflict in 1882–4. After 1884, of course, the French had formal control over the whole of Vietnam; but resistance did not die out, and in all the periods of intense opposition with which this article will be concerned, it is necessary to inquire into the links between Cochinchinese opposition and resistance movements in Annam-Tongking, or in exile. Second, however, we must take into account the evidence that some opposition to the French had its roots in the South, without any apparent connection with activities elsewhere. Such was the incident in Soc-Trang in 1883, where a Cambodian monk — but one who had Vietnamese as well as Cambodian followers — proclaimed himself *vua*: his claim to power, however limited, had no relationship to the claims of anti-French 'pretenders' of the Nguyen dynasty. We shall find that in some cases opposition movements were led by men whose horizons were barely wide enough to embrace the whole of Cochinchina. Third, the fact that this man was a Cambodian draws attention to the possibilities of concerted opposition to the French in Cochinchina and Cambodia, such as apparently occurred — though the details of the connection cannot be demonstrated — in 1885. Cochinchina had originally been ruled by the king of Cambodia (before the mid-seventeenth century) and its occupation by Vietnamese, and also Chinese, had left a number of areas still occupied by a Cambodian minority. This historical relationship between the colony and the Cambodian protectorate must always be borne in mind, especially when considering 'sectarian' opposition such as that of the *Dao-Lanh* movement.

Fourth, the relationship between religion and politics in this situation was of considerable complexity, and one not at all familiar to Western minds. In the Sino-Vietnamese tradition there was a deep-seated habit of doctrinal tolerance, which led to a highly eclectic approach to religion, favouring the existence of a wide variety of sects. But some of the sects became politically dangerous, and for that reason were persecuted from time to time. There was nothing unusual therefore in a religious sect-leader becoming the leader of a revolt against the government, in pre-French times; or in a man intending rebellion becoming a monk and acting under the cover of religion. After the arrival of the French, and the submission of the monarchy to an alien protectorate, it is not surprising that opponents of the French should look away from the established monarchy and its Confucian court, and seek both inspiration and an organizational basis among the various sectarian movements. These were to become an especially important feature of the development of nationalism among the peasantry of the South: much more so than in other regions of Vietnam.

Finally, mention must again be made of the presence of Chinese secret societies about which the French were also concerned during these years. In the letter quoted earlier, written in June 1882, the Governor of Cochinchina argued that there was no reason to suspect any connection between these societies and political movements against the French. But in December of the same year, the Governor's report on the state of affairs in Cho-Lon province included the observation that a Chinese rice-miller, known as a leader of the 'Heaven and Earth' Society (*Thien-Dia-Hoi*), was suspected of spreading anti-French propaganda.[8] And it was already known that Vietnamese as well as Chinese were being recruited to the secret societies. It would have been surprising if the secret societies had not sooner or later been drawn into the opposition movement against French rule. The more Vietnamese they became, the greater the possibility that it would happen, for their clandestine organizational network was of precisely the kind needed for effective resistance.

III 1905–8

It is not impossible that secret plotting against the French continued after 1885, but during the next twenty years only one such plot turns up in the records. In 1895, a number of documents were discovered at a village in Rach-Gia province which indicated an attempt to form a secret army, with the notables of the village serving as officers of one of its regiments. Fourteen men were interrogated, but it is not clear whether they confessed or what happened to them afterwards.[9] The plot coincided with the period of Phan Dinh Phung's last stand against the French in northern Annam, but apart from the use of the reign of Ham-Nghi for dating purposes, there is no positive evidence to connect the Rach-Gia episode with his resistance. Nor is there anything to link this incident with events in 1885 or after 1905.

The year 1905 was important, from the French point of view, mainly because it saw a revival of secret society activity and a new increase in crime, which continued into 1906. The Governor of Cochinchina, in his report of October 1906, recalled that the typhoon of 1904 (affecting My-Tho, Go-Cong, Cho-Lon and Can-Tho provinces) had led to serious economic difficulties, which had been made worse by more bad weather in 1905.[10] The growth of secret societies was seen as a direct response to this situation, since bad harvests forced numbers of men to leave the land and take to a life of vagabondage and crime. The situation became especially serious in Bien-Hoa province, where the country was terrorized by secret societies during the first half of 1906, until the chief leaders were arrested. But there was no fear of political repercussions, except perhaps in relation to one incident in Bien-Hoa province in May 1905, when an assembly of thirty people armed with knives led the local canton-chief to call in troops, who burnt down the house where they were meeting. On that occasion apparently one of those assembled claimed to have seen the Buddha and to have been instructed to proclaim himself *minh-hoang* ('bright emperor') of Cochinchina.[11] It appears to have been a purely local affair and to have had no repercussions elsewhere, and does not affect the Governor's overall judgement of the situation. Consequently, when the harvest of 1906–7 proved to be much better, and after a number of secret society leaders had been put away, the Governor felt justified (in his report of September 1907) in assuming that the situation was getting back to normal.[12]

His optimism proved unfounded. For one thing, secret society activity of a general nature (that is, not specifically political) continued in 1908 and 1909, notably in the province of Long-Xuyen.[13] But also the year 1908 produced the most serious political opposition the French had experienced since 1885. Moreover it manifested itself in all three main regions of Vietnam, and there was strong evidence that it was being coordinated from outside the country, in Japan. There is no necessity here to recount the careers of Phan Boi Chau, Phan Chau Trinh and Prince Cuong-De, who between them had established the *Duy-Tan Hoi* ('Renovation Association') during the years 1904–6, and had embarked on a policy of encouraging young Vietnamese to go to study in Japan. Nor is it necessary to describe in detail the anti-taxation demonstrations organized among the peasantry of Quang-Nam, Binh-Dinh and other provinces of Central Vietnam between March and June 1908, and the 'poison-plot' which was discovered among Vietnamese troops at Hanoi in July of that year.[14] We are interested particularly in the manifestation of this movement in Cochinchina.

The point at which the *Duy-Tan Hoi* first had some impact on the South is uncertain, but it must have been sometime before mid-1907. The most important representative of Phan Boi Chau and Cuong-De in the region would seem to have been Bui Chi Nhuan, a native of Tan-An province and a somewhat obscure figure who later withdrew to live in Siam.[15] More prominent in the newspaper accounts — when the plot was discovered — was a wealthy landowner of Rach-Gia province, and a French citizen into the bargain, Gilbert Tran Chanh Chieu. He was drawn into the new opposition movement sometime early in 1907, and in July of that year himself went to Hong Kong to meet some of the other members of the group. On his return, he wrote a pamphlet encouraging young men to go and study in Japan, and also circulated a number of 'seditious' poems. He became editor of a Vietnamese-language newspaper, the *Luc-Tinh Tan-Van*, and despite the lack of any formal freedom of the press was able to use it to print articles of a nationalist character. His programme was partly political, but partly also economic: he advocated the development of industry in Cochinchina, and early in January managed to gain the support of at least one Frenchman, who advertised his plans in the highly respectable *Courrier Saigonnais*. Together they appealed for French government help towards the establishment of a textile industry, but in view of French attitudes towards colonial economic protection it is hardly surprising that nothing was done.[16] That element of the programme could be made public, though hardly the related plan for an eventual boycott both of French produce and of the alcohol on which Indochinese finances rested. The promotion of study in Japan, on the other hand, was entirely clandestine; it was organized through a number of hotels at Saigon and My-Tho, which also served as recruitment-points where the future students could stay while waiting for a passage. It was to encourage such recruitment that the *Luc-Tinh Tan-Van* printed articles like that of the 23 January 1908, which recalled the legend of Nguyen Trung Truc's attack on Rach-Gia forty years previously. Nor should it be imagined that the efforts of Gilbert Chieu and his friends amounted to no more than a small side-show by comparison with the efforts of other regions. It is true that there were no peasant demonstrations in Cochinchina, nor any plots in the army; but it was recorded that of the 115 Vietnamese youths studying in Tokyo in 1908–9, as many as 75 came from Cochinchina.

Indeed it was the large number of Vietnamese going to Hong Kong from the port of Saigon which finally aroused the suspicions of the colonial government that there might be something afoot more serious than the mere spread of anti-French literature. Early in August 1908, the Governor decided to send a Chinese interpreter to Hong Kong with a couple of young Vietnamese, and he accompanied them all the way to Japan and back. On the return journey, one of them allowed him to have some incriminating documents. In the meantime, probably also in August, the arrest of a group of people who had been prophesying a Japanese invasion led the French authorities to uncover one of the group's 'cover' houses (a hairdressing saloon) and arrest its proprietor. Finally, towards the end of October, a whole series of arrests was made, including that of Tran Chanh Chieu himself, and also a 'bonze' named Lao-Su, whose rôle in the affair is obscure, but not entirely out of character given what we know of other Cochinchinese opposition groups.[17] It is conceivable that the group already had plans for a peasant rising against the French when a suitable time came, and possible that they intended to use the traditional religious figures of the 'bonze' (or *thay-phap)* to organize the villages. But when it came to a trial, it was difficult for the French to convict Gilbert Chieu even on the evidence they had. It was here that the cunning of the movement in choosing a French subject for its ostensible leader became clear. For, being a French subject, Chieu could be tried only according to strict French law, in which it was necessary to prove a definite intention to commit acts of rebellion. In the end, in April 1909, the French court had to bring a decision of *non-lieu* for lack of such proof.[18] Gilbert Chieu lost his honours but was allowed to go free — at which point he disappears completely from the pages of Vietnamese history.

In Cochinchina, as in Vietnam generally, the years 1905–8 were important because they saw the beginning of a new kind of nationalism in which the objective was some measure of modernization as well as independence. The purpose in sending students to Japan was to enable them to learn something of the methods used by the one Asian nation that had successfully countered the challenge of the West, as well as to bring them into more direct contact with the new Chinese nationalism of men like Liang Ch'i-ch'ao and Sun Yat-sen. Phan Boi Chau was the most distinguished propagator of their ideas in Vietnam, and Gilbert Tran Chanh Chieu, together with Bui Chi Nhuan, sought to apply those ideas in the South. But the fact remains that these were members of a very small group of educated men. Alone, there was not a great deal they could achieve. They spread their propaganda mainly among members of the bureaucracy and other educated people, presumably with the objective of undermining French control of the group on which the continuance of colonial government most depended. But such people were unlikely to take up arms against the French, and sooner or later they were liable to inform the latter about what was happening. As for the uneducated mass of the population, there is nothing to show that Chieu or Nhuan made any attempt to organize a mass following. In the villages, it was still the secret societies and the 'bonzes' who played the dominant rôle in local politics, and at this period they do not seem to have been harnessed to the political movement. If the French were sometimes more concerned about them than about 'l'affaire Gilbert Chieu', it was because they presented a serious obstacle to law and order — because they sought to ignore French rule rather than because they opposed it.

IV 1912–16

The events of 1908, though serious in Central Vietnam, were less threatening than those of the next period of crisis which the French had to face; and this was especially the case in Cochinchina. Once again what happened in the South had its parallels in the North and Centre: notably the bomb incidents of 1913 at Hanoi and Thai-Binh, and the plot of May 1916 at Hue, involving the young emperor Duy-Tan and a plan for revolt in Quang-Nam and Quang-Ngai provinces. But this time the South was the scene of the most serious trouble.

On the morning of 24 March 1913, home-made bombs were found at eight different places in the cities of Saigon and Cholon; none of them exploded, but they indicated a new effort at organized political opposition which the French had to defeat as quickly as possible. In fact they were already forewarned, for two days earlier they had arrested at Phan-Thiet a young man who called himself Phan Xich-Long (Phan 'Red Dragon') and whose real name was Phan Phat Sanh; and three days before that the Resident of Kampot province (in Cambodia) had visited a newly constructed temple there, with which Phan Phat Sanh was associated. These arrests, if nothing else, prevented the rising from proceeding according to plan. A few days later, on 28th March, about six hundred peasants dressed in white robes conducted a series of demonstrations against the French in different parts of Cholon, as a result of which over eighty people were arrested. The same day the police visited the houses of several people known to be involved in the plot, and further arrests were made. Several key figures in the rising escaped, but their organization was rendered impotent and the French could once again feel secure — for the time being. (They would have to face a continuation of the same movement, on a larger scale, in 1916.)

The trial of Phan Phat Sanh and his accomplices (some of whom were still at large) took place in early November 1913.[19] The prosecution was able to demonstrate that detailed preparations for a rising had been going on since at least September 1912, and that the first beginnings of the affair went back to mid-1911 or even earlier, when Phan Phat Sanh had met Nguyen Huu Tri and a man called Hiep at Tan-Chau (Chau-Doc province) and they had agreed to plot a rebellion under the cover of a religious sect. The focal points of the movement were the provinces of Cho-Lon and Tan-An, and that of Kampot just across the Cambodian border. It is not impossible that at the latter place the movement had even deeper roots, for in 1909 there had been an abortive march on the town by a group of Sino-Cambodian *métis* people, wearing white robes and claiming to be followers of a Cambodian prince living at Battambang who would lead his people to independence.[20] The affair of 1909 was limited, so far as one can tell, to Cambodia alone; by 1911–12, the Kampot area had been drawn into a Vietnamese movement.

Phan Phat Sanh himself was a native of Cholon, the son of a police agent and probably of Chinese descent; but he had connections with Kampot, and also spent part of the year 1912 in Battambang. In the latter part of 1912 he built a new temple ('pagoda') there, and in December made an application for a land-concession which was turned down. It was this temple that the local Resident visited in March 1913, and among the things he found there was a collection of white robes. These figure in the story as a sort of 'uniform' for the followers of the movement. In the meantime, by 1911 plotting was also going on in Cho-Lon province, led by Nguyen Huu Tri.

In November of that year he set up a sort of temple at a house in Cholon town in which he installed an old man as a 'living Buddha': a sacred person whom ordinary people were to venerate. When the old man died (February 1912), his remains became the focus of a cult — and this afforded a suitable cover for political preparations and the collection of money. Another leading figure in the movement was a village notable of Tan-Thanh (Cho-Lon province) who impressed his peasant following by declaring that in March 1913 a new Vietnamese king would descend from the sky at Cholon, and declared that only his followers would be saved. It was with this prediction in mind, presumably, that the demonstrators in the city on the 28th March undertook their task. Others of his following were set to work making bombs. But the 'king' who was to descend, having been proclaimed king at a banquet of his immediate entourage as early as October 1912, was none other than Phan Phat Sanh, or Phan 'Red Dragon', whom the French had already arrested. He was imprisoned in the Saigon Central Prison, and the plot crumbled.

Nguyen Huu Tri however managed to escape, and it was undoubtedly because of him that an attempt was made to free the 'Red Dragon' king three years later. In the early hours of the morning of 15 February 1916, a group of between one and three hundred Vietnamese, armed with staves and knives, came silently along the 'Arroyo Chinoise' and landed near the centre of Saigon, with the intention of proceeding to the Central Prison to free Xich-Long.[21] But the French were expecting trouble, though unsure from what quarter, and the police were soon on the scene. Some of the attackers reached the prison, but none penetrated its defences, and they soon had to flee. Ten of them were killed, as against one sentry at the prison; and sixty-five were arrested including their leader, Nguyen Huu Tri himself. It was later discovered that there had been meetings that night at various points in the provinces of Gia-Dinh and Cho-Lon, which had dispersed when news of the failure of the prison attack spread abroad; a plan to attack the electricity station never materialized. It was found, too, that there were plans for attacks on Vung-Tau (Cap Saint-Jacques) and in the provinces of Ben-Tre and Long-Xuyen: all apparently related to the Saigon plot. In the vicinity of Vung-Tau, the French had come across evidence of the plan earlier in the month, and had prevented it by making arrests. In Ben-Tre too, they had arrested a 'sorcerer' called Le Van Khanh in January and had thrown his followers into such confusion that they had staged their own local rising already, in the cantons of Minh-Thien and Minh-Thuan, as early as the 3rd–4th February; it had failed.[22] In Long-Xuyen province there were some serious local attacks between the 14th and 17th February, but order was soon restored. One further point of attack must be mentioned, which seems to have been less closely related to the others. About three weeks earlier, on the 25th January, a band of Vietnamese had made an attack on the prison at Bien-Hoa, in order to release a number of local men recruited for the army, following the decision in 1915 to send Vietnamese soldiers and artisans to the war in France. It too had been abortive and had led to a number of arrests.[23]

The fact that the French were at war with Germany at this time was an important reason why the events of 1916 were treated far more seriously than those of 1913: there was even talk of a German plan to attack Indochina, though it is more likely that the Vietnamese leaders themselves were simply using rumours of German action to inspire the peasantry, in much the same way as they had talked of Japanese action in 1908. The other reason why the 1916 events appeared a more serious threat to the French was that they were more widespread. In 1913, the only areas that appear to have supported Phan Xich-Long were the provinces of Gia-Dinh and Cho-Lon, and of course that of Kampot in Cambodia. In February 1916, the attackers in Saigon itself came from the provinces of Gia-Dinh, Cho-Lon, My-Tho and Tan-An, and a few from further afield; while there is clear evidence of a relationship between that attack and the plans of other groups in Ba-Ria (near Vung-Tau), Ben-Tre, Long-Xuyen and Tra-Vinh provinces; as well as the apparently independent attack on Bien-Hoa. The discovery of such a wide network of activity led the French to make diligent inquiries in all areas, and other anti-French societies were turned up in the provinces of Vinh-Long, My-Tho, Sa-Dec, Thu-Dau-Mot and Tay-Ninh. The French did their utmost to break up this network, and large numbers of people were arrested and tried before a Conseil de Guerre. Between five hundred and a thousand people in all seem to have been tried before the Conseil, between February 1916 and May 1917, and many of them were sentenced to death or various forms of imprisonment: for the attacks at Saigon and Bien-Hoa, at least fifty-eight were executed.[24] As a result, the anti-French movement in Cochinchina was crippled for about ten years.

The general character of the secret societies that were active in the years 1912–16 was explored in some detail by Georges Coulet, in a book published ten years later (1926); since he had access to many official papers not at present available, his account is very valuable, even though not easy for the historian to follow.[25] He emphasized both the diversity of the movement and the continuing importance of traditional elements, especially of a religious nature. The careful reader will find that many of the societies fall into one or another of four broad groups of secret organizations:

(1) First, there was the network of people directly associated with Nguyen Huu Tri and Phan Xich-Long. Their principal centres were in the provinces of Cho-Lon and Gia-Dinh, but by 1916 there were also followers (or associated groups) in the provinces of Thu-Dau-Mot and Tay-Ninh to the north, and those of My-Tho, Tan-An and Tra-Vinh to the south.[26] As we have seen, they also had links in 1913 with the town of Kampot. Their organization is referred to in different sources as the *Phat-Te* ('Buddha-Virtue') society, and the 'Pavillon du Dragon Jaune', Phan Xich-Long being the central figure in each case. In 1913, his followers wore white robes and turbans, which may also have had a religious significance. It may not be irrelevant that this organizational grouping coincides geographically with that of 1885, which had planned the attack on Saigon of February that year. Coulet says that the latter organization also had a religious character, being known as the *Phat-Duong* association; it too had links with Cambodia.

(2) Secondly, there were the societies which are known to have had direct connections with the notorious Cao Van Long (also known as Bay-Do and as Ma-Vang), who escaped arrest until March 1917 and whom the French regarded as one of the key figures in the events of February 1916.[27] He had his base at a temple on Nui Cam mountain (Chau-Doc province, in the far West), but the principal areas of his following appear to have been the provinces of Long-Xuyen, Ben-Tre and Ba-Ria; he himself was a native of Ben-Tre. All these areas had plans for action on 14–15 February 1916, although in Ba-Ria nothing actually materialized, and in Ben-Tre the rising of 2nd–4th February was premature. This suggests some kind of collaboration or alliance with the organization of Nguyen Huu Tri, though it cannot be traced in detail. Cao Van Long's own followers may well have been building up their strength for several years, for he is said to have built his temple in Chau-Doc either in 1904 or in the years 1910–12. But there is no indication of a direct connection between them and Phan Xich-Long, and their co-operation with the societies centred on Cho-Lon and Gia-Dinh may not have begun until the fiasco of March 1913. The fact that Cao Van Long had a temple suggests that this group had some religious element, but it is not easily defined. If so, it was probably Taoist: the cult said to have been practised on Nui Cam was that of the *tho-than*, which means simply 'soil-spirit'; but the temple was called *Nam Cuc Tuc*, which is difficult to identify in the absence of the Chinese characters, but might just possibly have meant 'Five Handfuls of Grain'. (One of the early Taoist political sects in China, in the late second century A.D., was called 'Five Bushels of Rice' — *wu-tou-mi* — and this acquired an importance in Taoist symbolism thereafter; but the Chau-Doc identification must remain tentative in the extreme.[28]) More easily demonstrable from the evidence is the relationship between the followers of Cao Van Long in Ben-Tre and the expression of economic grievances. Alone among the events of 1916, the rising in the cantons of Minh-Thien and Minh-Thuan had the character of a revolt against the rich, as well as against the French. In the course of two or three days, at least four village temples (*dinh*) were sacked and the archives destroyed, and at least twenty houses of village notables or rich Chinese were burnt down.[29] This was to become a much more prominent element in subsequent risings in Cochinchina; in 1916 it was unusual.

(3) The third group or network of societies was uncovered by the French in the provinces of My-Tho, Vinh-Long and Long-Xuyen, after the Saigon prison attack of 1916: there is nothing in the evidence to indicate any connection between these societies and that attack, except that we know some of the attackers came from My-Tho province.[30] It is not impossible that the group presently being discussed was quite separate from Nguyen Huu Tri's following, but its anti-French intentions are evident enough. Unlike the groups so far discussed, this one had its roots in earlier societies whose names suggest a Chinese origin: that is, *Nghia-Hoa* (Chinese *I-ho*: 'righteousness and harmony') and *Luong-Huu* (Chinese *Liang-yu*: 'good friends'). In Long-Xuyen province Henri Dusson's investigation of secret societies in 1909, arising out of an inter-society feud, revealed that the *Nghia-Hoa* was a branch of the *Thien-Dia-Hoi* ('Heaven and Earth Society'): among the places where it had members were two villages in which the investigations of 1916

revealed the formation of new societies in 1915, one of them called *Luong-Huu*.[31] In My-Tho and Vinh-Long provinces, there were at least three villages where *Nghia-Hoa* societies had emerged in 1910–11, and another with a society named *Luong-Huu*: by 1916 these same villages had societies with undoubtedly political names. In one case, the name was *Duy-Tan*, which had been adopted by the group of mandarins who had formed a secret anti-French group in Central Vietnam in 1904; in another it was *Phuc-Hung* ('Restoration'), the same name as that of a society of Vietnamese exiles at Canton formed in 1912.[32] It should be recalled at this point that the activities of Gilbert Chieu in 1907–8 had been centred on My-Tho province, and had been linked with those of the Central Vietnamese *Duy-Tan Hoi* and the exiles in Hong Kong and Japan. It is not at all impossible that in 1916 the same locality produced as association anxious to collaborate with the *Duy-Tan* group of Central Vietnam which was at that time plotting the coup which misfired in May of this same year; but this must remain a matter for speculation, since French action in February and March forestalled any plans for concerted action in Cochinchina. One thing however is fairly clear: by this time at least some of the previously non-political Sino-Vietnamese secret societies had been drawn into the nationalist movement.

(4) The fourth grouping consists of only two societies, both in the same canton of Sa-Dec province and both bearing the name *Dong Bao Ai Chuong*: 'Brothers (or Compatriots?) in Solidarity'.[33] The most important discoveries of the French were made at the temple of a 'bonze' called Phung (alias Nguyen Van Xu), and included a collection of the amulets bearing Chinese characters which were a feature of almost all the groups studied by Coulet. They also included a religious tract entitled 'Propagande de la Doctrine du Tiers-Ordre Bouddhique', suggesting perhaps some affinity with the religion which later came to be known as Caodaism. Whether the group had any plans for action in 1916 it is impossible to tell; none of the evidence suggests that anything serious happened in Sa-Dec province at the time of the Saigon prison attack.

So much for the main groups in Coulet's study. There were in addition at least two important 'affaires' which involved individual localities and less coherent organization. One was that of Mai Van Kiem's secret society in southern Tay-Ninh province, which terrorized that area from about September 1914 until the arrest of its leaders in February and March 1916.[34] It represented, like many of the societies of 1905–6, a serious threat to law and order; but it does not appear to have had any political ambitions. The second was the 'affaire de Bien-Hoa' which occurred on the 24–26 January 1916, and involved an attack on the prison there and an attempt to release people recruited for service in France shortly before. All the evidence suggests that it was a spontaneous reaction to the French policy of recruiting auxiliaries for the European war, and that the attackers had no connection with other organized opposition to the French; but in such circumstances it is always possible that connections existed which the French never uncovered.

The Bien-Hoa affair apart, the events of 1916 suggest a degree of coordination among Vietnamese secret associations such as had not previously been achieved in the growth of anti-French feeling. The followings of Nguyen Huu Tri and Cao Van Long extended over eleven provinces, from Chau-Doc and Long-Xuyen in the west to Ba-Ria in the east, a far wider geographical area than had been embraced by the movements of 1884–5, 1907–8 or 1912–13. The movement was held together, it would seem, by people who travelled around the country and were able to impress the peasantry either as 'bonzes' or as *thay-phap*, a term translated by the French as "sorcier" but meaning more literally 'method-master'. They distributed protective amulets among the peasantry, and collected subscriptions; sometimes they handed out 'brevets' of appointment to commissions in the nascent rebel army. But they lacked two things: a coherent set of political ideas, for they were still part of a traditional, semi-religious approach to society and saw no need for new ideas, merely for a seizure of power; and secondly they lacked any basis for centralized authority. They were able to coordinate the activities of a widely-scattered number of societies and to recruit new members; but — like all traditional secret societies in China and Vietnam — they were not able to impose the authority of a single centre over all the rest. The societies functioned as independent units each in its own locality. This reduced the possibilities of centralized coordination over a long period of time; but also it meant that when disaster came, as in February 1916, the various groups in different villages were not so dependent on a single centre that the loss of a few leaders could destroy the whole movement. The attempt at action had proved untimely, and some groups had to suffer for it. But in spite of the work of the *Conseil de Guerre*, enough survived beneath the surface for a revival to be possible at some future time. The question of continuity between the rising of 1916 and the events of the later 1920s is one that cannot at present be answered. But it is unlikely that the new leaders who emerged after 1925 had to start entirely from nothing in creating a new organization.

V 1925–31

The decade from 1916 to 1925 was a remarkably quiet period for the French in Cochinchina. They did not wholly solve the problem of law and order, and they had probably not uncovered all elements of the opposition movement of the previous few years; but they did not face any serious challenge to their rule at any time during this period. Important developments did take place, however, which would have their effects on the character of renewed opposition after 1926. Three developments deserve special mention: the growth of a French-language press in Saigon, the expansion of study by Vietnamese in France, and changes in the economy and society. French-language newspapers could be run by French citizens in the colony, including Vietnamese who had been granted naturalization, and were for the most part free of government interference. (Vietnamese-language newspapers were strictly controlled and censored.) Prominent amongst the early French-language newspapers owned by Vietnamese was *La Tribune Indigène*, founded in 1917 and by 1919 advertising itself openly as the organ of Bui Quang Chieu's Constitutionalist Party.[35] The Constitutionalists, while leading the way in the growth of a new kind of criticism of the French administration in Cochinchina, were content to demand reforms within the limits of the law. But they set an example for younger, more impatient men who by the mid-1920s were publishing less restrained ideas in French-language newspapers. Towards the end of 1923 a group which included Nguyen An Ninh founded *La Cloche Felée*, whose more vigorous tone brought it into conflict with the government by 1925. It was in this context that the young André Malraux founded an anti-government newspaper in Saigon in 1925.[36] Newspapers of this kind played an important rôle in awakening young educated Vietnamese of the region to the possibility of an attitude to the French other than one of mere grateful subservience. But they were, of course, limited in circulation and impact to the small minority who read French.

The second development of these years also relates to that minority, and especially to the even smaller minority who were able to study in France. Some were second-generation French-educated Vietnamese: that is, sons of people who had studied in French schools, if not in France itself. Such men could take French culture rather more for granted than their fathers had done and often attained a much deeper understanding of it, which made possible a more critical attitude towards French rule. The France to which they went, moreover, was itself in political ferment in the aftermath of the Great War. It had, too, a community of Vietnamese political exiles including Phan Chau Trinh, exiled there in 1911 after his release from Poulo Condore, who had an important influence on many younger men, notably the future Ho Chi Minh. Direct experience of living in France, combined with the discovery of new political ideas, made students increasingly aware of the French failure to live up to their own ideals in their colonies. Nguyen An Ninh, one of the leading Cochinchinese of his generation who studied in France between 1920 and 1925, was especially eloquent on the subject.[37] The experience of visiting France was also shared by a number of Vietnamese (perhaps 50,000 in all, many of them from the South) who went to France as auxiliaries or soldiers between 1916 and 1918: notable among them was Ton Duc Thang, a southerner who was later (1969) to become president of the Democratic Republic of Vietnam in Hanoi.

As for social changes in the period 1916–26, it is not possible here to attempt a summary of the social and economic history of Cochinchina during those years. But one development requires emphasis: the expansion of population, which was not yet great enough to fill the open lands of West Cochinchina but was nevertheless producing the beginnings of rural poverty in some localities, reflected in the fragmentation of property and the beginnings of a rural proletariat: features already familiar in North and Central Vietnam. The city of Saigon-Cholon was also growing apace: by 1931 it had a population of 256,000, and a proletariat which presented opportunities for political activity such as had not been exploited before 1926. In assessing its importance, however, one should always bear in mind that Vietnam is a country where men have always tended to retain their links with a home village, even when living in the town.

The year 1926 saw the beginning of a new excitement among the Vietnamese community of Cochinchina, and especially in Saigon. The previous year a new

Governor-General had been appointed, Alexandre Varenne, whose reputation as a socialist led both the Constitutionalists and the younger politicians to hope for new reforms. (Their disappointment on this score, inevitable in view of the conservatism of the French colonial officials, was an important factor in the growth of extremism in the next few years.) In March 1926, Bui Quang Chieu returned to Saigon from a visit to Paris having obtained no concessions in response to his demands for reforms. Not long afterwards, the death of Phan Chau Trinh (at last allowed to return to his native land in 1925) was followed by a massive funeral-demonstration and a strike of coolies at the rice-mills. And in April Nguyen An Ninh was arrested and tried for sedition and encouraging his fellow-countrymen to violence.[38] During the summer, Bui Quang Chieu sought to take advantage of all this excitement by reorganizing his party and founding a new newspaper, *La Tribune Indochinoise*. His efforts paid dividends, for in the elections to the *Conseil Colonial* in October of that year, all ten native seats went to Constitutionalist candidates on the first round.[39] The party was even making efforts at this period to establish a Constitutionalist movement across the whole of Vietnam, but was prevented from doing so by French refusal to recognize similar parties in Tongking and Annam.

Another movement which came to the fore in 1926, but whose political aims were for the time being concealed from view, was that of Caodaism. Its members were adepts of a powerful spirit which they called *Cao-Dai*, whose religion included spiritism, vegetarianism and elements from the three tradition Vietnamese religions, Taoism, Confucianism and Buddhism.[40] Between May and the end of 1926, the movement was permitted to open twenty or more 'oratories' (thirteen of them in Saigon and the neighbouring provinces of Gia-Dinh and Cho-Lon); and in November it inaugurated a temple or 'holy see' at Tay-Ninh which was to become the most prominent — not always the most important — centre of the new religion. During the next few years it made thousands of converts, and expanded into the Mekong provinces, with two other major centres at My-Tho and near Bac-Lieu; it was also important in Ben-Tre and Sa-Dec provinces. Indeed its geography, Tay-Ninh apart, had not a little in common with that of the 'secret societies' of 1916. It is impossible, in the present state of knowledge, to trace a direct connection between Caodaism and the societies discovered by the French ten years previously. But its use of religion in the interests of political organization is reminiscent of earlier movements. Whatever its precise origins, it belongs to the same tradition as the *Dao-Lanh* and *Phat-Te* of the 1880s and the period 1912–16 respectively. Interestingly, although the basic tenets and practices of the Caodaists can be traced to Chinese antecedents, it attracted a good deal of support from Cambodians. Until the religion was banned by the king of Cambodia in December 1927, there was a long series of pilgrimages to Tay-Ninh by Cambodian peasants from nearby provinces, culminating in a rally of ten thousand in November 1927. But for the time being the Caodaists revealed no political intentions; and the French, though suspicious, allowed them to carry on as a religion. Not until August 1929 did they forbid the opening of new 'oratories'; by which time there were said to be several hundred thousand adepts of *Cao-Dai*.

During the years 1927–8, the Constitutionalists continued to demand reforms, but to no avail; and the Caodaists continued to expand without taking any overtly political action. Meanwhile, the first activities of what can be reasonably called a revolutionary movement were beginning to affect Cochinchina. They had diverse sources. One important development was Nguyen An Ninh's decision to go beyond journalism and street demonstrations, to try and build up a secret association with branches in Saigon and the surrounding countryside, especially in his home district of Hoc-Mon (Gia-Dinh province). The organization may well have survived his own arrest and imprisonment in the autumn of 1928.[41] Other groups were associated with revolutionary bodies created elsewhere in Vietnam and by exiles in Canton, beginning in 1925. This was the period in which Nguyen Ai Quoc (better known as Ho Chi Minh) organized his Revolutionary Youth Association in Canton, seeking adherents in Central and North Vietnam; its operations in the South (Cochinchina) may well have been directed by Ho's own father, who died about 1930 at Cao-Lanh, a major centre of revolutionary activity along the Mekong.[42] By mid-1927, branches were also being established in Saigon by the *Viet-Nam Cach-Menh Dang* ('Vietnam Revolutionary Party'), later known as the *Tan-Viet* ('New Viet-Nam') party; and by the *Viet-Nam Quoc-Dan Dang*, the Vietnamese equivalent of the 'Left' KMT in China, founded in Tongking in 1927.

Such evidence as we have of these groups suggests that their activities, if not their memberships, were closely interrelated. Much of the evidence arose from a trial in 1930, following the discovery of a murder in the Rue Barbier, Saigon, in December 1928. In the interval between the crime and the trial, the French *Sûreté* arrested at least forty-five people who belonged to one or other of the revolutionary groups; they included the young Pham Van Dong, and Nguyen Duy Trinh, both of whom later rose to high office in the Democratic Republic of Vietnam.[43] This attack on the revolutionary organizations by the French authorities did not however destroy the network completely; the Communists in particular were able to continue building up their strength during 1929. It was later learnt that on the eve of the split in their ranks at a conference in Hong Kong in May 1929, they had nineteen cells and twelve attached associations in Cochinchina, with a total of a hundred party members and two hundred and seventy-five sympathizers.[44] This was very little by comparison with the scale of their organization and membership in northern Central Vietnam at the same date; but it may well have expanded further during the months following the healing of the split by Ho Chi Minh in February 1930.

This clandestine activity did not have many consequences on the surface of the life of Cochinchina during the years 1927–9. In 1927, the only serious left-wing challenge to the French came in some newspaper articles in *L'Annam*, the successor to *La Cloche Felée*, as a result of which the editor and staff were arrested and subsequently sentenced to terms of imprisonment.[45] In 1928–9, there were a number of strikes in Saigon, including one of barbers' boys in July 1928, and another of students at the Ecole Normale in May 1929.[46] But none of this amounted to a serious threat to French colonial order. Nor was the government seriously perturbed by an isolated outbreak of rural opposition in May 1927, led by a group of Cambodians, at the village of Ninh-Thanh-Hoi

(Rach-Gia province); fourteen peasants were killed, but there the matter rested, without serious repercussions elsewhere.[47] Rach-Gia was completely quiet in the disturbances of three years later.

It was not until 1930–1 that the French had to face a recurrence of the kind of widespread rural opposition that had taken place in 1916. When it came, though it could achieve little real impact on colonial power, it proved to be both more extensive and better organized than the movements of earlier years. The French blamed both Communists and Caodaists for the unrest, and even now it is impossible to know the extent to which it was planned, rather than merely exploited, by the Communist party cells. In this connection it is essential to appreciate that Caodaism was less than monolithic in its organization, and already there were probably important differences in attitudes to political and social questions between the Caodaists of Tay-Ninh, led at this time by Le Van Trung and Pham Cong Tac, and those of West Cochinchina about whose leadership and organization far less is known. An important figure in the latter group, and one who after 1945 was to throw in his lot with the Viet-Minh and the Communists, was Cao Trieu Phat; in November 1926, he had obtained legal recognition for his Indochinese Labour Party which was socialist in its general programme.[48] Thus while the Caodaists of Tay-Ninh were probably anti-Communist, those of West Cochinchina may have been more willing to participate in rural demonstrations. The fact that there was no trouble around Tay-Ninh should not therefore be regarded as significant for Caodaism as a whole. But the problem of precisely who was responsible for organizing the peasantry is perhaps less important than the fact of their unrest.

The demonstrations and attacks which occurred in Cochinchina were on a smaller scale than the more famous Nghe-Tinh Soviet rebellion in northern Central Vietnam in 1930–1, but they were significant in the political development of Cochinchina itself. Their main target was taxation. The first sign of unrest came at the beginning of May 1930, with two demonstrations at Cao-Lanh (Sa-Dec province) and Cho-Moi (Long-Xuyen province) in support of a demand for two months' postponement of the tax instalment due on the 1st May; there were further demonstrations in the same area on the 9th and 13th May. They dispersed after a promise that their demands would be considered, but on the 13th only after such a promise had been signed by the Administrator of Sa-Dec province. On the 27th May, the Governor of Cochinchina announced that taxes due on the 1st May could be paid on the 1st July.[49] However, on the 28th–29th May, the unrest entered a new phase when demonstrators at Cho-Moi and O-Mon (Can-Tho province) made more sweeping demands: including reduction of the personal tax, abolition of the market tax, and measures to reduce the price of rice. At Cho-Moi the militia were summoned and three peasants were killed; at O-Mon sixteen people were arrested. Similar demands were made by a further demonstration, in which red flags were carried, near the town of Vinh-Long on the 2nd June; more arrests were made on that day.[50]

Thus far the disturbances were confined to a region along the banks of the Mekong and Bassac rivers, but on the 4th June there were demonstrations in a new area: at Ba-Hom (Cho-Lon province) and Hoc-Mon (Gia-Dinh province), to the west and north of Saigon. Two demonstrators were killed at Hoc-Mon, and possibly one at Ba-Hom, as well as many arrested. The next day two people were killed when a crowd besieged the headquarters of the *délégation* at Duc-Hoa (Cho-Lon province).[51] As in the Mekong area, these incidents involved crowds of people numbering between four hundred and fifteen hundred on each occasion. This, moreover, was the area in which Nguyen An Ninh's association of 1927–8 had been strongest. It was by now clear to the French that they were dealing with more than localized, spontaneous objections to a particular tax, but rather with an organized movement whose leaders were challenging the whole basis of Cochinchinese society and French colonial rule.

Both in the Mekong area and in the provinces of Gia-Dinh and Cho-Lon, and also in Ben-Tre and Tra-Vinh, the disturbances reached their height during the months from August to November 1930. On the 31st July, new demonstrations occurred at Hoc-Mon and Ba-Queo (Cho-Lon province), at a place near Cao-Lanh, and at Cang-Long (Tra-Vinh province).[52] There were rumours in the Saigon press that the 1st August was to be a 'Grand Soir' for a massive Communist revolt, and appropriate cries of disdain when nothing happened on that day. But about the 22nd August, something approaching a general rising began to get under way. That night there were demonstrations and attacks on houses in the areas of Cao-Lanh, Hoc-Mon and various other places in Cho-Lon and Gia-Dinh provinces. By this time, too, the red flag and the hammer and sickle were very much in evidence in these areas: possibly it was at this stage that Communists began to predominate over Caodaists as organizers of revolt, and this could well be the reason why towards the end of August the Caodaist leader at Tay-Ninh (Le Van Trung) appealed to his own supporters to move from their homes in Gia-Dinh province and settle in the vicinity of Tay-Ninh.[53] Some Caodaists may well have joined the Communists in preference to such a move. Another sign of the growing violence of the disturbances was the series of attacks on village communal houses (*dinh*) and burning of archives which occurred at this time. Between the end of August and early October this happened in at least eight villages in the provinces of Cho-Lon, Gia-Dinh and Ben-Tre.[54] The spread of disturbances to Ben-Tre province came about the 2nd October, and in one of the incidents there a crowd carried a banner reading, 'Intervene in favour of the province of Nghe-An'.[55] By this time the Communists were influential enough to attempt coordination between their activities in Cochinchina and in northern Central Vietnam. Meanwhile in the Cao-Lanh area the peasants in revolt formed their own soviets. The details are not clear, but to judge from the reports of a subsequent 'submission' by over two thousand peasants the following January, there were four soviets in and around Cao-Lanh, each with between three and five hundred members: in some villages the whole population must have participated, but precisely how they used their brief tenure of local power is not known.[56]

The rising reached its peak in October and early November. On the 26th October the Communists felt confident enough to try and hold a political meeting in Saigon itself, but were quickly dispersed.[57] The French retaliated by gathering information about the Caodaists and Communists, raiding meetings, and making arrests.

They doubtless took advantage of the fact that most peasants had to work during the harvest season (November–February), and were able gradually to restore their control in the areas that had risen against them. And they were aided very often by village notables and canton-chiefs whose property was becoming as important a target of peasant demonstrations as taxation and French rule. The Constitutionalists were placed in an especially difficult position. Their own kind of opposition to the colonial government could be appreciated only by the educated élite, and meant little to peasants in revolt against their own village conditions; the Constitutionalists were thus not well placed to compete with the Caodaists and Communists for leadership of rural unrest. At the same time they were accused by completely pro-French Vietnamese (as well as by the French themselves) of having encouraged the rural unrest. This was the point at which Constitutionalism in Cochinchina began to lose its force.

By January 1931, the revolt had subsided, as one can see from the submission of the Cao-Lanh soviets. Communist activity continued in towns, and there were incidents in January at some schools and at the Nha-Be oil-depot south of Saigon; then on the 8th February they assassinated the chief inspector of the French police in Saigon.[58] But an attempted Communist rising at Nha-Be in March was soon suppressed; and renewed rural demonstrations in early May, in Cho-Lon and Ben-Tre provinces, quickly fizzled out. For reasons which could only be fully known to the Communists and Caodaists themselves, their capacity to co-ordinate and sustain a revolt had been broken for the time being. The events of the previous year had nonetheless been an important landmark in the process of opposition which was to culminate in the fulness of time in the Vietnamese revolution.

VI Conclusion

The character of Vietnamese opposition to the French in Cochinchina changed considerably between the 1880s and the 1930s. From the foregoing account of the principal events and organizations involved, it is possible to abstract four main themes of change which are of considerable importance in trying to understand the subsequent political development of South Vietnam: the growth of a *collaborateur* élite; economic change and conflict; new political ideas; and the development of organizations.

Collaboration versus opposition

There were always some Vietnamese willing to collaborate fully with the French: in the early days they were often Catholics, who had a predisposition to admire French culture and who had little to hope for but persecution under the rule of a vigorously Confucian monarchy. But in the 1880s they were still a small minority. By the 1930s they were both more numerous and more deeply imbued with French education and values.[59] Some were men who had acquired education, and through it administrative office (albeit not the highest offices), and were content to play their part in an ordered society; others were people, often neither educated nor holding office, who had found opportunities under French rule to acquire wealth and wished merely to enjoy it. The two factors operated at different levels: there were people of both kinds among the higher élite of Saigon, and also in each village. Village politics had often been a matter of faction-fighting, and the faction that supported the French gained accordingly. Thus there were influential people willing to defend the *status quo* in 1930. Whether we should call this pro-French group a 'bourgeoisie' is open to question, but their attachment to an order which depended on French rule is undeniable. Consequently any group which sought to oppose French rule by disrupting that order would find itself opposed by some Vietnamese as well as by all the French inhabitants of Cochinchina. In 1930, there were indeed notables and officials who supported the French against the demonstrating peasantry, and their loyalty was very valuable indeed to the French. Conversely, an increasing number of young Vietnamese who opposed the French felt that it was equally necessary to oppose the comfortable class amongst their own countrymen. This gave great impetus to revolutionary movements, especially the Communists.

2 Economic change and conflict

In itself, conflict between groups of Vietnamese who opposed and supported the French need not be interpreted in economic terms: the clan, which often cut across the difference between rich and poor, was very important, and in many cases two factions may merely have been carrying into politics a conflict which would have existed regardless of either the political or the economic situation. Nevertheless, there were economic developments which as time went on gave rise to more and more grievances; and on the whole they were the grievances of poor men either against French rule and taxes, or against wealthy Vietnamese.

The French increased taxes at an early stage in their rule, but in the South this was felt less keenly than in the poorer areas of Central and North Vietnam. When the Central provinces rebelled against high taxation and *corvée* labour in 1908, there is nothing to suggest that similar grievances were troubling the peasants of Cochinchina. In that region land was plentiful and the soil was rich; and even if the best new lands in the West were being taken by large concessionaires, there was not yet any serious overcrowding in the older-settled provinces. By 1930, however, this was ceasing to be true. It should not be imagined that the demonstrations of that year were in any way against the large concessionaires, or were occasioned by the fact that Cochinchina had a higher proportion of landlordship than other areas. On the contrary: the geography of unrest in 1930 shows that very little happened in the provinces of the far West where the largest estates lay. Nor was the revolt about tenancies and high rents: it was primarily against taxes, and on the large estates the tenant was protected by the fact that his landlord paid the tax.

As the Table below indicates, the provinces that were most disturbed in 1930, and in 1913–16, were those which had high proportions of landowners owning under 5 hectares of land, and very few owners with more than 100 hectares. The extreme case is that of Ben-Tre where 75 per cent of the province's 30,021 proprietors had

The geography of unrest, 1913–16 and 1930–31*

Province	Activity in 1913–16 (X)	No. of 'manifestations' in 1930–1	Percentage of Landowners in 1930 with under 5 ha.	over 100 ha.
Gia-Dinh	X	12	?	?
Cho-Lon	X	14	73%	0.3%
Tan-An	—	2	56%	9.7%
My-Tho	X	2	80%	0.4%
Ben-Tre	X	14	85%	0.2%
Tra-Vinh	X	2	80%	0.7%
Vinh-Long	(slight)	3	73%	0.9%
Sa-Dec	X	5	80%	0.4%
Long-Xuyen[+]	X	5	65%	1.7%
Chau-Doc	X	1	78%	0.2%
Can-Tho	—	3	60%	1.7%
Bac-Lieu	—	1	38%	4.8%
Rach-Gia	—	—	50%	3.7%

* Sources: For events of 1913–16 and 1930–1, as cited in text; for landownership figures, Y. Henry, *Economie Agricole de l'Indochine* (Hanoi, 1932).
[+] In Long-Xuyen, the cantons most seriously affected were An-Binh and Dinh-Hoa, where in 1930 as many as 85% and 79% of landowners (respectively) had under 5 ha.

under 1 hectare, and fewer than 1 per cent had over 50 hectares; even allowing for the widespread cultivation of coconuts in that province, these figures present a striking contrast to those for Bac-Lieu and Rach-Gia.[60] And it was in Ben-Tre that the first cases occurred, in 1916, of peasants attacking the village *dinh* or communal house in order to destroy the tax records. In the province of Sa-Dec, too, while the proportion of larger proprietors was a little higher, there were very many small owner-occupiers whose problem was too little land rather than too much rent; and this was especially true of the cantons round Cao-Lanh. Thus it would be wrong to see the outbreaks of disorder in 1930 as cases of direct conflict between tenants who were poor and landlords who had benefited from French rule. Rather they represented generalized discontent by small-holders of various kinds, against the government which forced them to pay taxes. But if land-hunger was among their motives, the Communist idea of a more equitable distribution of land would quickly appeal to them.

These remarks must be seen in their proper context: the situation of 1930. They do not apply to the economy as it developed over the next decade, following the impact of the slump in the rice trade. (That too, it should be mentioned, was not a factor in the events of 1930 itself: it came too late.) A recent study by Dr. R. L. Sansom has shown that there was a marked deterioration in the economic position of the Cochinchinese peasantry during the 1930s, principally for two reasons.[61] On the one hand, financial difficulties forced small men to borrow, and often they lost their land to others, thus increasing the proportion of tenancy in older areas. On the other hand, tenants found their rents increased, because landlords wanted to be able to export larger quantities of rice, at lower prices, in order to maintain their monetary income as far as possible at former levels. Thus by 1940, when there was a new revolt in the Mekong provinces, it is very likely that rents and tenancy problems, as well as indebtedness, were added to land scarcity and taxation as grievances amongst the peasantry.[62] It is probably no accident that the strength of the Communists in the area increased during the same period.

3 Political ideas

The cultural impact of the French on Cochinchina was considerable — greater indeed than on any other part of the country, for two reasons: first, French rule began earlier here, in the 1860s, and therefore lasted a generation longer than elsewhere; second, the withdrawal of the scholar-officials of the imperial government immediately the French took over meant that they had to educate officials of their own from the beginning.[63] There is also the fact that, in the historical development of Vietnam, the far south had been the most recently settled by Vietnamese and the least deeply influenced by Confucian education and ideas; this meant that there was slightly less resistance to French education here than farther north. The French, of course, were very conscious of their *mission civilisatrice* in their colonies; but their interest was in educating officials and professional people who would collaborate in the maintenance of French rule. It was only indirectly that French political ideas began to influence the thinking of those who opposed French rule.

To begin with, the framework of reference of those who opposed the French was wholly traditional. It was not entirely Confucian, for in general it was men less educated than the scholar-officials who took the lead. We have seen that an especially important rôle was played by priests, whom the French sometimes called *bonzes* and sometimes *sorciers*. They were, in general, not members of highly disciplined religious sects; often they were merely local spirit-healers, known to the Vietnamese as *thay-phap*, who had great influence in a particular locality but did not belong to any organization at all.[64] Their education was in traditional lore, often involving only one or two standard texts in Chinese characters; they could impress ordinary villagers with their capacity to draw amulets, but they had no highly articulated theory of society or politics. They were only gradually drawn into more sophisticated political movements, and probably with the simple idea of restoring Vietnamese independence under a tradition monarchical rule. More ambitious was the *thay-phap* who aspired to become a king himself: for example Phan Xich-Long in 1912–13. The important point however is that, whatever the level of their aspirations, such men were not challenging the French — or anyone else — on the grounds of any articulated political theory. They acted on assumptions rather than theories: assumptions wholly traditional in character.

Nor did the more elaborate organization of the Caodaists, who had a more disciplined framework of religious belief derived from a Chinese tradition of Taoism combined with apocalyptic Buddhism, carry with it a new political theory in and of itself. The organization would doubtless have stood them in good stead if by some miracle they had attained political power in the 1930s, but had they done so they would have ruled the country along essentially traditional lines, with their own hierarchy taking the place of scholar-officials.

It was among the French-educated élite that new ideas began to develop. Gilbert Chieu was probably not deeply imbued with French culture: but the ideas which he propagated came indirectly from the West, via Japan and the Chinese reformer Liang Ch'i-ch'ao. Ten years or so after his activities, the foundation of the Constitutionalist Party in 1917 represented a more direct French cultural impact on Cochinchinese politics. For its aims made sense only in terms of the political practices and assumptions of metropolitan France: it hoped to make the French live up to their own political ideals in administering and developing their colonies. It was when this hope proved impossible to fulfil through peaceful participation in existing institutions that a new generation of French-educated youth began to look for inspiration to French socialism: the methods as well as the ideals of the Revolution.

Between Nguyen An Ninh and Cao Trieu Phat on the one hand, and the more traditionalist of the Caodaists on the other, there was a widening gap by the 1930s. The followers of both were still simple people, to whom it probably mattered little whether they carried a Caodaist star or a Communist red flag in procession. But among the leaders, new horizons opened up: Bui Quang Chieu and Nguyen An Ninh were alike products of French education. Only time would tell whether it was to be Constitutionalism or Communism that would establish a new framework of political life, but by 1930 it was clear that traditional assumptions must be left behind.

4 Organization

Discontent, whether for economic or political reasons, was an ever-present factor in the situation of Cochinchina, for much if not all of the period of French rule. Discontent, moreover, generated new ideas about the kind of society there should be in Vietnam once the French had gone. But discontent and ideas alone could achieve little without some new form of organization with which to oppose the French. By the 1930s, the Vietnamese still lacked an organization strong enough to drive out the French, and it might well be argued that but for the Japanese occupation they would have had to wait another generation before giving adequate expression to their nationalist aspirations. Nevertheless, the period between 1880 and 1940 was a formative one in that it saw the emergence of new political organizations on a scale large enough to be able to take advantage of the situation which the Japanese advance, then defeat, brought about. It is impossible to discuss those organizations fully while confining our attention to one region of Vietnam: the Communists in particular had a nation-wide network as early as 1930. Our concern must be merely with organization at the local level, in the villages, which is where it was most important if any effective coordinated action was to be achieved.

The question of organization must be considered against the background of the Vietnamese tradition, in which there was a very strong sense of *order*, but not quite the same notion of *authority* as that with which we are familiar in the West.[65] So long as the monarchy continued to exist and to command the loyalty of all Vietnamese, there was a framework for order even though it could not always be sustained in practice. But the French conquest destroyed the traditional monarchy: although kings still ruled in Hue, under French 'protection', the monarchy gradually lost its place as a focus of loyalty for the Vietnamese who felt most strongly about expelling the French. The rôle of the scholar-bureaucracy in the service of the protectorate was also such that it could not act as a framework for nationalist organization. Even though some of the leading nationalists, especially in Central Vietnam, were educated in the Confucian tradition, their anti-French activities had to develop on the level of clandestine associations in which the methods of the traditional 'mandarin' were inappropriate. These changes affected the whole of Vietnam, but they were especially marked in the case of Cochinchina, which was ceded to France as a colony and which had no scholar-bureaucracy at all after 1867. This meant that opposition to the French must develop within some other kind of institutional framework.

There were three traditional institutions which could be used for the purpose, all of which were present in southern Vietnam in the 1880s: the secret society, the religious sect, and the *thay-phap* whose power was not part of any wider organization. We have seen that in the 1880s, the secret societies — mainly Chinese in membership but beginning to draw in Vietnamese — were not directly involved in Vietnamese politics. They may have originated as political associations in the context of the Manchu conquest of Ming China, but for the most part they had lost interest even in Chinese politics (until it was rekindled by Sun Yat-sen after 1900); they certainly had no immediately obvious rôle as the vehicle for opposing the French, unless and until the colonial government interfered with them. They were only gradually drawn into the nationalist movement, perhaps largely as a consequence of accepting so many Vietnamese recruits. The religious sect was more likely to become involved in politics, because it could so easily be used as a cover for political activity: the movement which called itself variously *Dao-Lanh* or *Phat-Duong* in the 1870s and 1880s was very much a case in point. There appears to have been a similar sect-organization involved in the support of Phan Xich-Long in 1912–16. As for the *thay-phap*, he could very easily be drawn into a sect-organization if one existed, and this had happened by 1916. But none of these organizations operated within a framework of strictly enforceable authority. Even the sect was based on the teachings of a master, in the present or in the past, not on any revelation of divine law capable of rigid interpretation and enforcement. The organization consisted rather of small groups of like-minded people, sharing loyalty — in the case of secret societies a very strong loyalty established by a brothers' oath and initiation rites — but not obeying any central authority. To establish a centralized leadership within such a framework was not easy; but such a leadership was essential if the Vietnamese were ever to be strong enough successfully to challenge the French.

By 1930, three new organizations had emerged which were capable of leading, if not controlling, larger numbers of people than had been involved in political activity in the past. The most traditional was that of the Caodaists, which by 1930 had 'holy sees' at Tay-Ninh, My-Tho and Bac-Lieu.[66] During the years after 1926 it built up a wide following, variously estimated at between 200,000 and a million adepts. But already by 1930 there were signs of disagreement within its ranks, probably over the proper attitude towards the Communists and towards violent methods. By 1932 it had split yet again, and ever since then only one faction of the movement has owed complete obedience to the most famous centre at Tay-Ninh. The movement had aspirations towards centralization and a single decision-making authority, but its structure was not strong enough to achieve that end. The second organization was that of the Communists, by which is meant in this case the adherents of Ho Chi Minh's 'Association of Revolutionary Youth' of 1925, out of which was born in 1930 the 'Indochinese Communist Party'. This too had its problems of unity, with a serious split in the leadership in 1929 which only Ho's intervention could heal the following year.[67] But both its political theory and its organizational structure were of a kind that made possible, indeed necessary, a kind of discipline which the Caodaists could not command. The Rue Barbier affair of 1928, moreover, showed that the Communists were prepared to go to extreme lengths to enforce discipline: it arose out of a party decision to execute a recalcitrant cell-leader.[68] In addition to discipline, the Communist organization had the advantage of a cell-system which, if properly administered, ensured that the detection of one small segment of party activities by the government need not lead to discovery of the whole network. The Communist movement thus had some of the features of traditional secret societies; but in addition it had a sense of political direction and a specific programme of concerted action.

Thirdly there was the organization of Nguyen An Ninh, which developed during 1927–8. Even now, it is impossible to say how close were Ninh's associations with the Communists of Ho Chi Minh's group. Initially, he probably operated independently of them but with a programme and organizational techniques that had much in common with theirs. After his arrest, it seems very likely that his followers were taken over by the Communist movement proper, for it was in their area that some of the most vigorous incidents of the 1930 revolt occurred. To judge from evidence relating mainly to Central Vietnam, the Communists made frequent use of the 'takeover' technique, in which they undermined the following of rival organizations and then proposed a merger.[69] Possibly they did this in relation to both the Nguyen An Ninh party and the left-wing Caodaists during the late 1920s and 1930s. On the other hand they may have been able only to attempt alliances with other groups, in which they themselves did not have the dominant voice.

The analysis of organization must inevitably be incomplete, for the records do not exist that would enable a full 'internal' history of the pre-1940 opposition movements to be written. One thing however is very clear. The various movements which have been the principal subject of the present article were able to make considerable progress in the development of an (ultimately) revolutionary organization. The Constitutionalists were not. They were an urban élite with superior education, and regardless of their decisions on tactics towards the French, they failed to organize an effective rural following. Had the French permitted the development of a proper electoral system and an effective legislative council or assembly, the Constitutionalists would have been forced to develop a new relationship with the peasantry. As it was, they were content to work within a system which was inadequate to fulfil their aspirations, while the support of the rural masses was drawn into other channels. After 1945, the principal conflict among Vietnamese in South Vietnam was between the Communists and the political sects, the two groups which had seized the only opportunities open to Vietnamese nationalists in the Cochinchina of the 1920s and 1930s.

Notes

1 Paris, Arch. Nat., Section d'Outre-Mer: INDOCHINE, A — 30 (53).
2 E.g. J. Chesneaux, 'Stages in the Development of the Vietnam National Movement, 1862–1940', *Past and Present*, no. 7 (Apr. 1955); G. Boudarel, 'Memoires de Phan Boi Chau', *France-Asie*, nos. 194–5 (1968).
3 As note 1; file also includes letters and reports of Le Myre de Vilers to the Minister of Colonies, 18 and 21 Dec. 1882.
4 *Ibid.*, INDOCHINE A — 50 (NF 445).
5 A. Schreiner, *Abrégé de l'Histoire d'Annam*, 2nd edn. (Saigon, 1906), p. 358.
6 *Ibid.*, pp. 408–10.
7 *Ibid.*, pp. 425–6; 434–5. Cf. also M. A. Osborne, *The French Presence in Cochinchina and Cambodia, Rule and Response (1859–1905)* (Ithaca, 1969), pp. 212 ff., which places the Cambodian revolt in the context of Cambodian court politics, and discusses whether it was in some respects a success for the king. It was certainly not a success for Si Vattha.
8 See note 3 above.
9 National Archives, Saigon: 'Rach-Gia, 9'.
10 *Courrier Saigonnais*, 22 Oct. 1906. *Cf.* reference to the typhoon of 1904 in Y. Henry, *Economie Agricole de l'Indochine* (Hanoi, 1932), p. 265.
11 Paris, Arch. Nat., Section d'Outre-Mer: INDOCHINE: A — 50, (NF 447).
12 *Courrier Saigonnais*, 21 Sept. 1907.
13 A serious case of inter-society rivalry in Long-Xuyen in July 1908 led the local procurator to make a thorough inquiry into the subject of Chinese societies, which was later published: Henri Dusson, *Les Sociétés secrètes en Chine et en Terre d'Annam* (Long-Xuyen, 1909).
14 On these events, see such works as G. Boudarel, 'Memoires de Phan Boi Chau', *France-Asie*, xxii (nos. 194–5) (1968); General Aubert et l'Etat-Major, *Histoire Militaire de l'Indochine Francaise* (Hanoi, 1930).
15 Paris, Arch. Nat., Section d'Outre-Mer: INDOCHINE: NF 28(2), which is the principal source for what follows on the events of 1907–8.
16 *Courrier Saigonnais*, 4 Jan. 1908.
17 Not much is known of him, but he is mentioned in G. Coulet, *Les Sociétés Secrètes en Terre d'Annam* (Saigon, 1926), p. 228.
18 *Courrier Saigonnais*, 22, 29 Apr. 1909; *L'Opinion*, 22–24 Apr. 1909.
19 The principal source used for the Phan Xich-Long affair of 1913 is the account of the trial in *Courrier Saigonnais*, 5 Nov. 1913.
20 *L'Opinion*, 24 Apr. 1909.
21 *Courrier Saigonnais*, 15 Feb. 1916; cf. Arch. Nat., Section d'Outre-Mer, Paris: A — 50, NF 28 (2).
22 On the Ben-Tre affair, see G. Coulet, *Les Sociétés Secrètes en Terre d'Armam* (Saigon, 1926), pp. 33, 326–32.

23 Coulet, *op. cit.*, pp. 343–9; *Courrier Saigonnais*, 28 Apr., 1–3 May 1916.
24 Coulet, *op. cit.* is based on the papers of the Conseil de Guerre, and includes a list of 'ordres d'information' in the various cases which it heard (pp. 392–5). His list covers 1,163 people, but not all of them came before the *Conseil* on specific charges, as can be seen from the accounts of trials that appeared in the *Courrier Saigonnais*.
25 Coulet, *op. cit.* His study is arranged under a number of analytical headings, such as the rôle of 'sorcerers', the rôle of religion, etc., in the various societies, without any attempt at a straightforward chronological and geographical account.
26 Coulet, *op. cit.*, pp. 33–4, 35–46, 88 ff., 213–5, 223–4, 240 ff., 273, 332–7.
27 Coulet, *op. cit.*, pp. 90–5, 158 ff., 326–32, 340–1.
28 Cf. Vincent Y. C. Shih, 'Some Chinese Rebel Ideologies', *Toung-Pao*, xliv (1956), pp. 150–226.
29 Coulet, *op. cit.*, pp. 326–32.
30 This is indicated by the lists of those arrested in the attack and tried in February and March: *Courrier Saigonnais*, 23 Feb., 15–17 Mar. 1916.
31 H. Dusson, *Les Sociétés Secrètes en Chine et en Terre d'Annam* (Long-Xuyen, 1909); and Coulet, *op. cit.*, pp. 199, 201, 212–3.
32 Coulet, *op. cit.*, pp. 34–5, 81, 106–10, 111–14, 168–9, 174–5, 199, 201, 208, 218, 237–8.
33 *Ibid.*, pp. 34, 83, 124 ff., 145 ff., 154–7, 178–81, 200.
34 *Ibid.*, pp. 315–25, 338.
35 For a more detailed account of this group see R. B. Smith, 'Bui Quang Chieu and the Constitutionalist Party in French Cochinchina, 1917–30', *Modern Asian Studies*, iii (1969), pp. 131–50.
36 Cf. W. G. Langlois, *André Malraux, the Indochina Adventure* (London, 1966).
37 E.g. Nguyen An Ninh, *La France en Indochine* (Paris, 1925), a tract of which there is a copy at the Ecole National de Langues Orientales Vivantes, Paris. On Nguyen An Ninh, whose father had been an active supporter of Gilbert Chieu in 1907–8, see Ralph Smith, *Viet-Nam and the West* (London, 1968), pp. 98 ff.
38 *Avenir du Tonkin*, 5 May 1926; cf. also the British Consul's report from Saigon, April 1926, which also refers to a student riot at the College de My-Tho about the same time.
39 *Tribune Indochinoise*, 10 Nov. 1926.
40 For a detailed account of the early development of Caodaism, see R. B. Smith: 'An Introduction to Caodaism, i: Origins and Early History', *Bull. of School of Oriental and African Studies, London*, xxxiii (1970), pp. 335–49.
41 Gouvernment-General de l'Indochine, *Contribution à l'Histoire des Mouvements Politiques de l'Indochine Francaise* (Hanoi, 1933–4), i, p. 44. This series will be refered to as *Contribution*.
42 J. Lacouture, *Ho Chi Minh*, Paris, 1967, p. 13; confirmed in conversations with Vietnamese in Saigon.
43 For detailed press reports of the trial, see *La Tribune Indochinoise*, 16–18 July 1930, and *La Dépeche d'Indochine*, 15–19 July, 1930.
44 *Contribution*, iv, pp. 19–20.
45 *Tribune Indochinoise*, 28 Oct. 1927, 28–30 March 1928.
46 *Contribution*, iv, p. 122; *Tribune Indochinoise*, 27 May 1929.
47 *Tribune Indochinoise*, 20–25 May 1927.
48 *Ibid.*, 22 Nov. 1926.
49 *Contribution* iv, pp. 124–6; *Echo Annamite*, 6 May, 28 May 1930; *Tribune Indochinoise*, 5 May, 14 May 1930.
50 *Contribution*, iv, p. 125; *Tribune Indochinoise*, 30 May, 2, 4 June 1930.
51 *Contribution*, *ibid.*; *Tribune Indochinoise*, 6 June 1930.
52 *Tribune Indochinoise*, 1 Aug. 1930. Cf. also *Dépeche d'Indochine* for the period which follows.
53 *Dépeche d'Indochine*, 28–30 Aug. 1930.

54 *Contribution*, iv, pp. 126 ff.; *Dépeche d'Indochine*, 13 Sept., 23–25 Sept., 4 Oct. 1930.
55 *Contribution*, iv, p. 127. The revolt in Nghe-An and Ha-Tinh provinces was at its height in this period.
56 *Dépeche d'Indochine*, 5 Jan. 1931.
57 *Dépeche d'Indochine*, 27 Oct. 1930.
58 *Dépeche d'Indochine*, 9 Feb. 1931.
59 For a fuller account of the élite see R. B. Smith, 'The Vietnamese Elite of French Cochinchina in 1943', to appear in a forthcoming number of *Modern Asian Studies*.
60 Y. Henry, *Economie Agricole de l'Indochine* (Hanoi, 1932).
61 Robert L. Sansom, *The Economics of Insurgency in the Mekong Delta of Vietnam* (Cambridge, Mass., 1970).
62 The details of the rising of November 1940 were not publicized at the time, and a proper study of the event must await the availability to scholars of the French archives of that time. It affected mainly the Mekong provinces, but its geography was by no means identical with that of the unrest of 1930.
63 Cf. M. E. Osborne, *The French Presence in Cochinchina and Cambodia, Rule and Response (1859–1905)* (Ithaca, 1969).
64 On the religious rôle of the *thay-phap* in more recent times, see G. C. Hickey, *Village in Vietnam* (New Haven, 1964), pp. 79–81.
65 This idea is more fully discussed in Ralph Smith, *Viet-Nam and the West*, cited earlier.
66 Cf. *art. cit.*, *Bull. of School of Oriental and African Studies*.
67 See *Contribution*, iv, pp. 21 ff.
68 Cf. above, note 43.
69 *Contribution*, i, consists of a long and detailed account by a member of a rival organization in northern Central Vietnam — the *Cach-Menh Dang*, known also by other names — and traces its loss of power in the area to the Communists during the years 1925–9. Although it is possibly not reliable in every detail (it was after all, a confession to the police), it gives a better idea than any other document of the character and atmosphere of Vietnamese revolutionary politics at this time. Unfortunately no comparable source exists for Cochinchina.

7 An introduction to Caodaism

Origins and early history

Source: *Bulletin of the School of Oriental and African Studies* 33(2) (1970), 335–349.

I

Few phenomena in the modern history of Asia can have been so completely mis-understood by Westerners as the Vietnamese religious (and political) movement known in European languages as 'Caodaism'. Based upon a syncretic approach to religion, in which a key role is played by spirit-séances, it has inevitably been regarded by Christian writers with the same suspicion (if not contempt) as occidental 'spiritualism'; and this initial lack of sympathy is compounded by the fact that the spirits who have revealed themselves at Caodaist séances include such familiar figures as Victor Hugo and Jeanne d'Arc. Then there is the show-piece temple of the Caodaists at Tây-Ninh, which drew forth Mr. Graham Greene's description of 'Christ and Buddha looking down from the roof of the Cathedral on a Walt Disney fantasia of the East, dragons and snakes in Technicolor'.[1] This superficial notion of the religious element in Caodaism fitted in very well with the cynicism of political observers, notably Bernard Fall, who saw in Caodaism no more than a political movement anxious to preserve its private armies and local power, using its religious ideas merely to dupe a credulous peasantry.[2] In these circumstances, it is perhaps not surprising that the real nature and origins of Caodaism have been lost from view, and even its history has never been adequately summarized in any Western language. The present article will attempt to fill the historical gap, by tracing the history of the religion from 1925 to 1936, and then looking at its origins and antecedents. A subsequent article (to appear in *BSOAS*, XXXIII, 3, 1970) will analyse the various beliefs which have been incorporated into this essentially syncretic cult.

To some extent Western ignorance about Caodaism is the responsibility of the Caodaists themselves. In the early days it was their deliberate intention to conceal their activities from the French, except in so far as it was necessary to offer the authorities a façade in order to obtain formal permission to open 'oratories' (*thánh-thất*). Moreover, it is in the tradition of Vietnamese religious sects to keep their innermost beliefs secret, not only from the authorities but from all outsiders. They did, it is true, put out a small amount of literature in French and English (especially around 1950–1, when there was a possibility that they might attract American support); but it is not easy to interpret correctly unless one is able to relate it to a wider background of Chinese and Vietnamese religious practices.[3] Moreover, it is very easy to be misled by these works into thinking that they contain the whole truth, whereas in fact they give only a few clues. It is only in recent years that a number of more detailed accounts of the early history of Caodaism have been published, in Vietnamese, and it is those works which form the most important source material for the present article. The author has probably not found all available writings of this kind, but in the present state of Western knowledge one may hope that it is excusable to publish an article based on incomplete material. The most important works used are a history of Caodaism by Đông-Tân, of which the first volume appeared in 1967; and a biography of Nguyễn Ngọc Tương published in 1958.[4] Another valuable source is the number of the bilingual *Revue Caodaïque* for December 1950, which contains some material about the early history of the religion.[5] In addition mention may be made of two Western-language accounts by people who were not themselves Caodaists: that compiled by the French colonial Sûreté in 1933–4,[6] and that written by the American anthropologist Dr. G. C. Hickey, relating particularly to the village of Khánh-Hậu (Long-An province) in the 1950s.[7] Finally, it is possible to glean a little additional information from contemporary accounts in the Sàigòn press, notably the *Écho Annamite* (1920–42), whose director was for a long time Nguyễn Phan Long, a sympathizer and eventually an active member of the Caodaist movement.

II

The formal inauguration of the Cao-Đài religion took place at a ceremony, near Tây-Ninh, on 18 November 1926. Tây-Ninh has remained ever since the most publicized centre of Caodaist activity, though not necessarily the most important at all periods. As a centre its scale has increased with the passage of time. The inauguration ceremony took place in the village of Gò-Kén, five km. south of the town of Tây-Ninh, where the Từ-Lâm Tự temple had just been built by a Buddhist monk, the *hòa-thư ợng* Giác-Hải, of Chợ-Lớn. He was a convert to the new religion, and had eagerly made over his new temple to its leaders; but the laymen who had subscribed funds to construct the temple were less happy with the arrangement, and consequently the Caodaists had to leave and find a new home as early as March 1927.[8] They moved to another village, Long-Thành, not far away, and began to construct a new temple of their own with funds donated by Madame Lâm Thị Thanh, a businesswoman of Vũng-Liêm (Mỹ-Tho), who was rewarded by becoming the first woman to hold high office in the Caodaist hierarchy, with the grade of *phô'i-sư*.[9] The present temple was presumably the result of this donation, though the date of its final completion is not recorded in any of the materials used for this study. But it was not merely the temple which made Tây-Ninh so important as a Caodaist centre. In August 1930 there were press reports that the Caodaist leader, Lê Văn Trung, had appealed to followers living in various parts of French Cochinchina to move to Tây-Ninh to settle on 500 hectares of land which the movement had acquired.[10] A description of the Caodaist settlement as it was in 1932 indicates that the movement had two 'concessions provisoires' at Long-Thành, amounting to 196 hectares (none of it rice-land) and in addition an unspecified area of rice-land at the village of Hiệp-Ninh, a little towards the north.[11] There were also workshops of various kinds, and the community living there had (in the early days at least) something in common with the self-sufficient communities favoured by Gandhi in India. Indeed, given the considerable interest in Indian affairs shown by some of the Sàigôn press at that time, it is not impossible that Gandhi provided the inspiration for the Tây-Ninh community. But in the details of its administration, as well as in its religious content, Caodaism was thoroughly Vietnamese. Nor is it likely that Gandhi would have approved the development of Tây-Ninh into a military centre, which was to happen in the years after 1945 when the Caodaists created their own private army.

In some respects Tây-Ninh was recognized by all Caodaists as the focal point of their religion. But it would be wrong to regard Caodaism as in any sense a monolithic movement, always focused upon a single centre; nor would it be correct to accept 18 November 1926 as the date of its first beginning. The history of Caodaism cannot be written in terms of the history of Tây-Ninh, nor in terms of the careers only of those Caodaists who played a leading role there.

The official 'founder' of Caodaism was a man who had very little to do with Tây-Ninh. He was Ngô Văn Chiêu (1878–1932), sometimes known as Ngô Minh Chiêu, a Vietnamese official in the French colonial administration of Cochinchina. The son of a rice-mill employee, he was born at Bình-Tây (Chợ-Lớn), but from the age of seven he lived with his aunt (his father's sister) at Mỹ-Tho. With financial help from a friend of the family, he was able to go to French schools (first the *collège* of Mỹ-Tho, then the Collège Chasseloup-Laubat in Sàigôn) and so to qualify for entry into the administrative service in 1899. But he was never able to study in France, and Vietnamese cultural and religious influence inevitably counted for much more in his life than his French education. Having served for 10 years in Sàigôn, he was transferred to a post at Tân-An in 1909, and remained there for a further decade. The remainder of his official career consisted of periods in Hà-Tiên (1920), on the island of Phú-Quốc (1920–4), and once again in Sàigôn (from 1924 till his retirement in 1931).[12] It was on Phú-Quốc that he first became an adept of the spirit 'Cao-Đài'.

The evocation of spirits was traditionally a common pastime amongst Vietnamese (as amongst Chinese) officials, but Ngô Minh Chiêu appears to have taken it more seriously than some, especially after about 1917 when he sought by this means to obtain a cure for his sick mother. About the period 1917–19, he used to attend séances at a temple at Cái-Khê (near Cần-Thơ), later known as the *Hiệp-Minh* temple, and it was then that the spirit called 'Cao-Đài Tiên-Ông' first appeared to him.[13] At Hà-Tiên, he made further contacts with that spirit, in séances at the tomb of Mạc-Cửu (the Ming refugee who had founded Hà-Tiên around 1690). But it was after he moved to Phú-Quốc that the Cao-Đài spirit began completely to dominate the life of Ngô Minh Chiêu. At *Tết* (8 February) 1921, he accepted an instruction to adopt the discipline of vegetarianism; and in April of that year he had the vision which led him to adopt the great Eye as a symbol of the Cao-Đài spirit.[14] By the time of his return to Sàigôn in 1924, he was sufficiently confident of the importance of this spirit to begin to convert his friends to its worship. Those who became adepts of Cao-Đài during 1925 were Vương Quan Kỳ, a fellow-official in Sàigòn; Đoàn Văn Bản, who was in charge of a primary school at Cầu-Kho (Chợ-Lớn) where he subsequently founded a Caodaist temple; and Nguyễn Ngọc Tưởng, an official at Cân-Giuộc (Chợ-Lớn).[15] Then in December of that year, Ngô Minh Chiêu was visited by a quite separate group of spiritist adepts, known as the *Phò-Loan* group, and it is from that meeting that we can perhaps date the beginnings of Caodaism as an organized movement. The following month (January 1926), the cult of Cao-Đài began to be organized under the leadership of Lê Văn Trung.

About some of the early converts little is known beyond their names and profession; but a few can be studied in greater depth. Notable amongst them was Nguyễn Ngọc Tưởng (1881–1951), an official of about the same generation as Ngô Minh Chiêu, and one whose career was in many respects similar. Born at An-Hội, near the town of Bến-Tre, he was educated in Chinese at home and in French at the *collèges* of Mỹ-Tho and Chasseloup-Laubat. He entered the administrative service in 1902, and from 1903 till 1919 served in his own province of Bến-Tre. Then from 1920 till 1924 he was district chief at a place called Hòn-Chông, not far from Hà-Tiên, where the population was mainly Chinese and Cambodian.[16] It was whilst he was there (and interestingly enough, these were the same years that Ngô Minh Chiêu spent on Phú-Quốc) that he began to lead an ascetic life and to study the religion of the *Minh-Sư* sect, with which Chiêu had also had connexions.[17] In 1924 he was transferred to the district office of Cần-Giuộc, where he remained till 1927: it is said in his biography that he was moved from Cần-Giuộc to the more remote district of Xuyên-Mộc (Bà-Rịa) as a result of his proselytizing activities for the new religion. In due course, towards the end of 1930, he would leave government service altogether to take up an administrative position at Tây-Ninh, where we shall meet him again.

The background of the *Phò-Loan* group is somewhat different, for they appear to have had no education in Chinese culture or religion, and apparently some of them were originally Catholics. We first meet with them in July or August 1925, when they were practising spiritism 'in the European manner': that is, using the ouija-board.[18] The two most prominent figures in the group were Cao Quỳnh Cư (1887–1929), a clerk in the railway office at Sàigòn, and Phạm Công Tắc (1893–1958), who held a similar position in the customs department. Phạm Công Tắc, and probably other members of the group, belonged to a slightly younger generation than Ngô Minh Chiêu and Nguyễn Ngọc Tưởng. He was born in Tân-An province, and had entered government service in 1910: he served in the customs department from then until January 1928, when he retired to devote all his time to religion. Although he was by no means a young man by 1926, he was not merely an organizer of spirit-séances, but also a medium himself.[19] This notwithstanding, his whole career suggests that he was more interested in politics than religion, though it is not clear whether at this stage he was already a supporter of the Vietnamese pretender, Prince Cường-Đề, then living in Japan. Certainly he had contacts with him later on, in 1941–2.

Finally, o something must be said of the career of Lê Văn Trung (1875–1934). He too was of roughly the same generation as Ngô Minh Chiêu, and to begin with they had similar careers.[20] Born in Chợ-Lớn province (canton of Phước-Điên-Trung), he was the son of a small farmer, but was able through hard study to gain entry to the Collège Chasseloup-Laubat whence he graduated in 1893. He entered the administrative service soon afterwards, and advanced by the normal stages until 1905. But in that year he left to enter a business enterprise, and when it succeeded he resigned his government position for good. Subsequently he was elected to the Conseil Colonial of Cochinchina, and later was chosen by the authorities to serve on the Conseil Supérieur de l'Indochine; he resigned from the latter in October 1925. By that time he had suffered some severe financial setbacks, especially in 1924; also, he had become interested in Caodaism. There are two different versions of his first attendance at a séance. According to one story, he was taken to a séance at Chợ-Gạo in June 1925 by his friend the Conseiller Nguyễn Hữu Đắc; the same account mentions that he was also a friend of the brother of Vương Quan Ký, one of Ngô Minh Chiêu's first converts.[21] The other version tells how Lê Văn Trung was introduced to a séance by 'a relative', who was a member of the *Minh-Lý* sect, and how the spirit of Lý Thái Bạch (Li Po, the T'ang poet) predicted a spiritual future for him: whereupon he gave up all his vices overnight.[22] Whatever the origin of his connexion with Caodaism, there can be no doubt that he was in touch with the *Phò-Loan* group by 18 January 1926, when a séance was held at his house attended by Cao Quỳnh Cư, Phạm Công Tắc, etc., and it is from that date that he appears to have begun the organization of Caodaism as a formal religious movement.[23]

It was Lê Văn Trung who in May 1926 sought government permission for the opening of 21 'oratories' in various parts of east and central Cochinchina, most of which had been permitted to open, under strict conditions for worship, by the end of the year.[24] It was he too who organized the petition of 7 October 1926, addressed to Le Fol, the Governor of Cochinchina, in which 28 Caodaists appealed for the official recognition of their movement as a religion.[25] Besides Lê Văn Trung, and also Madame Lâm Thị Thanh, the signatories included Nguyễn Ngọc Tương, Lê Bá Trang, and Nguyễn Ngọc Thơ (who by 1931 occupied the three highest offices at Tây-Ninh under Lê Văn Trung); two of Ngô Minh Chiêu's first converts, Vương Quan Kỳ and Đoàn Văn Bản; and also the five members of the *Phò-Loan* group. Two other names which figured prominently in the list were those of Lê Văn Lịch and Trần Đạo Quang, both of whom are described as *thày-tu* (religious masters). They are mentioned in another context by Gobron: Lê Văn Lịch as head of the *Minh-Đường* sect, and Trào Dạo Quang as head of the *Minh-Sư* sect.[26] Their presence in this list of October 1926 confirms the impression that at its roots Caodaism must have had some connexion with the *Minh* sects.

The letter of October 1926 was not, however, signed by Ngô Minh Chiêu himself. His connexion, with the *Phò-Loan* group and with Lê Văn Trung proved to be very short-lived. As one source put it, 'used to his solitude, he was annoyed by the influx of adherents, who bothered him'.[27] In April 1926 he had already decided not to become involved in the politics of the new religious organization, and handed over his leadership to Lê Văn Trung. Shortly afterwards he organized his own small following at Cần-Thơ, and for the remainder of his life he was associated only with that place. It was to Cần-Thơ (in fact, Cái-Khề) that he retired in 1931, and there that he died the following year. His followers became known as the *Chiếu-Minh* sect of Caodaism. But behind this apparent schism there was another distinction: between the 'inner' and 'outer; aspects of the religion, or between 'nonaction' (*vô-vi*, Chinese *-wu-wei*) and; 'salvation' (*phổ-độ*, Chinese *pu-tu*): it was in the nature of this type of religious movement that some of its members should go out into the world and proselytize, whilst others remained aloof from lay contact, and also from politics.[28] It is not necessary therefore to suppose an open quarrel at this stage in the development of Caodaism, although we cannot of course be certain that none had occurred. We do not even know whether Ngô Minh Chiêu attended the formal inauguration of the Cao-Đài religion, of which he was ostensibly the 'founder', at the ceremony at Tây-Ninh in November 1926.

III

The movement which had thus been launched expanded rapidly during the next three years. Lê Văn Trung, in a letter defending Caodaism against the attacks of Ernest Outrey (the Cochinchinese Deputy in the French Assembly), claimed in October 1928 that the religion had over a million adepts; but that was almost certainly an exaggeration. More credible is the report of 100,000 adepts in June 1927; and when a year later an article in *L'Opinion* suggested that there were as many as 700,000 adepts, even the less credulous Maurice Monribot agreed that there must be at least 200,000.[29] The number of oratories rose from about 20 at the end of 1926 to over 100 by 1931.[30] To begin with, the religion was mainly centred on east Cochinchina, but as time went on it became equally popular in the provinces of the centre (along the Mekong), and began to spread to the west (the Transbassac). Gobron, for example, notes that all the early séances took place at Chợ-Lớn, Cần-Gioc, Lộc-Giang, Tân-Định and Thủ-Đức: all places in the vicinity of Sàigòn.[31] And of the 21 'oratories' (*thánh-thất*) for which Lê Văn Trung sought government permission in May 1926, 13 were in Sàigòn and the provinces of Gia-Định and Chợ-Lớn, and another 2 in Tây-Ninh and Biên-Hoa; the remaining 6 were in provinces of the centre, Mỹ-Tho and Bến-Tre (2 each), Sa-Đéc and Vinh-Long.[32] But by 1932 there were said to be about 35,000–50,000 adepts in each of the provinces of Chợ-Lớn, Gia-Định, Bến-Tre, and Mỹ-Tho; by then, too, there were 'rival' Caodaist centres at Mỹ-Tho and Bạc-Liêu. Down to 1930, most Caodaists (with the exception of those in the *Tiên-Thiên* sect, of which we must treat separately) accepted in principle the hegemony of the 'holy see' (*tòa-thánh*) at Tây-Ninh. There seems to have been some kind of disagreement within the movement in 1928, as a result of which the 'oratory' of Cầu-Kho (Sàigòn) came to be regarded as a dissident centre, but this does not appear to have amounted to a major breach.[33] It was not until 1930 that a real split began to develop, which produced rival centres of Caodaism.

What happened in that year must be seen against the background of growing concern on the part of the authorities that Caodaism was merely a cover for nationalist and perhaps also Communist activities. The attack by Outrey in 1928 has already been mentioned. About the same period there were other attacks in the Sàigòn press: some *colons* merely objected that the spiritism of the Caodaists was a superstition unworthy of men who had at least some French education; others went further, seeing in Caodaism a disguised revival of the secret societies which had endangered the security of the colony in the years before 1916. One writer suggested that the temple at Tây-Ninh was built on the precise spot where two Frenchmen had been murdered during the troubles of 1866.[34] A feature of the religion which especially alarmed the authorities at that time was its popularity amongst Cambodians, many of whom came across the border on pilgrimages to the 'holy see 'during 1927. As a result, on 23 December 1927 the King of Cambodia issued an ordinance condemning the new religion as a heresy, and for the time being these pilgrimages came to an end.[35] Then in 1930 came the most serious unrest in Cochinchina since 1916, with many and frequent demonstrations by gatherings of peasants, which were obviously the work of some kind of organization. Whilst the most concrete evidence seemed to attribute the unrest to the Communists, it was alleged by several people that the Caodaists were equally involved.[36] In vain was it pointed out that the worst trouble was in the provinces of the centre, whilst Tây-Ninh remained completely calm.[37] Whatever secret relations may have existed between the Caodaists and followers of the Việt-Nam Communist Party or of Nguyễn An Ninh's secret society left no tangible evidence, and it is impossible to know whether or not Caodaists actually were involved in the demonstrations. But the crisis of these years was sufficient to make the government more watchful in its desire to keep organizations like Caodaism under control. This in turn forced the leaders of the movement to consider carefully their attitude to the authorities.

The occasion of the first major Caodaist split appears to have been a decision, sometime towards the end of 1930, that all dignitaries of the religion above the grade of *phòi-sư* should go to live permanently at Tây-Ninh. One of the three men holding that grade in 1930 was Nguyễn Văn Ca, whose home was at Mỹ-Tho and whose family was. it would seem, opposed to his commitment to the religion in this way. After considerable hesitation, during which time he is said to have visited the dissident 'oratory 'at Cầu-Kho, Nguyễn Văn Ca decided not to go to Tây-Ninh but to establish his own: 'holy see' (*tòa-thánh*) at Mỹ-Tho.[38] It was said that there had been a long-standing rivalry between Ca and Lê Văn Trung; it was also said that at this stage the Mỹ-Tho group had the tacit support of the French administration, and even implied that the latter was trying to use Nguyễn Văn Ca to create an alternative focus of loyalty amongst the Caodaist faithful in order to draw them away from Tây-Ninh. During 1931–2 rivalry between Tây-Ninh and Mỹ-Tho became acute, and it would seem that many adepts transferred their allegiance to Mỹ-Tho. It was at this point, in 1931, that Lê Văn Trung transferred his administrative responsibilities at Tây-Ninh to Nguyễn Ngọc Tương, who had taken over Ca's place as *chánh-phôi-sư*, when he had gone to live permanently at the 'holy see' late in 1930.[39] Tương was able to persuade another *chánh-phối-sư*, Lê Bá Trang, to return from Mỹ-Tho to Tây-Ninh in November 1932, and these two men worked in close collaboration for the next four years, but Tương was unable to heal the breach entirely.[40] In August of that year a council at Tây-Ninh issued a decree outlawing Nguyễn Văn Ca and his followers as 'rebels' against the 'holy see' (of Tây-Ninh). But it was evident from the poor attendance at the Tây-Ninh festivities to celebrate the anniversary of the religion in November 1932, that its support had dwindled away.[41] Moreover, in the meantime yet another 'holy see' had been created at a place called Giồng-Bướm, in Bạc-Liêu province. This was established by Trân Đao-Quang, who had been a high dignitary at Tây-Ninh from 1926 to 1928, but then had gone to live at Cầu-Kho, and eventually moved to Bạc-Liêu in 1931.[42] The centres at Mỹ-Tho and Bạc-Liêu were probably on good terms with one another, though there were doctrinal differences between them. Their new forms of the religion were called respectively the *Minh-Chơn-Lý* and the *Minh-Chơn-Đao*.

The crisis at Tây-Ninh had by 1932 produced serious internal disagreements between the leaders who remained there. The principal rivalry was between Nguyễn Ngọc Tương and Lê Bá Trang, on the one hand, and Phạm Công Tắc and Lê Văn Trung on the other. Phạm Công Tắc, who held the position of *hộ-pháp*, was head of the *Hiệp-Thiên Đài* (the organization of mediums), whilst Lê Văn Trung was the highest member of the administrative organization, the *Cửu-Trùng Đài*. As we have seen, Tương and Trang held the slightly lower grade of *chánh-phối-sư* in the latter organ. But in addition, by 1932 Phạm Công Tắc had created his own inner sect, the *Phạm-Môn*, which was named after his own family and consisted of at most 500 of his own closest followers.[43] The conflict came to a head during the first half of 1933. In January of that year. Lê Bá Trang and Nguyễn Ngọc Tương sent out a circular requiring adepts to obey the French administration. It was possibly at this time that Nguyễn Phan Long intervened with Governor Krautheimer to secure the reopening of 92 Caodaist oratories which had been closed: the date of that event is unfortunately not clear.[44] What is certain is that Tương and Trang saw some show of obedience to the French as essential if their 'holy see' was to recover its position. In April 1933, Phạm Công Tắc and Lê Văn Trung decided to use this fact against them, and held a secret council meeting to condemn Trang and Tương as 'Francophiles'. But they were not yet strong enough to carry the day: on 16 April a formal meeting of the *Thương-Hội* council was held at Tây-Ninh, at which Lê Văn Trung and Phọm Công Tắc were condemned (in their absence).[45] In September, Lê Bá Trang made complaints against Trung in the French tribunal at Tây-Ninh town, and actually went as far as to have another of his opponents Lê Văn Bảy arrested at Phnom-Penh.[46] The situation was such that by the end of the year Lê Văn Trung and Phọm Công Tắc had to come to terms with Trang and Tương, and an agreement was signed between them on 27 December 1933.[47]

Such an agreement was, however, of no permanent value in a situation of this kind, and it is not surprising to find that once he was strong enough to do so, Lê Văn Trung denounced his rivals once again. It would seem that Lê Bá Trang and Nguyễn Ngọc Tương were much weaker now than formerly, and in March

1934 Tương withdrew from Tây-Ninh. He went first into seclusion in Bà-Rịa province, then to his home at An-Hội (Bến-Tre), where he began to organize the creation of his own 'holy see' and the reform of Caodaism: he called his new branch of the religion *Ban-Chinh-Đạo*.[48] The first assembly of adepts at An-Hội had just begun in November 1934. when news arrived of the death of Lê Văn Trung at Tây-Ninh. Nguyễn Ngọc Tương now recalled the agreement which he said had been made between himself and other leaders as long ago as 1928, to the effect that he himself was to be the successor of Lê Văn Trung in the highest office of *giáo-tông*.[49] But Phạm Công Tắc. although not strong enough to seize the position of *giáo-tông* for himself (he remained *hộ-pháp* as late as 1950), was able to prevent Nguyễn Ngọc Tương from succeeding to it. It was at An-Hội, therefore, that Tương was inaugurated as *giáo-tông* on 9 May 1935.[50] In November of that year, Phạm Công Tắc held his own council at Tây-Ninh, at which he had himself proclaimed Lê Văn Trung's successor as Caodaist 'superior'.[51] Whilst the Tây-Ninh group alleged later that the Bến-Tre centre was supported by a mere few hundred adepts, the biography of Nguyễn Ngọc Tương insists that (to begin with at least), he was supported by 96 out of the grand total of 135 Caodaist 'oratories'. Whatever the truth of these claims, it would seem that by November 1936, Tắc had restored the fortunes of Tây-Ninh sufficiently to be able to attract 20,000 people there to celebrate the tenth anniversary of the religion.[52]

By 1935, therefore, the original group which had founded Caodaism at Tây-Ninh nine years earlier had split into four different and rival centres: Tây-Ninh, Mỹ-Tho, Bạc-Liêu, and Bến-Tre. In addition there was a dissident group at Càu-Kho (Sàigòn) which did not claim the status of a *tòa-thánh* or 'holy see'. But this does not account for all those who called themselves Caodaists at this period. There was in addition a sixth group which was probably quite as important but about which very much less is known, at least before 1936. It is sometimes referred to as the *Tiên-Thiên* sect of Caodaism; but it is also known as the *Tây-Tông* 'Western Sect', supposedly to differentiate it from the original group at Tây-Ninh which in this connexion (but in none of their own literature) is referred to as the *Đông-Tông* 'Eastern Sect'[53] Its leaders were Nguyễn Bửu Tài (b. 1882) and Nguyễn Hữu Chỉnh. Of the former, we know that he was a native of the Ba-Tri district of Bến-Tre province and that he became a school-teacher, first at Bến-Tre and later at Biên-Hoa. He also became interested in religion, and is said to have been a *tu-đơn*, a kind of religious practitioner. When Caodaism was founded at Tây-Ninh in 1926, Tài (who was apparently in touch with Ngô Minh Chiêu and Lê Văn Trung) founded his own new sect, the *Tây-Tông*, in his own province. If this account is correct, then one cannot say he split off from the Tây-Ninh centre. Chỉnh on the other hand, possibly in 1927, is said to have left Tây-Ninh in order to establish a sect of his own at Mỹ-Tho.[54] It would seem that the *Tiên-Thiên* was much less organized than the 'Eastern Sect', or at least less openly organized. It did not acquire its own *tòa-thánh* until 1957, when one was established at Sóc-Sải: at that period the sect seems to have expanded, whilst the Tây-Ninh Caodaists were in decline, and it was then that Nguyễn Bửu Tài finally took the title *giáo-tông*.[55]

Whilst the *Tiên-Thiên* sect seems to have had few if any connexions with Tây-Ninh in the 1930s, it would seem to have been in closer contact with the Caodaists of Mỹ-Tho and Bạc-Liêu, and also with the 'esoteric' group at Cẩn-Thơ. In 1936 these various groups formed a 'Caodaist Union', the *Liên-Hòa Tổng-Hội*, with its centre at Cầu-Kho (Sàigòn).[56] An attempt to create some kind of union had already been made two years previously, with the participation of Đoàn Văn Bản and Vương Quan Kỳ (both at Cầu-Kho), Nguyễn Văn Kiên (at Mỹ-Tho), Cao Triêu Phát and Trần Đạo Quang (both at Bạc-Liêu), and also several other people including Phan Trương Mạnh. But all these people belonged to what seems to have been essentially a single group anyway, since both the Mỹ-Tho and the Bạc-Liêu Caodaists had been associated from the start with the 'oratory' at Cầu-Kho. In 1936 two new elements in the situation made possible a more worth-while union. First, the initiative was taken by a leading *Conseiller-Colonial* Nguyễn Phan Long, whose sympathies with Caodaism had been well known since he defended the religion in his newspaper *Écho Annamite* in 1927, but who had not previously played any ostensible role in the movement. He now became openly a Caodaist, and presided over the *Liên-Hòa Tổng-Hội*. Second, this new union had also the participation of the *Tiên-Thiên* sect, and Nguyễn Bửu Tài and Lê Kim Ty were amongst those mentioned as its leading members. It is not clear how deep the union was, but they seem to have played a full part in the first achievement of the *Liên-Hòa Tổng-Hội*. which was to spread Caodaism to Tourane (Đà-Nẵng) and other parts of central Việt-Nam.[56]

Thus by 1936 one can discern three broad alignments in the Caodaist movement: the Tây-Ninh group. led now by Phọm Công Tắc, with an important branch in Phnom-Penh presided over by Trần Quang Vinh; the Bến-Tre group, led by Nguyễn Ngọc Tương; and the *Liên-Hòa Tổng-Hội*, embracing the *Tiên-Thiên*, the *Minh-Chổn-Lý*. and the *Minh-Chổn-Đạo*, whose followers were mainly in the centre and west of Cochinchina. Given the material at present to hand, that is as far as one can reasonably hope to take the attempt to compile a detailed account of the history of Caodaism. More recent developments can only be studied when more 'inside' information becomes available.

IV

One major question concerning the early history of Caodaism remains to be raised: that of its origins and antecedents. The whole tenor of Caodaist publications is to emphasize that this was a new religion, which suddenly burst upon the world in 1926 and attracted immediately a large following of ordinary people. But when we come to examine the doctrines of the religion it will be clear that there was much in Caodaism that had deep roots in Sino-Vietnamese tradition, and that it must be seen against the background of earlier religious movements. We know that several of the leading Caodaists had had religious interests and experiences before 1925–6, notably Ngô Văn Chiêu and Nguyễn Ngọc Tương. Did they do so entirely outside any previously existing religious organization? On the face of things, it seems unlikely.

The divisions in Caodaism, 1926–36

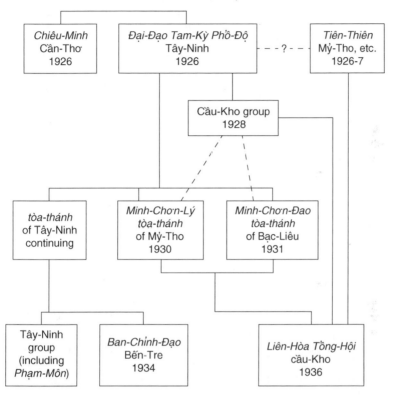

That secret organizations of a religious (and also political) nature had existed in South Việt-Nam in earlier periods is well known. They were particularly prominent in the periods 1860–85 and 1905–16. In the former period, the French conquest of Cochinchina was opposed most strongly by a group identified as a religious sect with the name *Đạo-Lành*.[57] Following a French decree of 1873 prohibiting that sect, it is said to have reorganized under the name *Đạo Phật Đường*. It was held responsible for 'rebellions' in Mỹ-Tho and other provinces in 1874 and 1878. and for the disturbances of 1885 which included an attack on Sàigòn.[58] But the French do not seem to have penetrated the organization of the movement, and there is no account of it in any printed or archival source-material I have seen. Concerning the secret society movement of the years 1905–16, which culminated in another abortive attack on Sàigòn, followed by a great many arrests, there exists the fascinating account by Coulet, based on detailed police records. But even there we do not have a detailed picture of whatever religious organization underlay the movement: Coulet gives only occasional translations of 'captured documents', and reproduces a number of amulets written in Chinese characters. The religious propaganda of Caodaism was certainly a new phenomenon amongst Vietnamese secret sects, and because we have no comparable material concerning earlier groups it is impossible to make detailed comparisons, in such matters as doctrine, ritual, or organizational hierarchies. We cannot say, therefore, to what extent (if at all) these earlier movements represent an earlier stage in the same line of development which eventually produced Caodaism. Nor is there so far any evidence to link the personalities of Caodaism with earlier movements: a fact which in itself proves nothing, of course, because it was unlikely that a newly organized sect would choose its leaders from amongst those whose leadership of the earlier movements was already well known to the police. There is, however, one interesting detail which should not be allowed to pass unnoticed, and which suggests that there may indeed have been connexions between these movements of different periods. In a Caodaist tract, published in French by Phan Trương Mạnh in 1950, there is a reference to a spirit-séance held at Cao-Lãnh in 1908, in which a message was received from the spirit of the 'laureate' (*thủ-khoa*) Huân, a leading figure in the revolt of 1874–5 which the French had attributed to the *Đạo-Lành* sect. The message, moreover, includes two references to the *Cao-Đài*.[59]

That same tract has another reference which suggests a slightly different line of inquiry in our search for Caodaist antecedents. Another amongst several earlier references to the *Cao-Đài*, cited by Phan Trương Mạnh, comes in a prayer which he says has been recited for about 40 years (i.e. since about 1910) by adepts of the religious sect called *Minh-Sư*.[60] We have already met references to this sect in the early careers of Nguyễn Ngọc Tương, who came into contact with, it around 1920. and Ngô Minh Chiêu, who is said to have been friendly with a high dignitary of the *Minh-Sư* around 1919.[61] But it was in fact only one of a number of sects of this kind which were associated with Caodaism. In the English edition of Gobron, there has been added a list of the various *phái* 'divisions' of the religion, including the *Minh-Chơn-Lý*, the *Minh-Chơn-Đạo*, the *Tây-Tông*, and so on, which is then followed by a list of the five *chi* 'branches' of Caodaism. together with the names of their heads: [62]

Minh-Lý	Âu Kích
Minh-Sư	Trần Đạo Quang
Minh-Tân	Lê Minh Khá
Minh-Thiện	'Dạt' and 'Mùi'
Minh-Đường	Lê Văn Lịch

We have already met two of these men in connexion with Caodaism: Trần Đạo Quang (later founder of the *Minh-Chơn-Đạo* at Bạc-Liêu) and Lê Văn Lịch. who were amongst the signatories of the letter seeking French recognition for the new religion in October 1926.[63] Concerning the *Minh-Đường*, the *Minh-Tân*, and the *Minh-Thiện*, there is no other information. But the *Minh-Lý* figures elsewhere in Gobron's account. It was to this sect that one of Lê Văn Trung's relatives belonged in 1925. and possibly through this connexion that Trung was first introduced to spirit-séances. At a later stage (the date is not given) we find Phạm Công Tắc insisting on the distinction between Caodaism and

'Minhlism': the latter 'is separated from us by a mystical and philosophical point of view'.[64] His vagueness on the actual doctrinal differences suggests that he had some political reason for making the distinction, but we have no means of knowing what it was.

All these references to the *Minh* 'branches' relate to the period after about 1919: they nevertheless seem to suggest that when Caodaism first emerged there already existed a number of sects in which some of its doctrines and rituals were already familiar. Might not these sects have existed for long before, and have provided the religious background to earlier movements? There is one last piece of evidence concerning the *Minh-Sư* which seems to point in that direction. Ngô Minh Chiêu, following his return to Sàigòn in 1924, spent a good deal of time at a temple in Dà-Kao (a suburb of the city) called the *Ngọc-Hoàng-Điện* 'Jade Emperor Palace'. That temple had been built in the years 1900–6, by a Chinese businessman called Lưu Minh, a member of the *Minh-Sư* vegetarian sect which in China was at that period dedicated to the cause of overthrowing the Manchu dynasty and restoring the Ming.[65] Do we have here a clue to the real roots of Caodaism?

Notes

1 Graham Greene, *The quiet American* (Penguin Books, 1962), 81.
2 B. B. Fall, 'The political-religious sects of Viet-Nam', *Pacific Affairs*, xxviii, 3, 1955, 235–53 .
3 The best-known of these works is G. Gobron, *Histoire du Caodaisme*, Paris, 1948 (English translation, Sàigòn ?, 1950); except where otherwise stated, references here will be to the English version, which includes additional material but omits an important chapter. See also Nguyễn Trung Hậu, *Lược-sử Đạo Cao-Đài: A short history of Caodaism* (in Vietnamese, French, and English), Tourane, 1956.
4 Đông-Tân, *Lịck-sử Cao-Đài*, *i. Phần Vô-Vi*, Sàigòn, 1967, referred to in subsequent pages as *Lịch-sử*; Anon., *Tiểu-sử Đức Giáo-Tông, Nguyễn Ngọc Tương*, Sàigón, 1958, referred to subsequently as *NNT*.
5 *Revue Caodaïque*, iiie An., décembre 1950; this periodical should be carefully distinguished from *Renie Caodaïste*, published in the years around 1930. I have not seen any copies of the latter, but it is cited in Gobron, op. cit., and in *Contribution*, vii (see n. 6 below).
6 Gouvernement-Général de l'Indochine, *Contribution à l'histoire des mouvements politiques de l'Indochine française*, vii. Le Caodaïsme, Hànội, 1934; referred to subsequently as *Contribution*, vii.
7 G. C. Hickey, *Village in Vietnam*, Yale, 1964, 66–73, 290–4.
8 *Écho Annamite*, 19 November 1926; Gobron, op. cit., 29.
9 *Contribution*, vii, 33–4.
10 *La Dépêche d'Indochine*, 28 and 30 August 1930.
11 *Contribution*, vii, 64–7.
12 There is a very full account of his life in Döng-Tan, *Lịch-sử*.
13 *Lịch-sử*, 53 ff.
14 ibid., 66 ff.; this episode is also mentioned briefly in Nguyễn Trung Hậu, op. cit., 7–8.
15 *Lịch-sử*, 82–92; Nguyễn Ngọc Tương is not mentioned there, but his conversion late in 1925 is indicated by *NNT*, 13.

16 *NNT*, 5–6.

17 ibid., 13.

18 *Lịch-sử*, 88 ff.; Gobron, 20–1, refers to this group without mentioning names.

19 The fullest account of Phạm Công Tắc's early career is in *Contribution*, VII, 87–90.

20 On Lê Văn Trung, see ibid., 27–32; also Gobron, 26 ff.

21 *Lịch-sử*, 91.

22 *Contribution* VII, 29–31, and Gobron, 26–7; both it would seem based, at this point, on material in *Revue Caodaï'ste*, no. 3, p. 345.

23 *Lịch-sử*, 91.

24 *Contribution*, VII, 81.

25 *Lịch-sử*, 108–10, gives the Vietnamese text of this letter and a full list of the actual signatories; there was an additional list of 247 adepts, but I have not seen any record of their names. Cf. *Contribution*, VII, 32, 81, where it is noted that no formal recognition of Caodaism was given at this time, despite Caodaist claims.

26 Gobron, 151; cf. *infra*, p. 349.

27 Gobron, 27.

28 *Lịch-sử*, 129 ff.

29 *Écho Annamite*, 13 June 1927; *La Presse Indochinoise*, 9 June 1928 (comment by the editor Monribot on an article in *L'Opinion*).

30 *Contribution*, VII, 80–1. Tây-Ninh controlled 105 *thánh-thất* in 1931, and 128 in 1932, but it is not clear whether 'dissident' oratories at that time are excluded from these totals.

31 Gobron, 28.

32 *Contribution*, VII, 81.

33 Gobron (French edition), 98 ff.: a whole section of this edition, relating to schisms within the movement during the period 1928–31, was omitted in the English version, for reasons which can only be guessed. Cf. also *NNT*, 20.

34 *La Presse Indochinoise*, 9 June 1928, citing a recent article in *L'Opinion*. The Frenchmen referred to were Captain de Larclauze and Lieut. Lesage, who were killed in an attack on Tây-Ninh by 2,000 Cambodians in June 1866; A. Schreiner, *Abrégé de l'histoire d'Annam*, Sàigòn, 1906, 277.

35 *Contribution*, VII, 35–7.

36 e.g. by R. Vanlande, *L'Indochine sous la menace communiste*, Paris, 1930, 118–19. For an account of the disturbances in Cochinchina, between May 1930 and March 1931, see Gouvernement-Général de l'Indochine, *Contribution à l'histoire des mouvements politiques de l'Indochine française*, IV, Hànội, 1934.

37 *Écho Annamite*, 23 May 1930.

38 Gobron (French ed.), 98 ff. There is a slightly different account in Hickey, op. cit., 292–3, which says that Ca left Tây-Ninh in 1931 after receiving a spirit-message instructing him to do so, and that he went first to Rạch-Gia before settling at Mỹ-Tho in 1932. Hiclcey's information presumably came from Caodaists he interviewed at Khánh-Hậu (Tân-An province), where the Mỹ-Tho sect had some members in 1958.

39 *NNT*, 21–4; the letter written by Tương to inform the Governor of Cochinchina of the change of direction is there reproduced, dated 1 September 1931.

40 *Contribution*, VII, 90.

41 ibid., 86–7, 90–1.

42 Gobron (French ed.), 101 ff.; cf. *Revue Caodaïque*, IIIe An., décembre 1950, 93–107.

43 *Contribution*, VII, 86–90.

44 ibid., 92; *Revue Caodaïque*, IIIe An., décembre 1950, 67–93.

45 *Contribution*, VII, 93; *NNT*, 31.

46 *Contribution*, VII, 94, 100.

47 *NNT*, 32–4.

48 ibid., 34, 37.

49 ibid., 41–5.
50 ibid., 48.
51 Gobron, 71–2.
52 ibid., 74.
53 The only account of the *Tiên-Thiên* sect which does more than merely note its existence is the biographical notice on Nguyễn Bửu Tài contained in a recent monograph of the former Bến-Tre province: Huỳnh-Minh, *Địa-linh nhơn-kiệt: Kiên-Hòa xưa và nay*, Gia-Đinh, 1965, 196–9.
54 Nguyễn Trung Hậu, op. cit., 20.
55 Hickey, op. cit., 293–4. The *Tiên-Thiên-* sect appears to have co-operated, closely with, the Communists since. 1960: one of its leading members, Nguyễn Văn Ngôi, sat on the Central Committee of the National Front for the Liberation of South Việt-Nam from 1961 till at least 1964; Douglas Pike, *Viet Cong*, Cambridge, Mass., 1966, 429.
56 Nguyễn Trung Hậu, op. cit., 20; *Revue Caodaïque*, IIIe An., décembre 1950, 67–92.
57 According to some sources (e.g. Coulet, 122 ff., cf. *infra*), this is *Đạo-Lành*, which would mean 'Religion of the Good'; "but according to others (e.g. a report by the Administrateur of Sóc-Trăng in 1883) it should be *Đạo-Lãnh*, which might mean 'Way of the Leader'.
58 A. Schreiner, op, cit., 315; G. Coulet, *Les sociétés secrètes en terre d'Annam*, Sàigòn, 1926, 122 ff.
59 Phan Trương Mạnh, *La voie du salut caodaïque*, Sàigòn, 1950, 48–9.
60 ibid., 48.
61 *Lịch-sử*, 57; cf. *supra*, p. 339.
62 Gobron, 151.
63 *supra*, p. 340, n. 25.
64 Gobron, 108 ff.
65 Vương Hồng Sén, 'La Pagode de l'Empereur de Jade à Dakao', *Notes et Documents* (*Bull, de l'Association Viet-Nam France*), janvier 1965, 26.

Part of the material on which this article is based was collected during a visit to Sàigòn in 1967, financed by the London-Cornell Project for East and South East Asian Studies, financed jointly by the Carnegie Corporation of New York and the Nuffield Foundation.

8 An introduction to Caodaism

Beliefs and organization[1]

Source: *Bulletin of the School of Oriental and African Studies* 33(3) (1970), 573–589.

The religion of Cao-Đài is fundamentally, and deliberately, syncretic. Since it includes Christ and Moses (but for some reason, not Muhammad) in its pantheon, the Western student might be tempted to see it as essentially an attempt to bridge the gulf between East and West by finding a sort of middle way between Christianity and Buddhism. It is possible that some Caodaists who have acquired a thorough Western education in France but maintained their religious belief do in fact see it in those terms, but most of the Caodaist literature indicates that the real basis of the syncretism is an attempt to bring together the three religions of the Sino-Vietnamese tradition. In this attempt, Christianity has only a peripheral position, and nothing has been adopted from Christian teachings that would seriously clash with the underlying doctrinal tolerance of East Asian religions. The most important feature of Caodaist syncretism is that it brings together elements of Taoist spirit-mediumship with a concept of salvation that was originally Buddhist. If any one of the three Sino-Vietnamese religions may be said to be dominant in Caodaism it is religious Taoism; but since the Caodaists themselves frequently refer to their religion as 'reformed Buddhism', that is a point which must be demonstrated rather than taken for granted. I propose to analyse some of the most obvious elements of Caodaism under four headings: spirit-mediumship; the Cao-Đài and other spirits; salvation and the apocalyptic aspect; and hierarchy and organization. A concluding section will deal briefly with the possible relationship between Caodaism and certain religious sects in China.[2]

I Spirit-mediumship

It is hardly surprising that in the account of Caodaism compiled by Gabriel Gobron, the spiritist element stands out very sharply, since he himself appears to have become aware of the Vietnamese religion through his interest in French spiritism.[3] Probably the same was true of Paul Monet and other Frenchmen who attended séances in Sàigòn and agreed to propagate the religion in France. This being so, neither is it surprising to find occasional references in Vietnamese writing to the European spiritist movement. French spiritism, as an organized movement, had come into being at the same period as the French moved into Cochinchina. Its founder, L. H. D. Rivail (1804–69), better known from 1856 till his death by the pseudonym Allan Kardec, was the proprietor of a school in Paris and a proponent of the ideas of Pestalozzi, at whose Swiss school he had been educated. He fell in with the fashion of playing with *tables tournantes* which developed in France about the years 1854–5; but he took it more seriously than most and in 1856 published a book, *Le livre des esprits*, consisting of answers to his questions about philosophy and ethics received at a number of séances.[4] It was followed in 1861 by his *Livre des médiums*, and in the meantime he launched the *Revue Spirite* at the beginning of 1858. By his death, he had created an organization capable of surviving him, which still existed in France in the 1920s. It was a distinctive feature of the spiritism of Allan Kardec (as opposed to Anglo-Saxon 'spiritualism') that messages from the beyond were always received in written form, by means of the *table tournante*, the 'ouija-board', or the *corbeille à hec.* Caodaism too accepted only this form of communication with spirits, and it would seem that these European methods were sometimes used at Vietnamese séances. In particular it is noted that the *Phò-Loan* group of Phạm Công Tắc, when it began to hold séances in 1925, practised the 'European method'; and it is worth recalling in this connexion that the ouija-board was perfectly suitable for the Vietnamese language, once it had begun to be written in the roman script of *quõc-ngũ'* instead of in characters.

However, it would be a serious mistake to conclude from the evidence of this connexion with French spiritism that the Caodaists, or any other Vietnamese, owed either the idea or their techniques of spirit-mediumship to the *mission civilisatrice*. The practice of spiritism can be traced far back into the past of the Vietnamese and Chinese traditions; and whereas in the West the orthodoxy of Christianity was thoroughly opposed to spirit-mediumship, as a black art, in China the Confucian orthodoxy never attempted to stamp out spiritism as such. De Groot, one of the few Western writers to be interested in the practice and not merely the texts of Chinese religion, was able to supplement his own observation of spirit practices in nineteenth-century Fu-kien by reference to several textual accounts of earlier times. A document relating to the T'ang period describes how 'it was customary for the people to take a wicker rice-tray and dress it with clothes, and insert a chop-stick into it by way of beak, which they caused to write on a platter covered with flour in order to divine'.[5] An early form, indeed, of the beaked basket. Further evidence of Chinese mediumship by means of 'automatic writing' is found in Mr. A. J. A. Elliott's account of spirit cults in Singapore, based on observations made in the years 1950–1; he emphasizes that it is quite separate from the 'speaking-kind' of mediumship, in which the medium talks while possessed by a spirit, which is the main subject of his book. He describes a technique in which a Y-shaped stick is held by two people, one of them a medium, and writes out messages on a tray of sand, one character after another. It is necessary, of course, to have an interpreter to identify the characters at great speed.[6] Sometimes, he says, this kind of mediumship leads to the formation of associations of people willing to follow the injunctions received by way of spirit-writing. Very often, however, the invocation of spirits has no deeper motive than the simple desire of those attending to ask questions about their own future. In China, under the Ch'ing (and doubtless earlier), scholars would consult the spirits in this way to find out whether they would pass the examinations: an example occurs in Wu Ching-tzu's *The scholars*, where the spirit of Kuan Yü, 'conqueror of the devils', foretold the future of one of the characters in the novel.[7] Another description of a Chinese spirit séance worth mentioning is one by W. A. Grootaers, who attended a Buddhist séance in Peking in 1948, when messages were received from three Buddhist deities of the Western Paradise.[8] It is clear that spirit-mediumship was not the monopoly of any one of China's three religions but was judged compatible with all of them.

There are no detailed accounts of Caodaist séances by outside observers like de Groot or Grootaers, and so no comparison can be made on that level. But it seems clear from the vocabulary of Vietnamese writings on Caodaism that they fit into the Sino-Vietnamese tradition. Two phrases occur noticeably often: *cầu-tiên* (Chinese *ch'iu-hsien*), meaning to 'invoke the spirits' (literally, 'immortals'); and *đàn-co'* (Chinese *t'an-chi*), meaning the place at which the séance took place, or perhaps more specifically the tray on which the spirits wrote their messages. The Caodaists appear to have used the word *co'* where the Vietnamese dictionaries (related most closely to the North Vietnamese dialect) would give *kê*; it seems to indicate a traditional Sino-Vietnamese technique of spirit-writing, but it is possible that the same word was used also for the European type of planchette as well. The use of the term *đàn* in this context, may have some significance; it is also the term used for the altar on which the imperial sacrifices to Heaven and Earth were made, and it is not inconceivable that spirit-mediumship originally partook of the nature of a sacrifice to spirits as well as communication with them. The terms *cầu-co'* and *cầu-đàn* also occur in the Caodaist literature.[9]

It would seem that there were certain places in Cochinchina that were especially noted as important *đàn* (or *đàn-tiên*) where communication with spirits could be most effectively made. One of these was at Cái-Khế (Cần-Thơ), and was where Ngô Minh Chiêu held some of his early séances in the period 1917–20 ; several *đàn* are mentioned there in the period 1907–37, notably the *đàn Quang-xuân*, which appears to have been subsequently renamed the *đàn Hiệp-Minh*. About 1931, Ngô Minh Chiêu established another, the *đàn Chiếu-Minh*.[10] Another famous centre of mediumship was Cao-Lãnh; at the *đàn* there, established early this century, it was well known that Lý Thái Bạch came to write verses.[11] There is no reference, in the documents used for the present study, to Caodaist séances being held there; but that possibility can certainly not be ruled out. Nor should it be forgotten that Cao-Lãnh was an important centre of unrest in 1930, in which Caodaists were accused of being involved. Indeed spirit-mediumship of this kind may well have been more wide-spread than any of the source material on Cochinchinese history before 1920 indicates. Phan Trương Mạnh mentions a séance at Cao-Lãnh in 1908, when *Thủ-khoa* Huân communicated a message.[12] Is it not possible that spirit-mediumship was also an element in the secret society activity of 1912–16, about which we have only French source material? Was there, for example, any connexion between spirit-communication and the making of the amulets which Coulet regarded as so important? There is one small clue pointing in that direction in Đồng-Tân's account of Ngô Minh Chiêu's early career: after he had sought a cure for his mother by invoking spirits, about 1917, Chiêu and a number of friends used a technique of spirit-writing in order to obtain amulets to be used for medicinal purposes.[13] The curious composition of some of the amulets illustrated by Coulet might be explained more easily, if they were actually produced at séances; but at present this can be no more than a speculative suggestion.

The 'theology' underlying the spirit-mediumship of the Chinese and Vietnamese tradition is a subject which has been very little studied, and which cannot be thoroughly investigated here. But there is one passage in Gobron which suggests that, in spite of his own emphasis on French spiritism, the Caodaist séances were based on Taoist beliefs about the nature of spirits. He indicates the importance of *âm* and *dương* (Chinese *yin* and *yang*) in the arrangement of offerings to the spirits; a little later he speaks of the *tam-tài*, or three essential elements of the universe (Heaven, Earth, and Man), and then of the three constituent elements of man: *tinh* 'matter', *khí* 'vital essence', and *thần* 'spirit, soul'.[14] This is the vocabulary of religious Taoism, and it was the Taoists in the Chinese tradition who knew most about how to deal with spirits of all kinds. Amongst their beliefs was the notion that the best person to communicate with spirits was a young boy in whom the *dương* 'male' element was very strong: such a medium was called *đồng-tử*, meaning literally a boy who had just attained puberty. The Caodaists also refer to their mediums as *đồng-tử*, though in practice they were by no means always young boys. It is unfortunate that no copy seems to be available, outside Caodaist circles, of the book which Ngô Minh Chiêu used as his source of the technique of mediumship. It is referred to under the title *Vân-pháp quý-tông*.[15] But the mere fact of reference to that manual indicates that the Caodaists depended mainly on Sino-Vietnamese knowledge of mediumship, and that the existence of such practices amongst a small minority of Frenchmen in the 1920s is merely incidental to an understanding of the religion.

II The Cao-Đài and other spirits

As with the techniques of mediumship, so with the identity of the spirits invoked, Western impressions of Caodaism tend to place special emphasis on the European figures whose spirits have entered into the séances, and far less attention has been paid to Chinese and Vietnamese spirits. Particularly prominent amongst the former is Victor Hugo; another often mentioned is Jeanne d'Arc.[16] Hugo's writings, especially *Les misérables*, made a deep impression on French-educated Vietnamese readers; and it would seem that he also had the reputation amongst Caodaists of having been himself interested in spiritism. (He was an exile in the Channel Islands during the 1850s and 1860s, but may well have indulged there in a pursuit which was fashionable in many parts of France at the time when Allan Kardec founded his movement.) But one cannot dismiss the possibility that the main reason why early Caodaists mentioned Hugo so frequently in talking with Europeans was a desire to impress them with their high degree of loyalty to French culture, and perhaps thereby to cover up the more essential features of their cult. For men like Ngô Minh Chiêu and Nguyễn Ngọc Tương, Vietnamese and Chinese spirits must surely have been more important than those of any Frenchman.

It is possible for almost any spirit to be invoked, or to reveal himself, at a séance; usually, it would seem, the name of the spirit is not known until it has been communicated, and Caodaists do not set out to obtain messages from particular spirits decided upon by themselves in advance. Obviously we have information about only a small number of the spirits who revealed themselves at Caodaist, and pre-Caodaist, séances in the period 1917–37. Moreover, it is likely that only politically unharmful spirits would be mentioned in published accounts of the early séances. Phan Trương Mạnh records a message received from the South Vietnamese patriot *Thủ-khoa* Huân at Cao-Lãnh in 1908; *Thủ-khoa* Huân being the leader of a famous rising against the French in Mỹ-Tho province in 1874.[17] It is not impossible, despite the absence of documentary evidence, that the Caodaists also received communications from spirits of that ilk. Might there, one wonders, be some significance in the fact that Ngô Minh Chiêu (on Phú-Quốc) and Nguyễn Ngọc Tương (at Hòn-Chông) developed their early interest in spirit-mediumship in places which had been associated with the resistance movement of Nguyễn Trung Trực in 1867–8?[18] This possibility can be the subject only of speculation; it is the religious and literary figures whose spirit-revelations appear in the published sources.

One of the most frequently mentioned of these is the Tang poet Li Po, known in Vietnamese as Lý Thái Bạch. According to Gobron, it was Lý Thái Bạch who appeared at the first séance attended by Lê Văn Trung in 1925; it was his spirit too which propounded the principal doctrines of Caodaism at a séance attended by several Frenchmen in January 1927.[19] Mention has already been made of the association of that spirit with the *đàn* at Cao-Lãnh. Clearly he was of considerable importance for the early Caodaists, for at Tây-Ninh his spirit was made 'titular' *Giáo-Tông* or head of the religion—earthly occupants of the office being regarded as merely temporary incumbents.[20] The reason for his prominence is not made clear in the Caodaist literature. The poet was however a well-known Taoist: Arthur Waley's short biography of him describes how in the 720s he met the Taoist master Ssu-ma Ch'eng-cheng (d. 735), patriarch of the *Shang Ch'ing* school, and also how he qualified for a Taoist diploma at a temple in Shantung about 745.[21] If nothing else, the importance of his spirit in Caodaism is another indication of the Taoist, as opposed to Buddhist, affiliations of the religion. Another Taoist spirit who is mentioned in Caodaist works is Kuan Ti, the Chinese god of war: in Vietnamese, Quan-Thánh-Đế-Quân. One of his messages, received by a Caodaist group in Châu-Đốc province at an unspecified date, is printed by Phan Trương Mạnh.[22] We know too that Ngô Minh Chiêu grew up very close to a temple dedicated to that deity, and that as an adult he venerated (*thờ*) Kuan Ti especially.[23]

The most important of all the Caodaist spirits was of course the one who called himself *Cao-Đài Tiên-Ông* 'His Excellency the Grandfather Immortal'. The term *Cao-Đài*, which in some contexts has the literal meaning of 'high tower' or 'high palace' is commonly used in Chinese as a term of deepest respect, and as such was chosen by the Protestant missionaries as a translation of Jehovah in the Old Testament.[24] *Tiên* (Chinese *hsien*) is usually translated as 'immortal'; but as we have seen, in the phrase *càu-tiên* it is used by Caodaists to mean 'spirit', where others might have preferred the word *thần* (Chinese *shen*). *Ông* is a Vietnamese word, without Chinese derivation, which in current usage often means simply 'Mr.', but in this context denotes extreme respect of the kind usually accorded to a grandfather. It is similarly used in other spirit connexions: for example. *Ông Táo* is the 'hearth god' found in some form or other in all Vietnamese households, whilst *Ông Cọp* is the Tiger in his spirit-manifestation, widely venerated by Vietnamese. The curious thing is that none of these words indicates any specific identity for the supreme Caodaist spirit: was this a spirit which never had any previous existence before his appearance at séances around 1919? Or can he be identified with a spirit already recognized by Taoists in China and Việt-Nam? The former impression is created by some accounts, which emphasize the gradualness of the way in which he revealed his identity to those who became his first Vietnamese adepts. Gobron, speaking of Ngô Minh Chiêu's invocation of spirits on Phú-Quốc in 1919 (an error for 1920), says that 'among the communicating spirits he discovered one named Cao-Đài. in whom he became particularly interested'.[25] This discovery is described in greater detail by Đông-Tân.[26] Gobron also reports the early séances of the spiritist group which included Cao Quỳnh Cư and Phạm Công Tắc in 1925: 'One of the communicating spirits became particularly noticeable by his high level of moral and philosophical teachings. This spirit, who signed himself under the pseudonym "AAA" [in fact, *A-Ă-Â*, the first three letters of the Vietnamese alphabet, with different diacritical marks] did not wish to reveal himself in spite of the entreaties of his hearers'.[27] The spirit did eventually reveal himself as the *Cao-Đài Tiên-Ông*. But Nguyễn Trung Hậu describes how this latter revelation came about, in greater detail than Gobron, and in so doing he indicates the real identity of the Cao-Đài spirit: at a séance on Christmas Eve 1925, this spirit announced his name as *Ngọc-Hoàng Thượng-Đế viết Cao-Đài giao-đạo Nam-Phương*. The English version of his account translates this as 'Emperor of Jade, alias Caodaist God for the South', but a more literal rendering would be 'Jade Emperor, Supreme Deity, alias Cao-Đài, religious teacher of the Southern Quarter'.[28] The *Cao-Đài Tiên-Ông* was in fact none other than the Supreme Being himself, and Đông-Tân confirms this by his references to the spirit as *Cao-Đài Thượng-Đế*. The Jade Emperor was the Supreme Being of the Taoist pantheon, a personal deity of the highest order. Đông-Tân also tells us that when Ngô Minh Chiêu returned to Sàigòn in 1924 he stayed some of the time at a temple in Đà-Kao called the 'Jade Emperor Palace', which seems to confirm his connexion with the cult of this deity.[29] That temple is arranged as a Taoist temple. Here again, careful study of Caodaism seems to indicate that its origins were Taoist.

III   Salvation and the apocalyptic aspect of Caodaism

It lies beyond the scope of the present study to attempt a full analysis of the spirit-messages, which form the principal source for all the details of Caodaist belief and symbolism. One element in those beliefs, however, is indicated by the very title of the religion, and is of key importance: the belief in salvation and in the imminent end of the world as we know it. It will be recalled that when Ngô Minh Chiêu parted company with Lê Văn Trung and the other Caodaist leaders in April 1926, the former established the *vô-vi* section of the religion, whilst the latter established the *phô-đô* section.[30] The full official name of Caodaism, as used at Tây-Ninh, at Bến-Tre, and also by the 'United General Assembly' of 1936, is *Đại-Đạo Tam-Kỳ Phổ-Độ* 'the Great Way of the Three Epochs (or Third Epoch) of Salvation'. The idea of three epochs of spiritual development is a Buddhist rather than a Taoist idea, at least in origin, and amongst Mahayanists is often associated with belief in the three Buddhas: of the past (Amitābha, Vietnamese Di-đà), of the present (Sâkyamuni, Vietnamese Thích-Ca), and of the future (Maitreya, Vietnamese Di-Lặc). Some Buddhists (by no means all) regard the 'coming of Maitreya' not as a distant event, of no immediate concern to the present, but as an imminent day of judgement which could come at any time. The essentials of this apocalyptic form of Buddhism were incorporated into Caodaism. But in place of the 'coming of Maitreya', the Caodaists believe in the inauguration of the third epoch by the Cao-Đài spirit (that is, the Supreme Being or Jade Emperor) at their séances, beginning around 1920. Since this 'epoch of salvation' has already begun, the salvation of souls is of the greatest importance for all mankind, but above all for the Vietnamese since it was in Việt-Nam that the Cao-Đài chose to reveal himself. The question of the precise meaning of the term *phô-đô* 'salvation' in the Buddhist context, and differences between it and the Christian idea of salvation, are matters which must be left to specialists in Chinese Buddhism.

Of the Caodaist writings used for the present study, those of Phan Trương Mạnh place the greatest emphasis on this apocalyptic element of Caodaism; it occurs more briefly in the short history of Nguyễn Trung Hậu. Both writers were associated with the *Liên-Hòa Tổng-Hội* of 1936, and by 1950 with the Institut Caodaïque in Sàigòn, rather than with the Tây-Ninh branch of the movement. There is not enough evidence, however, to conclude that the division between these two groups in the 1930s had any doctrinal cause. In 1950, Phan Trương Mạnh published (in French) a tract entitled *La voie du salut caodaïque*, which contained translations of some of the most important messages from the Cao-Đài and other spirits. One of these is particularly interesting since it outlines the creation of the world by the Supreme Being, and then goes on to describe the three *manifestations de la miséricorde divine*, or *alliances* (between the Supreme Being and Man?) which have occurred in the history of the world. The first of these saw the sending to earth of *les archanges des trois sectes*: Amitābha (Di-đà), the spirit Thái-Thượng, and the mythical first ruler of China Fu Hsi (Phục-Hi). In the second *manifestation*, made necessary by man's moral decline since the first, each of these three beings appeared again in a new form: Amitābha as the Sākyamuni

Buddha, Thái-Thượng as the sage Lao Tzu (Lão-Đam), and Fu Hsi as Tõ-Vuong, identified by Mạnh as Confucius. Here we have the figures usually recognized as the founders of the three religions united in Caodaism. The message goes on to explain how, also in this second 'epoch', God sent his only son to earth in the West, to reveal his teaching. In the third *manifestation* there is no indication of a triad, nor even a mention of Maitreya, who would have been the logical third manifestation of Amitābha and Śākyamuni. There is, however, a noticeable emphasis on the fact that the Supreme Being on this occasion chose to reveal himself to the Vietnamese, which made them a sort of chosen people.[31]

The central position afforded to the Thái-Thượng spirit and Lao Tzu in these triads may well signify that, as the founders of Taoism, they were slightly superior to the Buddhist and Confucian figures named. The Thái-Thượng spirit is mentioned in at least one other Caodaist context: Dr. Hickey found that he was one of the deities honoured by the Caodaists of the *Ban-Chinh Đạo* and the *Tiên-Thiên* sects in the village of Khánh-Hậu (Tân-An province): his festival was on the fifteenth day of the second lunar month, and the former sect referred to him as Thái-Thượ ng Lão-Quan.[32] The pattern of three sacred figures in each 'epoch' also suggests affinities with the *Tam-Thánh* 'three holy ones' of the Taoist pantheon.[33] It would seem that the Caodaists have combined into a single system the Buddhist concept of three ages and the Taoist concept of three deities, and in this respect their religion is a genuine fusion of at least two Chinese religions.

In another work, an article in the *Revue Caodaïque* of the Institut Caodaïque, Phan Trương Mạnh discussed the progress of the newly-dawned third epoch of salvation and predicted that the 'era of incarnation' would be superseded by the 'era of disincarnation' in the year 1978; a war of 18 years would then be followed by a golden age beginning in 1996.[34] It was in this article that he discussed the significance of the term *long-hoa* (Chinese *lung-hua*, meaning literally 'dragon-flower'), which symbolizes the forthcoming end of the world. The term also occurs in Nguyễn Trung Hậu's short history, where the three 'epochs of salvation'— described in approximately the same terms as those of Phan Trương Mạnh's tract—are called the three 'dragon-flower assemblies': *long-hoa hội*.[35] Dr. Topley found references to the dragon-flower as a symbol of the coming of Maitreya in her study of sects in Singapore. She explains that the third Buddha will judge men's souls whilst sitting under a tree of which the *long-hoa* will be the flower.[36] Phan Trương Mạnh attempted to deduce the date of the forthcoming end of the world (1978) from the structure of the two Chinese characters making up this phrase.

IV Caodaist organization

The pattern of three, and also patterns of five and nine, are reflected very strongly in the organization of Caodaism, as it is described both by the English edition of Gobron (relating especially to Tây-Ninh) and by Nguyễn Trung Hậu (presumably with reference to the groups associated with the union of 1936). Their accounts are not identical. According to Nguyễn Trung Hậu the three principal organs of the

religion were the *Bát-Quái Đài*, the *Cửu-Trùng Đài*, and the *Hiệp-Thiên Đài*.[37]
Gobron (or rather, the editor of the English edition) also lists three organs, but he
omits all reference to the *Bát-Quái Đài*; his third organ is called the *Cơ-Quan
Phước-Thiện*.[38] For reasons which will become apparent, I propose to regard the
former of the two frameworks as the more fundamental grouping of three organs.

(1) Bát-Quái Đài 'Eight trigrams palace'

Nguyễn Trung Hậu calls this the *vô-vi* 'non-action' palace, governed by the
Supreme Being (Thượng-Đế), which implies an association between this organ
and the *vô-vi* side of Caodaism established by Ngô Minh Chiêu in 1926 when
he withdrew, leaving Tây-Ninh to become the centre of the *phổ-độ* 'salvation'
side. This might explain why there is no mention of the *Bát-Quái Đài* in Gobron's
account relating specifically to Tây-Ninh. The union of Caodaists to which Nguyễn
Trung Hậu seems to have belonged did in fact include the *Chiêu-Minh* group at
Cần-Thơ, and hence had closer links with the *vô-vi*. The eight trigrams were
another element of traditional Chinese (Taoist) symbolism that was incorporated
into Caodaism. Nguyễn Trung Hậu reproduces a photograph of Ngô Minh Chiêu
in his white ceremonial robes, on which the eight trigrams are clearly inscribed.
They are also marked on the white robes worn by Nguyễn Ngọc Tương in at least
one picture taken after he had become *Giáo-Tông* at Bến-Tre.

(2) Cửu-Trùng Đài 'Nine spheres palace'

This organ, again according to Nguyễn Trung Hậu, is the 'palace of *hữu-hình*',
the material world. The phrase *cửu-trùng* is sometimes used to indicate the 'nine
spheres' of the universe, associated with the eight cardinal points and the centre;
it is also used in connexion with the nine steps before the imperial throne. In
Caodaism the *Cửu-Trùng Đài* is the administrative organ, or 'executive body', and
is headed by the highest-ranking Caodaist, the *Giáo-Tông*. An editorial addition
to the English version of Gobron lists the nine ministries (*viện*) amongst which the
various executive responsibilities were divided, from rites to education to public
works. Gobron's own account indicates a more important division of the *Cửu-
Trùng Đài* into three larger sections. Each of these three sections is identified with
one of the 'three religions': it also has a name and a colour, as shown in the table
which follows. The table also gives the names of the people who, under Lê Văn
Trung, occupied the highest filled positions in the three sections in 1931. Their
religious names comprise three elements: the name of the section (for it would seem
that individuals were assigned to a particular section for life); the personal (third)
name of the individual; and lastly the word *thanh*, meaning 'pure', which may
also have been an appellation for life, or may conceivably have reflected a status
which would change. Lê Văn Trung's religious name was Thượng Trung Nhựt,
which indicates that he belonged to the Taoist (*Thượng*) section; the element
Nhựt means 'sun'.[39] It is interesting to find that the colour symbolism recorded

by Gobron is found confirmed by one of the few published colour photographs of a Caodaist ceremony at Tây-Ninh, taken about 1961.[40]

The *Cửu-Trùng Đài*

Division	Colour	Religion	Functions	*phôí-Su* in 1931
Ngọc 'Jade'	red	Confucianism	personnel rites order	Ngọc Trang Thanh (Lê Bá Trang)
Thái 'High'	yellow	Buddhism	finance building works	Thái Thơ Thanh (Nguyễn Ngọc Thơ)
Thượng 'Supreme'	blue	Taoism	interior education charity	Thượng Tương Thanh (Nguyễn Ngọc Tương)

The *Cửu- Trùng Đài* embraces nine grades *(phẩm)* of adepts of the religion; the higher grades are limited in numbers, but their complements are not necessarily full at any particular date.[41]

Giáo-Tông	1
Chưở-ng-Pháp	3
Đầu-Su	3
Phôí-Su	36
Giáo-Su	72
Giáo-Hữu	3,000
Lễ-Sanh	no limit
Chức-Việc	no limit
Nho·n-Sanh	no limit

Gobron's list contains twelve grades, because he counted as a separate grade the three *Chánh-Phôi-Su* 'principal *Phôi-Su*', and also counted separately the three sub-grades within that of *Chức-Việc*.[42] The grade of *Chánh-Phôi-Su* was certainly in existence by 1931, when it was one of the highest effective grades since the higher ones were for the most part unfilled. Trần Đạo Quang, who had left Tây-Ninh in 1928 and later founded the *Minh-Chon-Đạo*, was apparently *Chưởng-Pháp* before he went, a high position which he may have owed to the fact that he was already a sort of priest at the time when Caodaism was inaugurated in 1926.[43] Before 1933, Lê Văn Trung himself was only a *Đầu-Su*, and he was the highest dignitary at Tây-Ninh in 1931, being followed by the three *Chánh-Phôi-Su* whose names are given in the table.

(3) *Hiệp-Thiên Đài* 'Union with heaven palace'

Nguyễn Trung Hậu says that this organ stands between the *Bát-Quái Đài* and the *Cửu-Trùng Đài*, being the 'palace' where the *Giáo-Tông* goes to communicate with the Supreme Being (*Đức Thượng-Đẽ*), and with the Buddhas (*Phật*), the Holy Ones (*Thánh*), and the Immortals (*Tiên*), in order to establish the way to salvation (*phổ-độ*) and the release of souls (*siêu-rỗi toàn-linh*). He goes on to say, 'the *Bát-Quái Đài* sets forth the *pháp* and establishes the *đạo*; the *Cửu-Trùng Đài* maintains the *pháp* and executes the *đạo*; the *Hiệp-Thiên Đài* protects the *pháp* and defends the *đạo*'.[44] The terms *pháp* and *đạo* are important for the structure of this third organ, because together with *thể* they occur as the names of the three sections (*chi*) into which it is divided. *Thể*, in this context, clearly means the material world; *đạo* probably means here the practice of religion; and *pháp* might be translated as 'rule' or 'method', since the translation 'law' implies a meaning closer to the Christian concept of divine law than is ever found in Chinese and Vietnamese religions. In fact, *pháp* seems to refer to the techniques or methods of mediumship, and the French version of Nguyễn Trung Hậu translates *Hiệp-Thiên Đài* as *palais de médiumnité*; the officials of this organ were probably all mediums. Thus Pham Công Tắc, who held the position of *Hộ-Pháp* by 1934 and still held that position during later years when he was referred to in English-language sources as 'Pope', was the chief medium. As such he could hold a position not open to Lê Văn Trung. There is no firm evidence of any overlapping of personnel between the *Hiệp-Thiên Đài* and the *Cửu-Trùng Đài*, though it is impossible to be certain that there was none at all, since full lists of office-holders are not available. Indeed the relationship between the two organs is an important problem upon which the sources I have used throw very little light. There is no indication of any correspondence between the three sections of one and the three sections of the other, nor any suggestion of any colour symbolism in the *Hiệp-Thiên Đài*. Nor is it clear which of the two bodies was superior in practice. It is not impossible that precisely this question was at issue in the conflict between Phạm Công Tắc and Nguyễn Ngọc Tương during the years 1932–5.

The *Hiệp-Thiên-Đài*

Pháp section ('Method', i.e. mediumship)	*Đạo* section ('Religious practice')	*Thể* section ('Material world')
(1) Heads of sections:	'Defenders'	
Hộ-Pháp	*Thượng-Phàm*	*Thượng-Sanh*
(2) 'Protectors'		
Bảo-Pháp	*Bảo-Đạo*	*Bảo-Thể'*
(3) 'Administrators'		
Hiển-Pháp	*Hiển-Đạo*	*Hiển-Thể'*
(4) 'Propagators'		
Khai-Pháp	*Khai-Đạo*	*Khai-Thể'*
(5) 'Continuators'		
Tiếp-Pháp	*Tiếp-Đạo*	*Tiếp-Thể'*

The third organ in the English edition of Gobron, the *Cơ-Quan Phước-Thiện*, is not mentioned by Nguyễn Trung Hậu, and not a great deal can be said about it.[45] Its name means literally 'Organ of Good Works', and it is described as a 'charitable body'. Twelve grades of membership are listed, the head being called *Phật-Tư*; the highest actual office-holder at the time of writing (1949–50) belonged to the seventh grade, *Chí-Thiện*, but his identity is not given. It seems that the principal work of this body concerned the development of the social community of Caodaists at Tây-Ninh, established in 1930, and it probably did not play any important role in the politics of the movement. The same addition to Gobron goes on to describe briefly the provincial hierarchy of the religion. There were at this time (1949–50) five *trấn* (provinces or circuits), each headed by a *Khâm-Trấn-Đạo* who must be of the grade of *Giáo-Sư*. Below them came, in order, the *châu*, the *tộc*, and the *hương*; and below that the hamlets. These terms are not exclusively Caodaist; *trấn* and *châu* are found in the vocabulary of traditional Vietnamese imperial administration at different periods; *tộc* means in other contexts 'clan' or 'lineage'; and *hương* (in Cochinchina) seems to have been interchangeable with *xã*, since the village officials are known as *hương-cả hương-chu*, etc.[46]

Finally, returning to the account of Nguyễn Trung Hậu, it is possible to note the existence of a number of different kinds of Caodaist assembly.[47] Starting at the lowest level and working upwards, they were (and presumably still are)

(i) *Hội-Nhơn-Sanh*: comprising the lowest grades of adept, up to and including the *Lễ-Sanh*; it is not clear whether its meetings involved the attendance at Tây-Ninh (or any other centre) of adepts from the provinces, but that would seem very likely.

(ii) *Hội-Thánh*: the 'Sacred Assembly', comprising the grades from *Giáo-Hữu* up to and including *Phối-Sư*. It is interesting to note that in Gobron's account of the elevation of Phạm Công Tắc to a position of leadership at Tây-Ninh in 1935, it is stated that he was entrusted with the task by the *Hội-Nhơn-Sanh* and the *Hội-Thánh*, and no higher councils are mentioned.[48] Conceivably it was by using these assemblies against the higher ones that Phạm Công Tắc had been able to outpace his rival Nguyễn Ngọc Tương.

(iii) *Thương-Hội*: the 'High Assembly', comprising the highest grades of the *Cửu-Trùng Đài*. upwards from *Chánh-Phối-Sư*. It cannot therefore have included more than ten people at any one time, and was probably much smaller than that.

(iv) *Đại-Hội Vân-Linh*: the 'Great Assembly of the Ten Thousand Souls', embracing all the other three assemblies. It was at a meeting of this assembly that Nguyễn Ngọc Tương denounced Lê Văn Trung and his group in June 1933, following on from an earlier denunciation in the *Thương-Hội* in the previous April.[49] It is mentioned on that occasion that the *Hộ-Pháp* (Phạm Công Tắc) was absent, which presumably implies that he could have attended. Since the assemblies are described in terms of the grades in the *Cửu-Trùng Đài*, it is once again difficult to know what their relationship was to the offices of the *Hiệp-Thiên Đài*.

V Chinese analogies

If nothing else, this discussion of beliefs and organization has shown that Caodaism, for all its claims to be an entirely new religion, has affinities with older religious movements. It seems indeed to belong to a sectarian tradition which developed in China over many centuries. This is reflected in the existence, both in

China, and amongst the overseas Chinese of the Nanyang, of a number of similar or related cults in the twentieth century. A notable example is the *Tao Yüan* sect (also known, in its charitable work, as the 'Red Swastika. Society'), which was established at Tsin-an in 1921 and which spread to the Nanyang during the 1930s.[50] It claims to unite five religions—Confucianism, Buddhism, Taoism, Christianity, and Islam—but at its core stands belief in a supreme spirit, not unlike the Cao-Đài spirit. In this case the supreme being is T'ai-i Lao-jen, who at a series of spirit-séances has revealed the truth and established the means to salvation. Neither the terminology of this religion nor its administrative structure resemble very closely those of Caodaism, but the similarity of the fundamental tenets of the two religions suggests that they belong ultimately to the same tradition.

Another sect, or group of sects, with some similarities to Caodaism, has been studied by Dr. Marjorie Topley in Singapore: they are known sometimes as *p'u-tu* (*phổ-độ*) sects, and sometimes by the name *Hsien-t'ien Ta-tao* (*Tiên-Thiên Đại-Đạo*).[51] The adepts of this group of sects place great emphasis on salvation through self-purification, abstinence, and vegetarianism, and like the Caodaists, they believe in the imminence of the third epoch of salvation. The Buddhist (or rather, Salvationist) element is much stronger here than in Caodaism, and the Taoist element is not at all prominent. The symbolic figure of three seems to relate entirely to the three epochs, and the greatest emphasis is on the three Buddhas, Dīpankara, Śākyamuni and Maitreya. Whereas the colour symbolism of Caodaism relates to the three divisions within the religious structure, in the *Hsien-t'ien* religion the three colours of blue, red, and white are related respectively to the three salvation periods. Dr. Topley is able to show, moreover, that the famous 'White Lotus' society of Chinese tradition originally belonged to a similar religion, in which white was the symbol of the coming of Maitreya. The sects which she found in Singapore traced back their origins far into the past: with some degree of credibility to the seventeenth-century patriarch Lo Wei-ch'un, but also far beyond that period to the sixth *Ch'an* (*Zen*) Buddhist patriarch of the T'ang period, Huineng. However, the line of patriarchs is not the only source of authority within the religion: there is also an element of spirit-mediumship, even here, and the adepts follow the dictates of a spirit called 'Mother' (*Wu-sheng Lao-mu*, also known under other names), who reveals her intentions at séances with the planchette. (This same spirit was also important in the cult of the Peking group one of whose séances was described by Grootaers as mentioned above.) Again there is no direct correspondence of terminology or structure between the *Hsien-t'ien* sects in Singapore and Caodaism in Việt-Nam, but the basic simlarities are obvious. Moreover, there exists in South Việt-Nam one branch or sect within Caodaism which calls itself the *Tiên-Thiên*.[52] Unfortunately very little is known of its beliefs or organization, which may not necessarily be identical with those described in the present article.

Reference has already been made to the writings of de Groot. He too found evidence of sects, in Fu-kien and elsewhere, which appear to have belonged to the salvationist-spiritist tradition. Two of them he describes in some detail, under the names *Hsien-t'ien* and *Lung-hua*.[53] Once again, neither resembles Caodaism in detail, but an indirect relationship might be postulated. Recent research into the history of rebellion in China has found evidence of sects of this kind in much earlier periods. As early as 515 and 613, for example, there were revolts in which belief in the apocalyptic coming of Maitreya played a prominent part; and the same belief is found amongst many of those who rebelled against the Yüan dynasty in 1351.[54] Revolt by a Taoist sect is found as far back as A.D. 184, when adepts of the 'Way of the Five Bushels of Rice' rose under Chang Heng and established a hierarchy held together by veneration of 'the Spirit' (*Kuei*).[55] No doubt the potentially rebellious political activities of the various kinds of sects that appeared in traditional China is part of the explanation why the Confucian officials sought to prevent them from developing; and precisely because of that, information about their internal organization and beliefs is so limited.

Caodaism, then, fits into a long religious tradition whose roots lie deep in Chinese history. The question naturally arises: how far was it Vietnamese at all, and how far was it merely a Chinese accretion? How, indeed, did it arise in Việt-Nam at all? One aspect of Caodaism deserves special emphasis in this respect: Caodaism was peculiar to the area which the French called Cochinchina. Where it appeared in central and northern Việt-Nam, it was as a result of attempts to spread it there from the south.[56] It was not therefore a direct product of the *Nam-Tiện* movement of the Vietnamese, by which that people gradually expanded to settle in areas further and further south, from the fifteenth century onwards. Nor should it be confused with other spirit-mediumship cults in other areas of Việt-Nam, such as those studied by Durand in Tongking, in which the medium was possessed by the spirit and spoke its words, rather than writing them down.[57] It seems highly probable therefore that the antecedents of Caodaism are to be found amongst cults introduced directly into Cochinchina by migrants from China. Such migration began in the seventeenth century, with the establishment of Chinese colonies at Bién-Hoa, Mỳ-Tho, and Hà-Tiên; and the first Chinese to settle in those places were none other than political refugees from a South China recently conquered by the Ch'ing, who were quite likely to have had connexions with secret religious societies. Other Chinese migrants followed, and by the late nineteenth century they were coming in considerable numbers. If not in the seventeenth century, then at some later date it would seem that the Chinese introduced the syncretic tradition to which Caodaism belonged, and in particular the *Minh* sects out of which it grew.[58] It will he recalled that the founder of the *Ngọc-Hoàng* temple at Đà-Kao was a Chinese; and Âu Kích, head of the *Minh-Lý* sect by 1950, was a *minh-hưo'ng*—half-Chinese, half-Vietnamese.[59] Nevertheless, the Chinese were quickly assimilated into the Vietnamese society of Cochinchina, and this would explain why any cult introduced by them could very easily become Vietnamese, accepted by people without any Chinese blood. The long establishment of sects of this kind in Cochinchina, combined with an element of 'Vietnamization', would also explain why the actual structure and terminology of Caodaism were quite different from those of similar sects elsewhere.

It will be evident that the foregoing study has not by any means answered all the questions that ought to be asked about the nature, origins, and history of Caodaism. My purpose has been to suggest lines of inquiry which might in time be followed up by other researchers. Nor should Caodaism be seen as of interest merely to specialists in the history of South Việt-Nam. It is very probable that in due course a comparative study relating it in closer detail to the various Chinese sects will also throw some light on the origins and development of the latter.

Glossary

Using Vietnamese sources it is not always possible to be certain of the Chinese characters corresponding to *quoc-ngũ'* words. The following, however, would appear to be the Chinese equivalents of the most important of the terms used in the foregoing article.

Bát-Quái Đài	八 卦 臺
Cao-Đài	高 臺
càu-tiên	求 仙
co·(kê?)	乩
Cửu-Trùng Đài	九 重 臺
Đại-Đạo Tam-Kỳ Phổ-Độ	大 道 三 期 普 度
đàn	壇
đạo	道
Giáo-Tông	敎 宗
Hiệp-Thiên Đài	叶 天 臺
Hộ-Pháp	護 法
long-hoa	龍 華
pháp	法
thê'	世
Thương-Đê'	上 帝
Tiên	仙
Tiên-Thiên	先 天
vô-vi	無 爲

Notes

1 For part I see *BSOAS*, XXXIII, 2, 1970, 335–49.
2 I am very much indebted to conversations with Dr. Marjorie Topley and Mr. Michael Saso for several of the ideas followed up in the present article; neither of them, however, should be held responsible for any particular statement herein, save where directly acknowledged; still less for any errors.
3 The word spiritism will be used here merely because it was preferred by the French spiritists, with whom the Caodaists had much closer contacts (and more in common) than with Anglo-Saxon 'spiritualists'.
4 cf. Allan Kardec (L. H. D. Rivail), *Oeuvres posthumes*, Paris, 1912, which includes a biographical memoir reprinted from *Revue Spirite*, mai 1869; and Allan Kardec

(L. H. D. Rivail), *The spirits' book*, translated with an introduction by Anna Blackwell, London, 1875.

5 J. J. M. de Groot, *The religious system of China*, repr., Taipei, 1964, VI, 1310.

6 A. J. A. Elliott, *Chinese spirit-medium cults in Singapore*, London, 1955, 140–5.

7 Wu Ching-tzu, *The scholars*, English translation, Peking, 1964, 126 ff.

8 W. A. Grootaers, 'Une séance de spiritisme dans une religion secrète à Péking en 1948' *Mélanges Chinois et Bouddhiques*, IX, 1948–51, 92–8.

9 For all these Vietnamese terms, see, e.g. Dồng-Tân, *Lịch-sử Cao-Đài, i. Phần Vô-Vi*, Sàigòn, 1967, referred to subsequently as *Lịch-sử*, 53 ff.

10 ibid., 53, 129 ff.

11 Huỳnh-Minh, *Cần-Tho· xưa và nay*, Gia-Định, 1966, 222.

12 Phan Trương Mạnh, *La voie du salut caodaïque*, Sàigòn, 1950, 48.

13 *Lịch-sử*, 57.

14 G. Gobron, *History and philosophy of Caodaism*, Sàigòn, 1950, 135, 124.

15 *Lịch-sử*, 57–8: Gouvernement-Général de l'Indochine, *Contribution à l'histoire des mouvements politiques de l'Indochine française*, VII, Hànôi, 1934, referred to subsequently as *Contribution*, VII, 54–5.

16 Gobron, op. cit., 46, 51 ff.; *Contribution*, VII, 58–9.

17 cf. *supra*, p. 576.

18 Nguyễn Phút Tần, *A modern history of Viet-Nam*, Sàigòn, 1964, 410–22.

19 Gobron, op. cit., 26, 31 ff.

20 ibid., 149 ff.

21 Arthur Waley, *The poetry and career of Li Po (701–762)*, London, 1950, 7, 29–31.

22 Phan Trương Mạnh, *La voie du salut*, 101–4.

23 *Lịch-sử*, 43, 58.

24 *Contribution*, VII, 27.

25 Gobron, op. cit., 19.

26 *Lịch-sử*, 59 ff.

27 Gobron, op. cit., 21.

28 Nguyễn Trung Hậu, *Lược-sử Đạo Cao-Đài: A short history of Caodaism*, Tourane, 1956, 8. The word *viết* is here the Vietnamese form of the Chinese *yüeh*, meaning 'to say' 'namely'.

29 *Lịch-sử*, 81–2; cf. *BSOAS*, XXXIII, 2, 1970, 349.

30 cf. *BSOAS*, 33(2) 1970, 341.

31 Phan Trương Mạnh, *La voie du salut*, 50–8; it is worth noticing that Dr. Topley found the pattern of three Buddhas in the sects she studied in Singapore, but with Dīpankara in place of Amitābha, *BSOAS*, XXVI, 2, 1963, 371.

32 G. C. Hickey, *Village in Vietnam*, New Haven, 1964, 69, 71.

33 For this comparison, and information about the Taoist *San Ch'ing (Tam-Thánh)*, I am indebted to Mr. Saso.

34 *Revue Caodaïque*, IIIᵉ An., décembre 1950, 67–92.

35 Nguyễn Trung Hậu, op. cit., 10–11.

36 M. D. Topley, *The organization and social function of Chinese women's chai-t'ang in Singapore* (unpublished Ph.D. thesis, University of London, 1958), 131.

37 Nguyễn Trung Hậu, op. cit., 17–19.

38 Gobron, op. cit., 153 ff.

39 *Tiếu-sử Đức Giáo-Tóng, Nguyễn Ngọc Tương*, Sàigòn, 1958, referred to subsequently as *NNT*, 19 ff.

40 *National Geographic Magazine*, CXX, 4, 1961, 464–5.

41 Nguyễn Trung Hậu, op. cit., 18.

42 Gobron, op. cit., 154.

43 *NNT*, 19; he belonged to the *Ngọc* division.

44 Nguyễn Trung Hậu, op. cit., 18.
45 Gobron, op. cit., 156–7.
46 ibid., 157–8.
47 Nguyễn Trung Hậu, op. cit., 19.
48 Gobron, op. cit., 71.
49 *NNT*, 31.
50 Hou Su Shuang, *Important points of Tao Yuan at a glance*, Singapore. 1932; I am grateful to Dr. Topley for drawing my attention to this source.
51 Marjorie Topley, 'The Great Way of Former Heaven: a group of Chinese secret religious sects', *BSOAS*, XXVI, 2, 1963, 362–92; the subject is treated more fully in her unpublished thesis cited above, p. 581, n. 36.
52 cf. *BSOAS*, XXXIII, 2, 1970, 345–6.
53 J. J. M. de Groot, *Sectarianism and religious persecution in China*, repr., Taipei, 1963, I, ch. vi–vii.
54 Y. Muramatsu, 'Some themes in Chinese rebel ideologies', in A. F. Wright (ed.), *The Confucian persuasion*. Stanford, 1960, 246–8.
55 Vincent Y. C. Shih, 'Some Chinese rebel ideologies', *T'oung-Pao*, XLIV, 1–3, 1956, 150–226.
56 Nguyễn Trung Hậu, op. cit., 21 ff., deals at some length with the mission to establish Caodaism in central Việt-Nam from 1937 onwards. There were also a few Caodaists in Hảiphong and possibly Hànội.
57 M. Durand. *Technique et panthéon des médiums vietnamiennes*, Paris. 1959.
58 cf. *BSOAS*, XXXIII, 2, 1970, 348–9.
59 According to a relative.

9 Bui Quang Chiêu and the Constitutionalist Party in French Cochinchina 1917–30[1]

Source: *Modern Asian Studies* 3(2) (1969): 131–150.

THE years 1916–17 were something of a turning-point in the development of Vietnamese nationalism. In Cochinchina an abortive attack on Saigon central prison in February 1916 was followed by a great many arrests and the virtual destruction, for the time being, of the network of secret societies which had grown up in many of the colony's provinces during the previous decade. Many members of such societies were brought before special military tribunals (justified by the fact that France was at war in Europe) and sentenced to death, exile, or long terms of imprisonment. In Annam another abortive plot, probably quite separate, was hatched at Huê in May 1916, involving the kidnapping of the boy-emperor Duy-Tân; but he was found by the French two years later, before a projected rising in the provinces of Quang-Nam and Quang-Ngai could get under way. The leader of the plot, Trân Cao Vân, was executed along with three others, and the deposed emperor was exiled to the island of Réunion.[2] These events in Cochinchina and Annam brought to a halt, for a time at least, the activities of secret nationalist groups which, drawing their initial inspiration from Japan, had been increasing in strength since about 1905. In Tongking there were also secret associations, mostly acknowledging the leadership of Phan Bôi Châu who was then in exile at Canton, and strongly influenced by the revolutionary methods of Sun Yat-sen. But there also, their last important operation for several years occurred in September 1917, when Luong Ngoc Quyên escaped from prison at Thai-Nguyen and was able to control the town for a week, before being driven out and committing suicide.[3] Phan Bôi Châu himself was arrested by the Chinese the following year.

It was in these circumstances, with the French enjoying firmer control in Indochina than they had ever done before, that there began to emerge in Saigon a rather different kind of political movement led by men who were prepared to use constitutional methods to try to force the colonial government to live up to its own expressed ideals. It began with the foundation, in August 1917, of a French-language newspaper, *La Tribune Indigène*. The publication of newspapers, or any other literature, in the Vietnamese language was subject to severe restrictions and constant censorship, but publications in French were permitted. There had long been a number of daily and weekly newspapers serving the French community in Saigon, and one of them at least was quite outspoken in its criticisms of established authority: namely *La Cochinchine Libérale*, which had been founded in 1915 by Jules-Adrien Marx. But by now there was also a growing number of people in Saigon who, although Vietnamese by birth and mother-tongue, were French by education and in some cases nationality. The small minority who had French citizenship were as free as any other citizen of that country to found a French-language newspaper, and it was one of them, Nguyên Phu Khai, who founded *La Tribune Indigène*.[4] Khai, a native of Ba-Ria province, had been educated in France as a protégé of Pierre Loti, but on his return home had decided against taking a place in the French colonial service. He argued that his countrymen had for too long been obsessed with the idea of *fonction*, whether in the old mandarinate or in the service of the French, with the result that they had come to be exploited economically by the Chinese just as firmly as they were ruled politically by the French. If the country was ever to make any progress, its first need was not for political independence, but for economic modernization, which meant that Vietnamese would have to go in for other occupations besides government service. It was in this spirit that Nguyên Phu Khai had himself helped to establish the first Vietnamese-owned rice mill at My-Tho in 1915, to compete with the Chinese.[5]

His views were shared by another Cochinchinese who was probably the prime mover behind the foundation of the newspaper and the real leader of the group which supported it. This was Bui Quang Chiêu (1873–1945), the second son of Bui Quang Dai, a native of Mo-Cay in the delta province of Bên-Tre whose family had a strong tradition both of Confucian scholarship and of opposition to the French.[6] Chiêu himself went to a French school and, despite some reluctance on his father's part, he jumped at the opportunity to go and study abroad. He went first to Algiers, where his protector was the ex-emperor Ham-Nghi whom the French had exiled thither in 1888; and then on to France itself. Returning home in 1897, he entered the service of the Government-General of Indochina on the eve of Paul Doumer's reforms, and not long afterwards was assigned to the *Service Agricole*. Having specialized in agricultural engineering, and particularly in the study of sericulture, he was in a position to rise much higher in the colonial service than the clerks and interpreters who made up the bulk of the native membership of the service. By 1913 he was addressing the *Société des Études Indochinoises* as an expert on the subject of silk.[7] Since he was employed by the Government-General and not by the Government of Cochinchina he was posted in various parts of the Union, and in the early years of the present century he was at Huê. He may well have met there his famous near-contemporaries, Phan Bôi Châu (1867–1940) and Phan Châu Trinh (1872–1926), who in 1904 were among the founders of the *Duy-Tân Hôi* ('Reformation Association'). Chiêu, however, was separated from such men by a wide educational gulf, for whereas he had been successful in the French system of Cochinchina, they had received the Chinese education necessary to prepare them for the mandarinal examinations of Annam. It is most unlikely that Chiêu participated in the *Duy-Tân* movement, but he was probably aware of its existence and of the attempts it was making during the years 1905–8 to persuade young men to leave home and study in Japan. His own view appears to have been that since Vietnam could not hope to succeed in modernizing its economy and society without outside aid, it might as well learn from the French as from the Japanese. By 1906 Chiêu was working in Hanoi, and in August of that year he was mentioned as first president of a *Société de Secours Mutuel* founded by Cochinchinese residents in Tongking.[8] The mutual help association is a characteristic Vietnamese organization, and indeed the secret societies whose political activities so much alarmed the French had as one of their primary purposes the object of enabling members to lean upon one another in time of need. The French were prepared to permit associations which had no political purpose, and Bui Quang Chiêu did much to promote the development of legal societies of this kind. Some years later, back in Saigon, he played a leading role in the creation of an association of former pupils of the Collège Chasseloup-Laubat, as well as in the expansion of the *Société d'Enseignement Mutuel* which had originally been founded by the Frenchman A. Salles. By 1918 he was president of both.[9] It was out of societies of this kind that the Constitutionalist Party was created.

From April 1919 the front page of *La Tribune Indigène* bore the legend 'organe du Parti Constitutionaliste', but the party appears to have been founded at the same time as the newspaper, with Chiêu as its effective leader and with probably only a small group of intimates as members. Both its objects and its methods are indicated by its name. It hoped to achieve, through the action of the French themselves, reforms which would lead to the modernization of the country and a greater degree of liberty for its inhabitants. As early as 1908 Phan Châu Trinh had appealed to the French Governor-General to treat the people more favourably if he wished for their support; but he did so in very general terms, apart from a plea for the reduction of taxes.[10] The Constitutionalists on the other hand were interested in obtaining specific reforms, and the columns of their newspaper were full of discussions about what those reforms should be. No normal manifesto of the Party's aims survived from this early period, but they were probably much the same as those expressed by Diêp Van Cuong in a speech of September 1917 before the *Conseil Colonial de la Cochinchine* of which he was one of the six native members.[11]

Diêp Van Cuong (1876–1918) was born in Bac-Liêu province but had settled at Bên-Tre and must have been an acquaintance of Bui Quang Chiêu if not actually a member of his party; he might have become more prominent in the movement had he not died in January 1918.[12] In this speech he set forth six specific demands for reform: first, the transformation of the traditional *xa* (the local 'commune') into proper municipalities with elected councils; second, the abolition of what remained of the traditional mandarin system in Cochinchina and its replacement by a more modern administrative hierarchy; third, a reduction in the number of minor Vietnamese functionaries, and substantial increases of salary for the rest; fourth, the appointment in every canton of a *juge de paix* independent of the executive power; fifth, a reform of the naturalization law to make it easier for Vietnamese to become French citizens; and sixth, the expansion of native representation in the *Conseil Colonial* to give an equal number of French and Vietnamese representatives, with the latter elected on a much wider franchise.

The Constitutionalists' hopes were raised by the fact that in 1917 the new Governor-General of Indochina was Albert Sarraut, whose public statements suggested that he might be willing to apply in earnest the colonial philosophy of 'association', and to interpret it in a sense which would mean genuine progress for the colony. In some respects what Bui Quang Chiêu and Diêp Van Cuong wanted was *assimilation* rather than *association*: the introduction that is, of more rather then less French-style modernity. But they also wanted French-style constitutional progress, and in the circumstances of 1917 there was more chance of achieving that from associationist politicians than from assimilationist administrators. As it turned out, Sarraut was more interested in educational reforms than in administrative or political changes, and devoted most of his energies towards achieving for Tongking and Annam the kind of French education that already existed in Cochinchina; in the process he abolished the traditional examinations, and established a university at Hanoi.[13] The Constitutionalists, therefore, although they themselves were not uninterested in education, still had not achieved any of Cuong's aims by the time Sarraut's term as Governor came to an end in 1919.

About the middle of 1919 they returned to a theme which had long been dear to the heart of Nguyên Phu Khai, namely the Chinese domination of Cochinchina's economy. On 28 August *La Tribune Indigène* published an announcement that there was to be a boycott of the Chinese, and two days later a *Société Commerciale Annamite* was founded, with Khai as president.[14] Its vice-presidents were Nguyên Chanh Sat, editor of the Vietnamese-language *Nông Cô Min Dam* (a weekly journal which ran from 1901 until 1924), and Trân Quang Nghiêm, a small businessman; it held its first meeting at the premises of the *Société d'Enseignement Mutuel*. In October there followed the creation of a *Banque Annamite*, and early in November the boycotters organized a *Congrès Économique de la Cochinchine* attended by representatives from sixteen of the colony's twenty provinces.[15] However, congresses proved easier to organize than mass economic action, and the Chinese had too firm a grip on the rice trade to be seriously disturbed by anything less. By mid-1920 the boycott had died away, and apart from drawing into commercial activity a few more Vietnamese than there had been before, it achieved little economic change. Nevertheless it proved that the French-educated elite of Cochinchina were capable of organizing themselves, and they gained from it experience which was to prove valuable later.

A second venture of the Constitutionalists about the same time was their campaign on behalf of one of the candidates in the election for the *député de la Cochinchine* which took place on 1 December 1919. Being a colony, Cochinchina was represented in the French National Assembly, but only French citizens were entitled to vote. The two principal candidates were Ernest Outrey, formerly a high-ranking official in the colony, and Paul Monin, a liberally inclined lawyer who had lived in Saigon for many years; the Constitutionalists supported Monin, but he got only 396 votes against 1,486 for Outrey. Even the Vietnamese elite of Saigon was by no means united behind Monin: Outrey had the support of a group calling itself the *Société des Annamites Citoyens Français*, led by (another) Diêp Van Cuong, who was later to come in for strong condemnation by the Constitutionalists.[16]

It was clear that some French-educated Vietnamese would never stand out against the conservative French *colons*, even within the limits allowed by the law. The Constitutionalists themselves were later regarded by more extreme groups as being pro-French, but they were not sufficiently docile for the liking of Outrey. Moreover, between 1917 and 1924 they were virtually the only organized political group in Cochinchina, at a time when opposition of any more extreme kind would have been rigorously suppressed. During those years they were able to increase their following within the Vietnamese community. In 1920 another French-language newspaper was founded in Saigon by Vietnamese. This was *L'Echo Annamite*, whose effective founder was Nguyên Phan Long, although he did not become editor until two years later. His connexion with Bui Quang Chiêu before this time is not clear, but already in 1919 he had demonstrated his sympathy for *La Tribune Indigène* by contributing to it a serialized story entitled *Le Roman de Mademoiselle Lys*, into which he incorporated his reflections on the problems both of individuals and of the colony whose culture was partly French and partly Vietnamese.[17] Another event of 1920 may be noticed in passing: the creation in Paris, in November of that year, of an *Association Mutuelle des Indochinois*. One of the founders was Nguyên Phu Khai, who seems to have been in France from 1920 to 1923; others included the physician Dr Lê Quang Trinh, and the lawyer Duong Van Giao.[18] At this date there were far more Vietnamese willing to support an organization of this kind than were prepared to follow Nguyên Ai Quôc (that is, Hô Chi Minh) into the French Communist Party which he helped to found at Tours the following month.

About the middle of 1921 *La Tribune Indigène* began a new campaign for the reform of the *Conseil Colonial* and the extension of Vietnamese representation. By this time Sarraut had been succeeded as Governor-General by another 'associationist', Maurice Long, who held the position from 1920 till his death in 1922. It was no doubt owing to his liberal attitude that the campaign for reform met with some success, in the shape of the decree of 9 June 1922, which increased native representation on the *Conseil* from six to ten, and expanded the Vietnamese electorate from about 1,500 to over 20,000.[19] At that time, however, the effective French membership was increased to fourteen so that they still held a majority; and 20,000 was not a large electorate out of a population of over three million. The first elections under the new regulations were held in October and November 1922, and the ten native members elected included a number of Constitutionalists. Most prominent among them was Nguyên Phan Long, who became Vice-President of the *Conseil* as well as the Party's chief spokesman there; he sat for the constituency which included Saigon.[20] Another field in which Maurice Long was prepared to make changes welcome to the Constitutionalists was education. Between the end of 1918 and the end of 1922 the number of primary schools in Cochinchina was increased from 905 to 1,017, and a third secondary school, or college, was created at Cân-Tho.[21] But the pace of development was not maintained, and a few years later we find Bui Quang Chiêu pointing out that although the number of pupils in schools in Cochinchina had risen more than tenfold between 1904 and 1924, the total of 72,809 for the latter year was not a very large proportion of the

600,000 children of school age.[22] The Constitutionalists began therefore to found 'free schools' under their own management. In 1923 Nguyên Phan Long opened a *pensionnat* at Gia-Dinh, and about the same time Bui Quang Chiêu founded a similar school known as the *An-nam hoc-duong* at Phu-Nhuân on the outskirts of Saigon.[23] But the French administrators were less than enthusiastic about all this educational expansion, and in September 1924 a decree severely restricted the creation of private schools. Nevertheless Bui Quang Chiêu's school still existed in 1927, when Ta Thu Thau, subsequently leader of the Trotskyist Communists in Cochinchina, was a teacher there before his departure for France.[24]

During the years 1923–4, the political temperature in Saigon began to rise as the Constitutionalists found themselves increasingly alienated from the French conservatives who at that time controlled the Cochinchina government. Maurice Long's successor as Governor-General was the more cautious Merlin (against whom there was an attempt at assassination when he visited Canton in June 1924); and the new Lieutenant-Governor of Cochinchina, Maurice Cognacq,[25] who was appointed in February 1922, was a conservative with long experience in Cochinchina. The first major clash between Cognacq and the Constitutionalists came in November 1923, when Nguyên Phan Long spoke out in the *Conseil Colonial* against proposals for a new Saigon port convention which would make it a virtual monopoly in French hands. He spoke eloquently but was unable to prevent its passage through the *Conseil* by a majority of fourteen votes to seven.[26]

During December and January the Constitutionalists carried on a campaign of meetings and speeches to try to obtain a reversal of the decision, and for the first time something like public opinion was aroused in Saigon. A Vietnamese-language periodical, *Nam-ky Kinh-tê Bao* ('Economic Journal of Cochinchina') was closed down early in 1924 for ignoring the censorship on this issue.[27] The government argued that it was a political matter, whereas the Constitutionalists claimed that it was purely an economic question; but there was no doubt which side was the stronger, and the government won the day. Much of the bitterness of the opponents of the port convention stemmed from the fact that in the *Conseil Colonial* some of the native representatives had voted for it, notably Dr Lê Quang Trinh, who had been given Constitutionalist support in the election of 1922. He was sharply attacked in the columns of *La Tribune Indigène*, and in March 1924 he replied in kind by founding a newspaper of his own, *Le Progrès Annamite*. The conflict ended in litigation, and Lê Quang Trinh was fined in the *Tribune Correctionnel* for defamation.[28]

Le Progrès Annamite was Saigon's fourth French-language newspaper run by and for Vietnamese. A third had been founded in December 1923 by Nguyên An Ninh and Phan Van Truong: *La Cloche Fêlée*. Like Bui Quang Chiêu and Nguyên Phu Khai, Nguyên An Ninh (1900–43) had been educated in France and had absorbed French political ideals.[29] But he belonged to a new generation and was much more impatient than the older men. To begin with, he espoused their aims of constitutional progress, but already by 1925 he was writing of the possibility that if those aims could not be achieved quickly by peaceful means, it might be necessary to resort to violence.[30] The Constitutionalists found themselves in 1924 steering a middle course between those of their countrymen who followed the lead of Diêp Van Cuong and Lê Quang Trinh in supporting the conservative *colons*, and those who were beginning to think of violence. Their philosophy is summed up in the words of an article that had appeared in *La Tribune Indigène* in mid-1923:[31]

> Il y a deux façons de conquérir la liberté: par le canon ou par la culture; nous sommes pour la culture.

In terms of French politics, Bui Quang Chiêu appears to have been a member of the *Parti Radicale et Radicale-Socialiste* of which a branch was formed at Saigon in August 1924. This was not sufficiently far left for Nguyên An Ninh, who later became a Communist, but it was too much for Outrey. It was probably the latter's doing that at the beginning of January 1925 Chiêu was transferred to a post in Cambodia; he was evidently a disruptive influence in Saigon and better out of the way.[32] In February, *La Tribune Indigène* was closed down. In the meantime, in Paris, Duong Van Gaio and a sympathetic Frenchman Georges Grandjean formed a *Groupe Constitutionaliste* and persuaded Phan Châu Trinh to become its president. It played some part in the moves which led the French government to allow Trinh to return to Saigon (though not to his native Annam) later in 1925.[33]

During most of 1924 the Constitutionalists had no official organ, although Nguyên Phan Long's *Echo Annamite* continued publication. For a few months in the summer, and again in the winter of that year, however, another newspaper carried on a series of attacks against Cognacq's policies and general corruption: the *Indochine* of Paul Monin and André Malraux.[34] Between mid-June and mid-August 1925 it opposed the Governor so vigorously that he had it closed down by intimidating every printer in Saigon. It reappeared in November, as *L'Indochine Enchaîné*, using type smuggled in from Hong Kong, and ran for another couple of months. Malraux himself went to Hong Kong at this time, and also paid a brief visit to Canton. Both places were in the grip of the strike movement which inaugurated China's second revolution, and it is against the background of these events that one must see the growing concern of Cognacq and his friends about opposition movements in Cochinchina. It is not certain at precisely what stage they became aware that in June 1925 the Comintern agent Nguyên Ai Quôc founded his Vietnam Revolutionary Youth Association at Canton.

It was beginning to look as though the government of Cochinchina would tolerate no opposition of any kind, and make no serious reforms either, when in July 1925 the new government in Paris appointed as Governor-General of Indochina the socialist Alexandre Varenne. There was hope once again that the demands of the Constitutionalists might be met, and it was not wholly destroyed by the public interview between the newly arrived Governor-General and Nguyên Phan Long in November when Varenne made it clear that it would be impossible to grant full civil liberties immediately.[35] His first real test was the affair of Phan Bôi Châu, who had recently been sentenced to forced labour for life following his arrest in Shanghai in June. There was a public outcry, alike in Paris, in Saigon and in Hanoi; and in due course Varenne reached his decision that the veteran nationalist should be released, but allowed to live only at Huê and not to travel either within the country or abroad.[36] About the end of the year Bui Quang Chiêu decided to go to Paris himself, and to join forces with Duong Van Giao in a bid to convince the government in Paris of the desirability of reforms.

Their aspirations are recorded in an article they contributed in 1926 to the Belgian review, *L'Essor Colonial et Maritime*.[37] They were six in number: first, basic civil liberties, including freedom to write without censorship in Vietnamese, freedom of assembly and association, and freedom to travel without special permission; second, expansion of the educational system, to give the Vietnamese proper opportunities of higher education; third, an increase in the number of native officials, with responsibilities and remuneration appropriate to their education; fourth, proper representation of Vietnamese, both in Indochina itself and in the National Assembly, and the creation in Paris of a new *Commission d'Études Indochinoises* to advise the government, with elected representatives from the colony; fifth, reform of the judicial system, and the application to Indochina of social and labour legislation current in Metropolitan France; and sixth, the suppression of the monopolies of alcohol and opium. Such demands made an impact on some Frenchmen, such as Georges Garros whose book *Les Forceries Humaines* appeared the same year, and young radicals like André Malraux. But they made very little impact on the government, and Chiêu returned to Saigon in March 1926 empty handed.

He was greeted on the quay by a demonstration of French *colons* opposed to his ideas, but a few days later there was a counter-demonstration in his support by members of the movement of younger men that had come to be known as *Jeune Annam*. Not long afterwards the death occurred of Phan Châu Trinh, and his funeral on Easter Sunday was made the occasion for a demonstration by 25,000 people in procession and a strike by the coolies of the rice-mills in Cho-Lon. Pupils in a number of schools wore black mourning-bands, and when this was prohibited and the prohibition was ignored, a number of boys were expelled; at My-Tho there was a clash between the pupils of the college and the local militia.[38] Two members of *Jeune Annam* were arrested and given prison sentences in a Saigon court on 23 April: Nguyên An Ninh got two years for prophesying a violent struggle against the French, and Lam Hiêp Châu one year for publishing sedition in the sole issue of a new newspaper, itself also called *Jeune Annam*.[39] The conservative *colons* went further, and took steps to try to remove Varenne from his Governorship. On 27 May, Outrey introduced a motion of censure against him in the Chamber of Deputies. Varenne was defended by the Minister of Colonies and the motion was rejected, but the fact that he was now at loggerheads with many of his administrators meant that he had little opportunity of making major reforms.

In August 1926 the Constitutionalists refounded their newspaper, under the name *La Tribune Indochinoise*, and a new period of vigorous activity began. Bui Quang Chiêu was now formally the director of the paper, and its administration was in the hands of Nguyên Kim Dinh, who also ran a Vietnamese-language newspaper *Dông-Phap Thoi Bao* from 1923 to 1929. (A not unimportant result of all the newspaper activity from 1917 was the creation in Saigon of a body of men with considerable journalistic experience.) An item in the second number of the new organ gives some indication of the state of Saigon politics at this time. At a recent meeting of the *Conseil Colonial* a French liberal called Gallet had introduced a motion for a *'rapprochement Franco-Annamite'*, which Nguyên Phan Long and the Constitutionalists had supported. But five of the Vietnamese members joined most of the French in opposing it and it was thrown out. It may well have been this vote which determined the Constitutionalists to win control of all native seats in the *Conseil*, and that is what they achieved in the elections of October 1926: all ten Constitutionalist candidates were returned, and Bui Quang Chiêu joined Nguyên Phan Long as a member.[40] This was to be the high-point of the party's success.

So far we have been concerned almost exclusively with political developments in Cochinchina, where the laws permitting some degree of opposition to the government in a French-language press were far more liberal than was the case in the protectorates of Annam and Tongking. In these latter regions the French-educated elite was much smaller, and even its leading figures like Pham Quynh (1892–1945) were more attached to the old Confucian tradition than their counterparts in the South. During the period 1917–26, while Bui Quang Chiêu and his friends were developing a more radical French-language press in Saigon, Pham Quynh took the lead in promoting a periodical literature in *quôc-ngu*, the Romanized form of Vietnamese, within the limitations of a censorship which virtually precluded any political content. He did however also found a French-language newspaper, *France-Indochine*, in 1922 and was interested in some of the things which preoccupied the Cochinchinese Constitutionalists. In the summer of 1926 he proposed the formation of a legal political party in Tongking and Annam which would co-operate with the French in promoting the moral, economic and intellectual development of the community. He won over Phan Bôi Châu to this idea, but not Varenne, and legal recognition was withheld. A new party was in fact founded at Tourane (Da-Nang) in September 1926, the *Parti Progressiste du Peuple Annamite*, but it did not meet Pham Quynh's approval and it was not long before it was completely infiltrated by extremists.[41] Bui Quang Chiêu was apparently approached by the founders of this latter party, but he refused to participate, possibly fearing that the extension to Annam and Tongking of political movements begun in Cochinchina might result in an extension to the latter of the very restrictive political and press regulations of the protectorates. The Constitutionalist Party therefore, although it now called itself 'Indochinese', continued to limit its activities to the South. Some years later, in 1933, Pham Quynh participated in the attempt at a 'constitutional' government at Huê under the new emperor Bao-Dai, but Ngô Dinh Diêm was probably right in his opinion that the experiment would never lead to real independence, constitutional or otherwise.[42]

In the years 1927–28 there was inevitably some rivalry between the Constitutionalists and the less moderate *Jeune Annam* group; however it had not yet reached the point where the former dissociated themselves from the activities of the younger men. In March 1927 *La Tribune Indochinoise* criticized Nguyên An Ninh and Trân Huy Liêu (later prominent in the Viet-Minh) for organizing a separate demonstration at the tomb of Phan Châu Trinh some days before the anniversary of his death, and accused them of taking the hero's name in vain.[43] But this did not represent a serious breach. By this time Ninh, who cannot have served his sentence of the previous year in full, was organizing a new secret society in the Cochinchinese countryside, the Hope of Youth Party, which was virtually Communist both in its aims and its techniques; if the Constitutionalists knew of it, they did nothing openly to reveal its activities to the French Sûreté.[44] In April or May 1927, *Jeune Annam* issued an appeal for French withdrawal from the colony, to be followed by the election of a Vietnamese Parliament and full independence; and amongst the names put forward for membership of a *Commission d'évacuation* was that of Bui Quang Chiêu. There is nothing to suggest that he or any of the others had given permission for their names to be mentioned in this way, but when he was challenged by a conservative French newspaper to state his position, Chiêu refused to dissociate himself entirely from the appeal; he said merely that young men were always impatient.[45] Again, in July when Phan Van Truong, director of the newspaper *L'Annam*, was charged with incitement to revolt, *La Tribune Indochinoise* went to his support. The affair dragged on until March 1928, when Truong was sentenced to two years' imprisonment: immediately Bui Quang Chiêu nominated him as a candidate in the election for the *Député de la Cochinchine* the following month, and conducted a campaign on his behalf, which won him 175 votes despite his sentence.[46] (Outrey was, as usual, elected by a vast majority.) The columns of the *Tribune* continued also to plead the cause of lesser men caught up in situations where French injustice seemed likely to prevail. During the first half of 1928, for example, it sought to defend a peasant family in Bac-Liêu province which had refused to surrender its land to a fraudulent Chinese money lender, with the consequence that a French gendarme and three members of the family had been killed in an affray.[47]

By the end of 1928 however, it was becoming more and more difficult for the Constitutionalists to avoid dissociating themselves from more extreme groups. In the next two or three years they were able to survive only by pro-claiming their moderation to the point of losing all influence over the extremists. On the government side, Varenne was succeeded by Pasquier in 1928 and the conservatives were once more in control. During the autumn of 1928 and the first half of 1929 they began to crack down on as many secret organizations as the Sûreté was able to unearth. Nguyên An Ninh's activities were by now no longer as secret as he wished, and in October he was arrested and sentenced some months later to three years' imprisonment.[48] Then in December came the Rue Barbier murder in Saigon, leading to the arrest of about forty-five members of Communist and other secret organizations operating in Saigon, including incidentally Pham Van Dong who already had a position of some importance in the Revolutionary Youth Association. They were kept in prison until their trial in July 1930, and most of them remained in prison for a good while after that.[49] The press was also carefully watched by the Sûreté, and a number of journalists were arrested and fined: Duong Van Loi for example, a former contributor to

La Tribune Indigène and now an editor of *L'Echo Annamite*, was fined by a Saigon court on 1 June 1929; and a fortnight later the police arrested Cao Hai De, editor of a new French-language paper *L'Ere Nouvelle*.[50] The younger journalists were nevertheless becoming bolder, notably Diêp Van Ky who founded the Vietnamese-language *Thân-Chung* in 1929, only to see it closed down in March of the following year.[51]

It was much easier however to make arrests in Saigon than to keep control over secret activities in the villages. That the colonial authorities had by no means succeeded in destroying the new opposition movement in the countryside of Cochinchina became apparent in the months after May 1930, when there was a series of demonstrations and riots in the Mekong provinces and in the country to the north of Saigon. Initially they were in support of a demand for relief from taxation, but as time went on they became extreme. The Communists (who had founded the Vietnam Communist party in Hong Kong in February 1930) claimed credit for these disturbances, even though they may not have been entirely responsible. The unrest was less serious here than in northern Annam, particularly the province of Nghê-An; but it went on for a considerable time, and it was not until about June 1931 that Cochinchina was wholly quiet again.[52] Some of those most obviously involved were arrested and sent to Poulo Condore or into exile further afield. If the disturbances themselves can be compared in some respects with the secret society movement of 1916, so also can their aftermath which was the disruption of the movement that created them, and a consequent period of calm.

As for the Constitutionalists, they could do little but insist that they themselves were not responsible; some of them went even further and argued that they themselves were bourgeoisie, and therefore as much a target for the Communists as the French themselves. The truth may have been a little more complicated, for the line taken by *L'Echo Annamite* during the crisis seems to suggest that some of the Constitutionalists supported the early demonstrations in May and June 1930 and the peasants' demands for tax relief following a typhoon in West Cochinchina, and that they only became alarmed when the extremists among the demonstrators insisted in going further.[53] But even if this were the case, the effect of the disturbances as a whole was to prove that the Communists and other extremists had a much greater influence in the countryside than the Constitutionalists, and at the same time to make impossible for the future any real alliance between the two groups. The Constitutionalists would henceforth be dismissed by many Cochinchinese as pro-French.

It would be wrong however to suppose that Constitutionalists and Communists were the only two groups competing for a position of strength in Cochinchina at this time. A third element in the situation was the federation of sects which had combined to establish the Cao-Dai religion.[54] It had been inaugurated at a temple in Tây-Ninh province in October 1926, and by the end of that year it had about twenty 'oratories' in eight provinces. Its titular head, Lê Van Trung (1875–1934), was a near contemporary of Bui Quang Chiêu and a fellow-pupil at the *Collège Chasseloup-Laubat*; he had been a member of the *Conseil Colonial*, and later the representative of Cochinchina in the (nominated) council which advised the

Governor-General at Hanoi, a position from which he resigned in 1925.[55] But there were younger men in the background, notably Pham Công Tac (d. 1958) who had links with the exiled prince Cuong-Dê still living in Japan, and the Tây-Ninh branch of the movement was strongly pro-Japanese from about 1937. The movement was indeed extremely diverse, which is not surprising since it was really a federation of sects. It is possible that already by 1930 some of its followers were collaborating with the Communists, at a time when Lê Van Trung was exhorting his followers to come to settle at Tây-Ninh so as to avoid persecution by the Communists. Other Caodaists were supporters of the Constitutionalist Party: for example, Lê Kim Ty who was one of the *Tribune* list of candidates for the Saigon Municipal Council in 1929; and Trân Quang Nghiêm, whom we met as a vice-president of the anti-Chinese boycott in 1919.[56] There is nothing to suggest that Bui Quang Chiêu himself was ever a member; but Nguyên Phan Long, who denied that he was a Caodaist in 1930, was taking an active part in one section of the movement by 1937.[57]

However, even if there was some overlap of membership between the Constitutionalist group and the Caodaists, the latter represented a political technique which was quite different from constitutionalism. They did not necessarily wish to use violence, nor were they necessarily opposed to a constitutional system of government if Vietnam became independent. But they themselves adopted the technique of the secret society, which was in many respects a continuation or revival of the movement of 1913–16. The contrast between the Caodaists and the Constitutionalists demonstrates perhaps better than anything else the true significance of the latter: that they tried to introduce into Vietnamese politics a new political method, derived from their French education. They did so within the framework of such a narrow franchise and such limited opportunities for education that inevitably their method was able to establish itself only in Saigon and perhaps the provincial towns. In the villages their methods made little sense yet, and so the countryside was left to the secret societies, whether Caodaist or Communist. The gulf between the moderation of the Constitutionalists and the extremism of the other groups tended very often to coincide with the gulf between town and country. Unfortunately for the Constitutionalists, Vietnam is a country whose political fate is on the whole decided in the villages, rather than the towns. The Constitutionalists, despite some internal differences inevitable in a situation where things were not going their way, were still able to win seats in the *Conseil Colonial* as the elections of 1930 showed. But it was no longer enough. The one chance of Cochinchina's developing a Parliamentary system with the same kind of spontaneity as did British India, depended on the villages being absorbed into a constitutional system during the 1920s and 1930s. The reform of 1922 represented a step in that direction, but it was not followed up. When the French eventually left the colony they did not leave behind them any basis for rural democracy, and the election of village councillors was no substitute for a tradition of electing representatives to sit in Saigon. Perhaps in 1931, when the disturbances in the countryside had died down and many of the people who created them were in prison, there was still a possibility for the colonial government to allow reforms to take place and so make possible constitutional development along lines comparable to that of British India. But nothing was done.

The comparison with British India is not so unreasonable as events in Vietnam since 1945 might lead one to suppose; it was one which the Constitutionalists themselves made, for one of their principal sources of inspiration during the 1920s was the career of Gandhi. In 1929, Bui Quang Chiêu and Duong Van Giao went to Calcutta to attend the National Congress. They also took the opportunity to visit Tagore's university at Santiniketan, although they did not meet Tagore himself until later in the year when they persuaded him to call briefly at Saigon on his way home from Japan.[58] Chiêu wrote a series of articles in *La Tribune Indochinoise* praising both Gandhi and British policies in India, which drew forth the criticism from Babut's *Révue Franco-Annamite* that Gandhi was out of date and that it would be a long time before Bui Quang Chiêu toured Indochina in bare feet.[59] The implication that the Constitutionalist leader was himself far more Westernized and progressive than Gandhi was fair. Nevertheless by 1930 Chiêu was probably seeking a marriage of Eastern tradition with Western modernity to a far greater extent than had been the case in 1917. Gandhi himself, interestingly enough, had by this time quite a different attitude to Britain from that which had led him to organize an ambulance unit in Europe in 1914 and to oppose any movement for home rule until the war was over.

One factor in Chiêu's changing outlook was no doubt the failure of successive French governors to respond to his demands. Another may have been his long stay in France itself, from 1932 to 1941, as Indochinese representative in the *Conseil Supérieur de la France d'Outre-Mer*. By the time he returned home, on the eve of the Japanese Occupation, the Constitutionalists had long since ceased to dominate the Saigon political scene. The initiative had passed to younger men, and even in the *Conseil Colonial* three Trotskyists had roundly defeated their Constitutionalist opponents in the elections of 1939, only to be arrested a few months later when the French authorities clamped down on all Communists.[60] In 1942 *La Tribune Indochinoise*, along with other newspapers unacceptable to the Japanese, was closed down. Its last numbers reflect very well the changing pattern of Bui Quang Chiêu's thought during the preceding decade. In July he wrote of the war between Japan and the Anglo-Saxon powers:[61]

C'est la conséquence logique d'un antagonisme irréductible où, à des causes morales, viennent s'ajouter celles d'ordre économique quasiment insoluble.

And in September he discussed favourably the trend towards learning Chinese characters and studying the Vietnamese past: '*nous avons trop négligé notre propre pays*'.[62] Had he, at the age of seventy, come at last to regret his faith in the France to which he had travelled with so much enthusiasm half a century before and whose values he had embraced and tried to put into practice? Perhaps so; but his tragedy was not yet complete. With Ta Thu Thau he might have found a rapprochement, but with the Viet-Minh there could be none. In September 1945, as the Viet-Minh provisional committee was being forced by Anglo-French action

to abandon Saigon, Chiêu was taken from his house at Phu-Nhuân, and executed—
a fate which he shared with Ta Thu Thau as well as with the pro-Japanese Hô Van
Nga and Pham Quynh.[63] In 1945 Constitutionalism was no longer, for the time
being, a practical alternative to the violence of war.

That the Vietnamese themselves should have all but forgotten the Constitutionalist part is not perhaps surprising, for in the changed circumstances of the years
after 1945 it was difficult to recall the political realities of the 1920s and very
easy to dismiss as pro-French the policies and attitudes of men who took French
power for granted and sought only to change the details of their situation. With the
exception of some of the Cochinchinese who co-operated with the French in the
Autonomous State of 1946–49 and the Associated State of 1949–54 (one of whom
was Nguyên Phan Long, Prime Minister for a few months in 1950), none of the
leading figures in Vietnamese political life since 1945 has owned to any connexion
with or admiration for the Constitutionalist Party. However, the neglect of their
movement by Western students, at a time when enormous American resources are
being devoted to the establishment and protection of constitutional democracy in
South Vietnam is more remarkable. The *Conseil Colonial* of Cochinchina was the
nearest thing French Indochina had to a democratic institution in the Western
sense, and the Constitutional Party was the only group with any real interest
in developing it into a truly representative assembly with power to bring about
the country's gradual modernization. If nothing else about the Party holds any
interest for American scholars, they might at least enquire into the reasons for
its failure.

Notes

1 Some of the research for this article was done during a visit to Saigon under the auspices
   of the London–Cornell project for East and South East Asian Studies, financed jointly
   by the Carnegie Corporation of New York and the Nuffield Foundation.
2 G. Coulet, *Les Sociétés Secrètes en Terre d'Annam*, Saigon, 1926, analyses the events
   in Cochinchina of 1913–16 in some detail; on the Huê plot, see *Courrier Saigonnais*,
   17 May and 5 June 1916.
3 Lê Thanh Khôi, *Le Viêt-Nam, Histoire et Civilisation*, Paris, 1955, p. 390.
4 M. Khai still lives in Saigon and I was fortunate enough to meet him there in September
   1967; my information about his career is based partly on our conversation then.
5 *La Cochinchine Libérale*, 6 July 1915; the editor was strongly in favour of the move.
6 I am indebted for much information about Bui Quang Chiêu's life to his daughters in
   Saigon, who were kind enough to spend several hours talking to me about his career.
   In the account which follows, however, I have tried as far as possible to document all
   events.
7 *Courrier Saigonnais*, 25 February 1913.
8 *L'Avenir du Tonkin*, 22 August 1906. The society had 110 members.
9 *La Tribune Indigène*, 25 April and 27 June 1918.
10 Part of the letter is printed in Duong Dinh Khuê, *Les Chefs d'Oeuvre de la Littérature
   Vietnamienne*, Saigon, 1966, pp. 351–3.
11 *La Tribune Indigène*, 24 September 1917.

12 *La Tribune Indigène*, 21 and 28 January 1918. A former government official, he sat on the *Conseil Colonial* from 1904, and is to be distinguished from his namesake referred to below.

13 Khoi, *op. cit.*, p. 403.

14 *La Tribune Indigène*, 28 August and 4 September 1919.

15 *La Tribune Indigène*, 7 October and 4 November 1919.

16 *La Tribune Indigène*, 18, 27 November and 2 December 1919.

17 *La Tribune Indigène*, May 1919, *passim*.

18 *La Tribune Indigène*, 17, 24 February 1921; Lê Quang Trinh was elected president.

19 *Rapport du Gouverneur de la Cochinchine, 4ᵉ trimestre 1922*, National Archives, Saigon: S.L. 366.

20 *La Tribune Indigène*, 17 October 1922.

21 *Rapports,* etc., as note 19 above; 1ᵉʳ *trimestre 1919* and 4ᵉ *trimestre 1922*.

22 Georges Garros, *Forceries Humaines, l'Indochine litigieuse, esquisse d'une entente Franco-Annamite*, Paris, 1926; *Documents annexés*.

23 *La Tribune Indigène*, September 1923.

24 *La Tribune Indochinoise*, 31 August and 7 September 1927.

25 Walter G. Langlois, *André Malraux, the Indochina Adventure*, London, 1966, pp. 93–5, etc.

26 *La Tribune Indigène*, 13, 20 November and 1 December 1923; cf. also 22 January 1924. I. M. Sacks says that the opposition to the convention was successful, but I find no record of it being withdrawn ; his source on this is the newspaper *La Lutte* for 1 November 1934, ten years after the event; F. N. Trager (ed.), *Marxism in Southeast Asia*, Stanford, 1960, p. 113.

27 Nguyên An Ninh, *La France en Indochine*, Paris, 1925, p. 17.

28 *La Tribune Indigène*, 11–13 December 1923; 18 March 1924.

29 For an account of his early career, see *L'Avenir du Tonkin*, 5 May 1926. Ninh appears to have been in France in 1921–3, but it is doubtful whether he left with a qualification.

30 In the tract cited in note 27 above.

31 *La Tribune Indigène*, 26 June 1923.

32 *La Tribune Indigène*, 3 January 1925.

33 *La Tribune Indigène*, 31 January 1925.

34 The story of this newspaper, and of Malraux's other activities in Indochina, has been told by W. G. Langlois in the work cited above, note 25.

35 Langlois, *op. cit.*, p. 178.

36 For a report of the trial see *L'Avenir du Tonkin*, 23–25 November 1925; all later sources say that Châu was sentenced to death, but this was not so.

37 And reprinted by G. Garros, *op. cit.*, note 22 above.

38 Report of the British Consul in Saigon, F. G. Gorton, April 1926.

39 *L'Avenir du Tonkin*, 5 May 1926.

40 *La Tribune Indochinoise*, 10 November 1926.

41 Gouvernement-Général de l'Indochine, *Contribution à l'Histoire des Mouvements Politiques de l'Indochine Française*, I, Hanoi, 1933, p. 17. The new party was not given legal recognition by the authorities.

42 Ph. Devillers, *Histoire du Viet-Nam de 1940 à 1952*, Paris, 1952, pp. 63–4.

43 *Tribune Indochinoise*, 14 March and 4 April 1927.

44 *Contribution*, etc. (as note 41), I, p. 44.

45 *Tribune Indochinoise*, 27 May 1927; *La Presse Indochinoise*, 5, 12 June 1927.

46 *Tribune Indochinoise*, 25 July and 28 October 1927; 28 March, 16 and 24 April 1928. Also sentenced to imprisonment in this case was Nguyên Khanh Toan, who spent some time in Moscow in the 1930s, and later became Deputy Minister of Education in Hanoi.

47 *Tribune Indochinoise*, 30 April–11 May and 20 June 1928.

48 On 8 May 1929, *Tribune Indochinoise*, 7 February 1930, review of events of the previous year.

49 *Tribune Indochinoise*, 16–18 July 1930.
50 As note 48.
51 *Echo Annamite*, 25 March 1930.
52 A list of the disturbances is contained in *Contribution*, etc., IV, pp. 124 ff.; a short account of the events of 1930–31 will be found in Ralph Smith, *Viet-Nam and the West*, London, 1968, pp. 104–8.
53 Cf. Nguyên Tân Duoc's reply to an attack on the Constitutionalists by *La Dépêche d'Indochine*, in *Echo Annamite*, 7 June 1930.
54 For a brief account of the religion, see Smith, *op. cit.*, pp. 71–6. Fuller details will be found in *Contribution*, etc., VII, which is devoted entirely to Caodaism.
55 *Thân Chung* (Saigon newspaper), 14 and 21 March 1966. Unlike Chiêu, Trung had not been educated in France; there is no evidence that he was ever active in the Constitutionalist Party.
56 G. Gobron, *History and Philosophy of Caodaism*, Saigon, 1950, p. 150; *Revue Franco-Annamite*, I, July 1929, pp. 9–11; *Revue Caodaique*, 1950, pp. 93–107.
57 *Echo Annamite*, 16 January 1930; *Luoc-Su Dao Cao-Dai, Histoire Sommaire du Caodaisme*, Tourane, 1956, p. 20.
58 *La Tribune Indochinoise*, 29 June 1929; cf. Nguyên Dang Thuc; *Asian Culture and Vietnamese Humanism*, Saigon, 1965.
59 *Revue Franco-Annamite, I*, Hanoi, 1 July 1929, pp. 3–6 and II, 16 July, pp. 1–5.
60 Devillers, *op. cit.*, p. 69.
61 *La Tribune Indochinoise*, 13 July 1942.
62 *La Tribune Indochinoise*, 28 September 1942.
63 Devillers, *op. cit.*, p. 181.

10 The Vietnamese élite of French Cochinchina 1943

Source: *Modern Asian Studies* 6(4) (1972): 459–482.

I

IT is well-known that the French colonial theory of *assimilation*, even though it could never be carried out completely in practice, implied the development in French colonies of an indigenous élite of people prepared to accept both French culture and a (subordinate) role in the running of the colony. In French Cochinchina, this élite was especially important owing to the circumstances of the conquest, between 1860 and 1867, when most of the Vietnamese scholar-officials who had ruled the area previously, withdrew and refused to co-operate with the Europeans. The French had no choice but to create an élite of their own, and begin to educate it in French ways. The process has been discussed in detail in a recent study by Dr Milton E. Osborne, which takes the story of colonial rule in southern Viet-Nam down to about 1905.[1] During the first four decades of the twentieth century, this élite continued to grow and develop, so that by the 1940s it had become the key element in Cochinchinese society so long as colonial rule might last. The purpose of the present article is to examine the composition and role of this élite about the end of the period in which France could take its presence in Indochina for granted.

An élite can be defined in various terms. Some would argue that, in the proper sense of the term, no society subject to foreign domination can have an élite, the topmost positions being reserved for the colonial rulers themselves. Any group willing to collaborate with the foreigners must, by so doing, surrender the right or ability to lead the rest of society in a direction chosen entirely by themselves. Others would suggest that in such a situation the true élite is that of the nationalists who lead resistance movements against foreign domination. From this point of view, the social groups to be discussed in the pages that follow would have to be regarded as something less than an élite. Their importance in the modern history of south Viet-Nam, however, cannot be denied; and ultimately terminology must be regarded as less important than historical significance. With that preliminary caution, it is possible to define the élite with which we are concerned in terms of three principal criteria: education (especially in French); administrative or professional functions, arising from collaboration with the colonial government; and economic rewards, ownership of property, etc. It will be advisable to see these criteria in the context of Vietnamese traditional society, and not solely in terms familiar to students of Western society.

In pre-French Viet-Nam, as in pre-revolutionary China, the same three criteria had been of fundamental importance. To a far greater extent than in the pre-nineteenth century West, official advancement within the bureaucracy depended on education and success in an examinations system rather than on the mere possession of property. Very often, wealth derived from office rather than the other way round. As a result, there was a strong inclination on the part of a rising family to seek education and office, and not to move in the direction of economic enterprise that would lead directly to an increase in wealth. Property in any case tended to be communal, within the family or clan, and there was little in the way of legal security to protect private wealth from a jealous monarchy. The tendency to prefer education and office to business activity was thus deeply engrained in Vietnamese society before the French came, and it was only gradually left behind. Consequently, although the French-educated, *collaborateur* élite is sometimes called a bourgeoisie, its leading figures were not usually men who had risen to prominence through independent economic efforts. They were people who owed their success very largely to French approval, obtained through attendance at French schools and colleges, or through service in the administration. Even those who did acquire wealth without office tended to do so through opportunities for corruption or money-lending rather than through productive enterprise. Such a social pattern fitted in very well with French ambitions for their colony, which did not include independent economic development on a grand scale. In short, the Vietnamese élite of French Cochinchina was very much dependent on the French, perhaps inevitably so.

II

The French-educated élite of the 1940s in Cochinchina was both more numerous and more diverse than the handful of people who had been thoroughly committed to French culture (and power) in the early days of colonial rule. Dr Osborne mentions by name only about a dozen Vietnamese prominent in French service in the period 1860–85; and whilst they probably do not include all those with any knowledge of French learning at that time, they certainly include all those recognized by the French as truly an élite. The situation of that time contrasts very sharply with that of the last quarter-century of complete French rule (1920–45), which is well reflected in a biographical handbook printed in 1943, bearing the title *Souverains et Notabilités d'Indochine*.[2] Of the individuals included in it 141 were natives of French Cochinchina, and they represent a fair cross-section of the people in the Vietnamese élite whose loyalty to France was (or was believed to be) beyond question. An analysis of this group of people will provide us with a valuable starting-point in the effort to understand the character of this element in Cochinchinese society. Eight of the 141 were women, who will be treated separately in due course: let us concentrate first on the 133 men.

They belonged to a wide range of age-groups, and it will be useful sometimes to distinguish between those born at different periods. The following figures indicate their age-distribution:

Born 1860–79: 50.
Born 1880–99: 70.
Born 1900 or later: 13.

The first group, aged over 63 years in 1943, were all men who had retired from regular occupations, though many of them still served on various kinds of committees and councils. They were, of course, representative of stamina as much as of any other quality; many of their contemporaries who had had equally notable careers were already dead. The youngest age-group, men under the age of 43 in 1943, is also peculiar in that it includes only those of that generation who had distinguished themselves whilst young: eleven of the 13 had been educated in France. The same generation included many people who, had French rule continued longer, might have qualified for inclusion in a handbook of this sort at a later stage in life: officials in the administrative service, for example, did not usually reach the higher grades till they were fifty or older. In many respects, therefore, it is the middle group which is most representative of the Cochinchinese élite in general, and some attempt must be made in what follows to compare the pattern within this group with the pattern overall.

It will be useful to approach these 133 men and eight women through a number of different aspects of their life: in particular, their education (and religion), their offices and careers, and their wealth. The economic aspect must be left till last because it is there that the information in the biographies is least helpful. Under each heading it will be necessary to place the information about this sample of members of the élite against the wider background of social categories in Cochinchina.

Education. Information is given, or can be deduced, about the French education of 109 of the 133 men named in the handbook. In addition to those whose schools or qualifications are specified, they include 31 men whose education is not indicated specifically but whose careers imply some measure of education in French—mostly teachers or officials in the administrative services. The information is summarized in Table 1: the figures there relate to the highest level of education attained by each individual, which means that no account is taken of attendance at, for example, the Collège Chasseloup-Laubat, by men who later went on to study in Hanoi or in France. It is possible, in fact, to distinguish three broad levels of educational attainment in the table, all of them higher than that which the French referred to (in Cochinchina) as *premier degré*. First there was the level of the *deuxième degré*, which included several institutions in Saigon and one at My-Tho. The most important of them was the Collège Chasseloup-Laubat, founded in 1874 and named after the former naval minister whose persuasive voice had been responsible for French retention of Saigon in 1862.[3] Its *diplôme supérieur* was the primary qualification for entry into the administrative services of Cochinchina and the Government-General of Indochina, and since many of the people named in the

Table 1 Educational background of 109 members of the Cochinchinese élite in 1943

Place of education, etc.	Whole group	Those born 1880–99
France, etc.	27	13
École de Droit (Saigon, then Hanoi)	8	6
École de Médecine, Hanoi	3	3
Hanoi: other institutions	4	4
Collège Chasseloup-Laubat, Saigon	19	11
École Normale, Gia-Dinh	3	3
Institut Taberd, Saigon	3	3
Collège d'Adran, Saigon	1	—
Collège de My-Tho	2	—
Other specified institutions	2	1
Institution unspecified	6	2
Career implying some education in French	31	15
Total:	109	61

handbook were officials, it is not surprising that it figures prominently in the table. Many of those who studied in France or in Hanoi, and also some of the 31 men whose education can only be deduced, had probably also attended there. In addition to its Vietnamese section, the college was also the school for the sons of Frenchmen in Cochinchina and a few Vietnamese boys attended as sons of men who had acquired French citizenship. By the early twentieth century therefore, the college was much more important than the three other major secondary schools in Saigon. Two of these had been founded privately in the early years: the Collège d'Adran (1862), which was a Church school but had originally been endowed with seventy government scholarships; and the Institut Taberd (1874), intended originally for *métis* children. (It is not clear whether the three men of the 1943 handbook who had studied there were actually of *métis* descent.) A fourth Saigon school, founded somewhat later but growing in importance by the 1920s and 1930s, was the Lycée Petrus Ky, named after the first Vietnamese scholar to write extensively in French and in the Romanized form of Vietnamese.

Another early foundation which appears in the table was the Collège de My-Tho, which appears to have offered a lower level of education than the Collège Chasseloup-Laubat since many pupils proceeded from one to the other. In the early years of French rule, before about 1900, it was possible to go directly from the My-Tho college into the administrative service, but later on an education there ceased to be regarded as a qualification for entry on its own. Mention must also be made of the École Normale des Instituteurs at Gia-Dinh, just outside Saigon, founded in 1895 for the purpose of training teachers in schools of the *premier degré*. By about 1920 it had nearly 200 students, and some indication of the size of its task may be gleaned from the fact that there were then nearly 950 primary schools in the whole of Cochinchina. But the fact that only three people in the 1943 handbook had attended the École Normale suggests that it was seldom the path to membership of the higher élite. A number of other institutions of secondary education grew up during the 1890s, notably the École des Mécaniciens Asiatiques; but none at all of their former pupils figure in the handbook. It would be wrong therefore to suppose that the 133 men who do appear there represent more than a small proportion of the Cochin chinese who had received a French education beyond the most elementary level. They are an élite within an élite.

Some of the 133 *notabilités* of 1943 had been educated outside the colony of Cochinchina: some in France, but some too in Hanoi. Thirteen of them had received the most advanced stage of their education in Hanoi, and another two had attended the École de Droit during the period before it was moved to Hanoi in 1917 (on the foundation of the University of Hanoi). Of these thirteen, none belonged to the oldest of our three generations (those born before 1880), and very few to the youngest group which was composed mainly of young men educated in France. This should not, however, be taken as an indication of a rise and then a decline in the importance of Hanoi as a centre of education for Indochina during the French period. On the contrary, the university there expanded considerably during the 1920s and 1930s, and by 1940 it was increasingly common for children of parents who had gone no further than Chasseloup-Laubat to be sent to Hanoi. That expansion, however, came too late to be reflected in the 1943 handbook, where only the very distinguished amongst those born after 1900 were qualified for inclusion. These were for the most part educated in France, whereas younger men educated only in Hanoi would probably not emerge into prominence until later in life, after 1943. The expansion of the schools and faculties at Hanoi, even though their standards were inferior to those of French universities, reflects a gradual increase in the educational level demanded of aspiring officials after 1917.

That the general level of French education within the Vietnamese élite was gradually rising during the colonial period is also reflected in the numbers who had attended university in France. Of the 27 men in the table who fall into this category, eleven belonged to the youngest age-group. Only three belonged to the oldest group. Of the latter, two were sons of leading Catholics who had supported the French from the beginning, namely Le Phat Anh and Do Huu Try; the other was Bui Quang Chieu, whose father had opposed the French conquest but who was selected by the colonial government to study abroad. These three were not the only people of their generation to study in France; by 1943 they were old men, and others of their age-group were already dead. But they were part of a smaller and more privileged group than their counterparts of the generation born after 1900.

Dr Osborne notes that there were ninety Vietnamese studying in France as early as 1870, but these would seem to have been mainly Catholics attending secondary schools; few if any were able to enter universities.[4] By 1900 it was probably less usual for young boys to study in France, as the quality of schools in Saigon improved; but the number of university students was increasing, and almost all the 27 men in the table are known to have received university degrees. By the 1920s and 1930s, indeed, some Vietnamese were authors of doctoral theses. As regards subjects of study, which are specified in all but three cases, it is interesting that the 27 included eleven scientists, engineers and agronomists, six medical doctors and dentists, and seven graduates in law or commerce. None were students of the faculty of letters, although we know that some Vietnamese did study at the Sorbonne in the 1920s, notably the socialists Nguyen An Ninh and Phan Van Hum: such politically dangerous characters were hardly likely to find their way into a handbook like that of 1943, and we must continue to bear in mind this limitation of the source material. By the 1920s French education was by no means synonymous with loyalty to France.

One of the most interesting conclusions to emerge from this brief analysis of the educational background of the 1943 *notabilités* is the relative unimportance of the Catholic Church in their education. On the secondary level, far more were products of Chasseloup-Laubat than of the clerical institutions named after Adran and Taberd; and only one of the 109 people in the table (appearing under 'other specified institutions') had been educated at a seminary. Of those educated in France, too, only three or four followed the Catholic route to Marseille: most were educated at wholly secular institutions. Whatever the role of the Church in the early years, it would be a mistake to suppose that French cultural influence was wholly dependent on religion in the twentieth century, at least in Cochinchina. In Annam and Tongking the role of the Church was probably greater. It may well have been the case, in those areas, that Catholics were more ready than others to take up French in preference to traditional learning, at least before the 1920s. One must be careful not to apply too readily the results of the present study of Cochinchina to Viet-Nam as a whole.

Office and professions. The 1943 handbook gives fairly full information about careers, and it shows that 106 out of the 133 Cochinchinese men were, or had been, in either official posts or professional occupations. Amongst those with a professional training, most were in employment of some kind (usually, but not always, in government service), and no more than about half a dozen were in professional practice completely independent of any organization. These figures seem to support (not necessarily to prove, in themselves) the impression that Vietnamese saw education as the path to office, and hardly ever a means to independent enterprise, in business or any other field.

Information about these 106 people is summarized in Table 2; again the overall figures are compared with those for the middle age-group. It is possible to divide them into four main categories of career.

(1) *General government service.* This is by far the most numerous category, including over half of both the whole group and the middle age-group. Most of the 62 people involved served, or had served, in Cochinchina itself, even though some were employed by the Government-General and were theoretically liable to be posted elsewhere in the Indochinese Union. Five people, however, all but one in the oldest age-group, worked for the governments of the Protectorates of Annam and Tongking. One of the most distinguished of them was Tran Van Thong (1875–19?), a native of Bien-Hoa who entered the administrative service of Tongking in 1907 and rose to be governor (*tong-doc*) of Nam-Dinh province,

Table 2 Official and professional careers of 106 people in the Cochinchinese élite, 1943

Career	Whole group	Those born 1880–99
General Administrative Services:		
(a) Cochinchina and Government-General	57	35
(b) Protectorates of Annam–Tongking	5	—
Military service	5	3
Teaching	14	7
Medicine	8	7
Legal service or practice	4	2
Agronomy, engineering, etc.	6	—
Canton-chiefs	7	2
Total:	106	56

with the high rank of *dai-hoc-si*. Another, His Excellency Nguyen Van Hien (1877–19?), entered the government of Annam in 1894 and after a number of provincial appointments rose to be minister in charge of the palace between 1926 and 1932. But these were exceptional men, and in later generations there was either less need or less opportunity for men born in Cochinchina to follow their example. For most, government service meant working in Cochinchina, but usually (at least at the higher of the levels open to Vietnamese) in a province other than one's own.

A not untypical career, of an official especially noted for his loyalty to France, was that of Tran Van Mang, born in Saigon in 1899. He attended, in succession, the Collèges of My-Tho and Chasseloup-Laubat, and obtained his *brevet* in 1917. Having entered the administrative service of the Government-General, he was soon afterwards sent to study at the École de Droit (Hanoi), from which he graduated in 1921. He then spent some years in an official post in Hanoi, before returning to a number of posts in Cochinchina. Having passed through the grade of *tri-huyen*, he was made a *tri-phu* in 1928. In 1930—during the demonstrations and near-revolt of some Cochinchinese provinces—he was sent on a special mission to Cao-Lanh to calm the area. Finally in 1936 he was given the highest kind of office he could expect under colonial rule, as *délégué* of Ba-Tri (Ben-Tre province); and in 1937 he rose to the highest grade in the service in Cochinchina, that of *doc-phu-su*. He was still in service in 1943, and had been honoured with the Order of the Dragon in 1941. He applied for, and was granted, French citizenship in 1928. Such men were essential to French rule in Viet-Nam, and were—in French eyes—amply rewarded for their services. But none was entrusted with the highest responsibilities. Not until 1945, after the Japanese interregnum (March–August 1945), did the French promote a Vietnamese to the office of provincial administrator: their choice fell on Nguyen Van Tam (born 1895), who had entered the administrative service in 1913, become a French citizen in 1927, and rose to be *doc-phu-su* in 1934 after being made *délégué* at Cai-Lay; he was now made *administrateun* of Tan-An province, and subsequently became prime minister of the Associated State of Viet-Nam (1952–3).[5]

The 57 people of this kind who appear in Table 2 were, of course, merely the cream of the administrative services. In 1938–9 there were as many as 159 Vietnamese officials in the *cadre supérieur* of men serving in Cochinchina, and there were perhaps another dozen or so people—for example interpreters—in appointments of a similar status.[6] Since the 1943 handbook includes many retired officials, of whom there was an indeterminate number at any one time, it seems unlikely that the 57 men named there would amount to more than a fifth or a quarter of the officials and former officials in the highest grades. In addition there would be a very much larger number of Vietnamese employed in lowly clerical positions, who may be said to belong to the élite insofar as they had some education in French, but who were never going to rise into positions of any prominence. Here again, therefore, we are dealing only with an 'élite within an élite'.

(2) *Military service.* Vietnamese were being recruited to serve under French leadership from the very earliest days of colonial rule, but only at the lowest levels. Apart from those Vietnamese who, later on, joined the French army, there was very little opportunity to rise to a position of any importance through a military career. Not until 1950 were the French willing to permit a wholly Vietnamese army with its own officers. Nevertheless, the 1943 handbook includes five Cochinchinese who had had military careers, though some of them may have been included more for their activities after retirement than for their military activities. Two military men are worth mentioning by name. Thai Van Chanh, born in Can-Tho province in 1874, entered the French army in 1893 and served in Madagascar (1900–5) and on the Ivory Coast (1905–8), then ended his career on active service in Europe from 1914 to 1916. He became a French citizen in 1896, and gained the *Croix de Guerre* in 1911 and the *Légion d'Honneur* on retirement. After returning to Viet-Nam he bought a salt-works and some land, and also became an active Buddhist, so that by 1943 he was vice-president of the Buddhist Studies Association. Of a much younger generation, Nguyen Van Xuan (b. 1892) was the first Vietnamese to attend the École Polytechnique (promotion of 1912). He served in the French army in the First World War, being decorated at Verdun, and rose to the rank of Lieutenant-Colonel of artillery, obtaining French citizenship on the way. After the Second World War he became an active politician, and was prime minister, first of Cochinchina and then of Viet-Nam, between 1947 and 1949. He was, indeed, the first of a new kind of Vietnamese military officer which was to assume considerable importance in the political life of South Viet-Nam after 1954. But amongst the élite of 1943 he was virtually alone.

(3) *Professional service.* In the fields of general administration and military service, the French did no more than create in Viet-Nam their own versions of something that had existed in pre-French society. Those men who entered the former, in particular, did no more than substitute for the traditional education of a Confucian scholar some measure of French general education, on the whole of a more elementary kind. But the French also introduced the idea of professional skill, based on specialized education in a selected field of study. To the extent

that they permitted or encouraged Vietnamese to acquire an education of that kind, they had an important impact on both the culture and the techniques of government of the country. We have seen already that 27 of the 1943 *notabilités* were educated in France, and many of those specialized in a particular branch of professional study, notably agronomy, engineering, medicine, dentistry, commerce and law. A few others acquired specialized training of a less advanced sort at Hanoi, especially in medicine. Moreover, this type of education was becoming more common during the 1920s and 1930s. But only a small minority saw it as leading to independent professional practice, and they were probably men who had other sources of income, for example land. An outstanding figure amongst these exceptions was Dr Nguyen Van Thinh (1888–1946), who had studied at the Institut Pasteur in Paris and had written a doctoral thesis on beri-beri; but he was a large landowner as well as a physician. He entered politics in 1926 as a Constitutionalist, founded the Democrat Party in 1937, and in 1946 became head of the French-sponsored government of 'autonomous' Cochinchina; his tenure of the office ended in suicide.[7]

Most of the 18 professional men in Table 2 (excluding teachers, for the moment) were in some kind of institutional employment, and many were in government service. The oldest of them, and not the least distinguished, was Bui Quang Chieu (1873–1945), who had graduated from the Institut National Agronomique in 1897 and had been in government service from then until 1926 when he entered the *Conseil Colonial* as leader of the Constitutionalist Party.[8] Agronomy became increasingly popular as a field of study in the 1920s, and several of the youngest *notabilités* had qualified in it: for example, Chau Tam (to judge from his name, of Chinese origin), who qualified at the same institute in Paris in 1933 and then studied rice techniques in Italy before entering the Service d'Agriculture at home; in 1939 he became director of the École de Riziculture at Can-Tho.

(4) *Teaching.* Some of those who had acquired specialized qualifications, as well as some with merely a general education, became teachers—also a traditional activity for scholars in pre-French Viet-Nam. The teacher was held in almost as high regard as the scholar-official, especially in his own village. The growth of educational institutions under French rule has already been indicated, and these had to be staffed by educated men of one level of attainment or another. The fourteen teachers in the table clearly represent no more than the tip of an iceberg. Two examples will indicate the kind of teachers who qualified for inclusion in the 1943 handbook. Nguyen Thanh Giung, born in Sa-Dec province in 1894, was educated at Chasseloup-Laubat and then at the University of Marseille, obtaining the *doctorat-ès-sciences* in 1923. In 1926 he became *professeur* at the École Normale des Instituteurs, and subsequently had posts at Chasseloup-Laubat and the Lycée Petrus-Ky, before becoming director of the Collège de My-Tho. Tran Van Giang, on the other hand, born near Tay-Ninh in 1874, went no further in his education than attending the Collège Chasseloup-Laubat (1892–5) and then served as an *instituteur* at Saigon and Tay-Ninh, until he became inspector of schools in Tay-Ninh from 1926 to 1931. He is included, presumably, for his administrative work in the latter capacity, and it was for that that he was made an honorary

tri-phu on his retirement. The majority of the teachers in the handbook were in appointments at state schools, but one who was not deserves brief mention: Luong Van Hau (born 1897), who studied at the École de Commerce Supérieure in Hanoi and then taught at various private schools of commerce in Saigon, before opening a school of his own in 1930; he combined teaching with work as an accountant for several business firms.

(5) *Canton-chiefs.* Seven of the 1943 *notabilités* held the more lowly official post of *chef de canton*. But whereas the officials of the larger units of local administration were appointed by the central government from amongst its regular servants, the canton-chief was a local man selected from amongst the leading inhabitants of the villages within his canton. A representative career from those included in the handbook is that of Nguyen Duy Hinh (born 1874), of the village of Dai-Dien (Ben-Tre province). He held various appointments within his commune (*xa*), rising from *bien-lai* in 1893 to become *xa-truong* (village manager) in 1901, and *huong-su* (adviser on regulations) in 1904. He was canton-chief for twenty-three years (1913–36), and when he retired was given the honorary title of *doc-phu-su*; in 1942, he received membership of the *Légion d'Honneur*. He may well have owned lands, for he seems to have been a man of some substance, noted for his charitable work; but there is nothing in his biography to suggest that he owed his position in any way to education. In this respect, he and the other six canton-chiefs in Table 2 differ markedly from the rest; they may well have known French, but they did not need to be well educated (even by Cochinchinese standards). These men were not part of the higher élite, in this sense; and indeed, only a very small number of them appear in the handbook. There were over two hundred cantons in Cochinchina, and only seven of them were included: far fewer than the proportion of higher officials included. The collaboration of such people was nonetheless vitally important for French rule, and their position in local society was very important. It would perhaps be best to regard them as the top level of an élite of a different kind from the French-educated élite whose life centred upon Saigon and the main towns. Yet to do so might be to run the risk of making too great a distinction between the two groups, for there were sometimes family relations between them. Nguyen Duy Hinh is a case in point: one of his sons, Nguyen Duy Quan (b. 1906) was educated in France, and with a *licence en droit* and *diplôme des hautes études commerciales* he entered government service and obtained, in 1935, an important appointment in the imperial service at Hue. Bui Quang Chieu was also the son of a canton-chief and honorary *doc-phu-su.*[9] In social terms, therefore, one cannot regard canton-chiefs as belonging to a separate class from the French-educated urban élite.

Wealth. The handbook of 1943 is much less helpful when it comes to a discussion of the economic circumstances of its *notabilités*, and a thorough analysis is not possible. One can observe that 17 of the 133 are specifically stated to have landed property or to be occupied mainly in the management of family estates, but it is hardly likely that these were the only people drawing part of their income from land. The paucity of economic information makes it impossible, unfortunately, to make any assessment of the extent to which education and office brought economic rewards. All we can do is to notice a small number of individuals in the handbook whose principal activity was the management of an estate or a business enterprise. The most outstanding example was Truong Van Ben, who must have been one of the richest Vietnamese of his day; he was a native of Cholon, born in 1883, and conceivably was of Chinese extraction. He is described as an '*industriel*', having been one of the leading figures in the move to develop Vietnamese industries in the period around 1918: at that time he had started a rice-mill and oil-mill, and in 1932 he added to them a soap-factory. In the interval he was director of the Société Rizicole de Thap-Muoi, which owned 10,000 hectares, from 1925 till 1932. In 1931 he was mentioned as owning 18,000 hectares, but it is not clear whether the estate was his personal property or merely that of a company.[10] He never held any office, but in 1918 he was elected to the *Conseil Colonial*; and two years later he was a member of the *Chambre de Commerce*, of which he was vice-president from 1932 to 1941; from 1924 he also served on the committee which managed the port of Saigon. Very few non-official Vietnamese can have enjoyed so much success in the economic field. There were, however, a few people named in the handbook who inherited the fruits of success from their parents and who were able to live a life of leisure. One such was Jacques Le Van Duc, born in 1887 in My-Tho province of a Catholic family. His father had been in the administrative service from 1884 till 1919 and had played an active role in the suppression of secret societies in the later part of his career; Le Van Duc himself, educated at the Institut Taberd and the university of Marseille, served for a brief while as *commis-gréffier* in Saigon before retiring in 1913 to manage the family estates. Thereafter he was noted mainly for his endowment of three new schools and his travels in Europe and Asia. It is perhaps surprising that the 1943 handbook does not include more than a small handful of people of his type. One possible explanation is that in many families the estates were looked after by eldest sons who did not aspire to education or office but stayed at home to live a life quite different from that of their brothers: a life less likely to bring them into prominence in Saigon circles. Interestingly, Bui Quang Chieu was a younger son whose elder brother, Tru, lived at Mo-Cay and appears to have acquired neither a French education nor any kind of office. Here, perhaps, we have a part of the explanation why the information in the handbook is so weak on the subject of property and wealth; it was too complex a subject to be covered in biographies of individuals.

Nor is it easy to fill in this gap by reference to other sources. The materials at present available do not enable a comprehensive analysis of the wealth and property of the Cochinchinese élite; perhaps no such materials exist, for it was not the habit of Vietnamese landowners to advertise the details of their business life, and it was probably not of great concern to the French authorities to pry too closely into their affairs. The only statistical source which has any bearing on the problem is Y. Henry's survey of the agrarian economy in 1930.[11] In the fourteen provinces he covered, he found as many as 244 people registered as owners of over 500 hectares of riceland. But it was not his concern to identify them as individuals, and in view of the fact that his survey is based on the ownership-figures of cantons and villages, it is impossible to know whether he avoided the danger of counting some owners twice. Nor is it possible to know what proportion of the owners were Frenchmen. One thing, however, is clear: by far the largest number of these estates of over 500 ha. were situated in the provinces of the West, notably Rach-Gia, Bac-Lieu, Long-Xuyen and Sa-Dec. Those were the areas that were being opened up in the 1920s and 1930s, and it was likely that a successful Vietnamese official or businessman would invest his money there. The situation was, however, changing all the time, and one cannot be sure that the pattern of 1930 was the same as that of 1943. For one thing, economic pressures in the 1930s were making landlords charge proportionately higher rents, and forcing smallholders to borrow money at high rates of interest. Much land changed hands, and there was an opportunity for ruthless men with money to invest to acquire estates in all parts of the country, not just in the new lands of the West.

As in the fields of education and office, it is necessary to observe that not all major landowners appear in the 1943 handbook, and indeed the few individuals whose careers as landowners are most easily studied are not included there. A case in point is that of Tran Trinh Trach (born 1874), who was still living at the time of the land-reform of 1956–7, when he was reputed to own as much as 28,000 hectares.[12] He had begun life in a poor Chinese family of Bac-Lieu province, and had become a government clerk in 1898. As an interpreter between French officials and Chinese merchants, he had enough opportunity for private profit to retire in 1903 and buy some land. Money-lending enabled him to make ever greater profits, and by 1930 he had built up an estate of 15,000 hectares, to which he added a further 10,000 during the 1930s. His very absence from the 1943 handbook suggests that wealth alone was not a criterion for inclusion.

Before proceeding further, we should pause to mention briefly the eight women of Southern Viet-Nam who appear in the 1943 handbook. Five of them appear merely because they were wives, widows or other relatives of notable men. In a special category of her own, there was Madame Nguyen Huu Hao: a daughter of Le Phat Dat, who had been one of the most prominent of the nineteenth-century *collaborateurs*. She had married Nguyen Huu Hao, who belonged to another Catholic land-owning family, but who had died in 1937; their daughter was chosen to be the wife and empress of Bao-Dai. She thus belonged to an élite-within-the-élite of Cochinchinese families which had both great wealth and the highest social acceptance in French eyes. Another of these five women was the grand-daughter of another early *collaborateur*, Tran Ba Loc, and had married a son of the famous Petrus Truong Vinh Ky. On the other hand three women amongst the eight could justify inclusion by their own professional careers. One was a medical doctor, trained in France and at Hanoi; the second was a teacher at the École de Jeunes Filles in Saigon; and the third was an actress, Le Thi Phi, who had emerged as the leading lady of the Vietnamese *cai-luong* (reformed) theatre which flourished from the 1930s. Although, as is well known, Vietnamese women had enjoyed a role of some importance in the background of Vietnamese social and political life, it was a considerable innovation for women to leave home before marriage and be educated for an independent career. These three

professional women therefore represent the first beginnings of a very important.
trend indeed.

III

The handbook of 1943 has provided us with a basis of biographical detail for the
discussion of the main characteristics of what might be called the 'higher élite' of
French Cochinchina. Two groups of people, however, have not yet been discussed
but must be regarded as belonging to the élite in a wider sense. One is a group
which does in fact have a few representatives in the handbook: namely those people
who belonged more to the traditional culture than to the nascent French culture
of Viet-Nam, but were regarded as loyal to France. The second group is that of
people who had a French education, but were not at all 'loyal' to France: on the
contrary, they sought to oppose French rule.

Amongst the first group may be mentioned the three Buddhist priests in the
1943 handbook: all three were directors of temples ('pagodas') in the Saigon–
Cholon area, and their careers were all similar. Huynh Van Phuoc, for example,
born in Gia-Dinh province in 1883, entered the Giac-Vien temple at Cholon at
the age of seven, and spent practically the whole of his life there. In 1941, he
reached the highest Buddhist grade in Viet-Nam, that of *hoa-thuong*; and in 1943
he was director of the temple. In his own career he had no connection at all with the
French-educated élite we have been discussing; but it is not impossible that he was
related to men who became officials or entered professions. Precisely why these
three Buddhist monks should have been singled out, from amongst the very large
number of directors of temples in Cochinchina, is far from clear; conceivably it
was because of their relatives. Two other people may also be mentioned as part of
this category: not monks, but men whose education had been in Chinese. Of Thai
Xuan Lai, we know only that his education was in Chinese, and that in 1935 he
was made an honorary *doc-phu-su* and admitted to the *Légion d'Honneur*. His
career is not specified; he was born in Can-Tho province, and it is not impossible
that he was in fact a leading member of the Chinese community. Nguyen Chanh
Sat, born in Chau-Doc in 1869, may also have been of Chinese descent; but he
was also a scholar, who did much to try to bridge the two cultures, traditional and
modern. Until 1906, he was mainly a teacher of Chinese; thereafter he went into
journalism and publishing, translating numerous Chinese books into the romanized
script, *quoc-ngu*, and for a time editing the newspaper *Nong Co Min Dam*. But by
1943 he was an old man, and it is not easy to parallel his career in the younger
generations in Cochinchina: amongst well-known literary figures, indeed, he has
more counterparts in North and Central Viet-Nam than in the South.

Buddhism is not the only religion represented in the 1943 handbook. Surpris-
ingly perhaps, only one Catholic priest born in Cochinchina is included there:
namely Nguyen Ba Tong, born in Go-Cong in 1868, who in 1935 became the first
Vietnamese bishop at Phat-Diem (Tongking). But the handbook also includes a
number of men who, though the fact is not stated, are known to have belonged to
the new Cochinchinese sect of Caodaism.[13] In accordance with the precepts of that

religion, their priesthood in it permitted them also to have a career outside (unless they were very high dignitaries), so that the people concerned appear as retired officials. Vo Van Thom (born 1868, in Vinh-Long province) was an interpreter in the *Service Judiciaire* from 1890 to 1915, and then a member of the *Conseil Colonial*. In 1926 his wife became a disciple of the founder of Caodaism, Ngo Van Chieu, and two years later he himself became active in the movement at Can-Tho. Nguyen Van Kien (born 1878, My-Tho province) served in the administration from 1898 till 1932, and retired as an honorary *doc-phu-su*; soon afterwards he is found as leader of the Caodaists of My-Tho province, though he was suspected by his rivals in the religion of allowing himself to be used by the French authorities to split the sect into two camps. Possibly others named in the handbook also adhered to Caodaism.

Not all the dignitaries of Caodaism were likely to find acceptance with the French, however, for many of them had shown by 1942 that they were anti-French and pro-Japanese. Some were even imprisoned by the government. For in Caodaism the traditional Vietnamese relationship between religion and politics found new expression, and it proved especially attractive to men to whom French education did not mean political commitment, as well as to some who found that it did not lead to personal success. Two of the most important Caodaist figures in 1943 were Nguyen Ngoc Tuong and Pham Cong Tac. Nguyen Ngoc Tuong (1881–1951) had a career not at all unlike those of many of the 57 administrators included in the handbook: he attended the colleges of My-Tho and Chasseloup-Laubat, then entered the administrative service in 1902; he had risen to the grade of *tri-phu* by 1930, when he retired to devote all his time to religion. He was of good family and education, and in other circumstances his headship of the Caodaist temple at Ben-Tre which he had founded in 1934 might well have qualified him to be regarded as belonging to the élite. His great rival in the movement, Pham Cong Tac (1893–1958), who became head of the sect at Tay-Ninh in 1934, was also a former administrative employee, but on the more lowly level of clerical work. He had retired in 1926 to play a leading role at Tay-Ninh, and by 1943 was in prison for his pro-Japanese sympathies.

The Caodaists, to a considerable extent, were turning away from their French education and seeking satisfaction in a new interpretation of a traditional religion. Other Vietnamese with a French education, especially amongst those who had been to French universities, turned away from both traditional culture and the opportunity for advancement under colonial patronage; often they became left-wing politicians. It is impossible to make the same kind of systematic analysis of their careers as was attempted for the *notabilités* of the handbook, but a few examples are well-known. Outstanding is the case of Nguyen An Ninh (1900–43), who attended the University of Hanoi briefly about 1918, before going on to study law in France. He returned with his *licence* in 1925, but by then he had already played a part in founding a French-language radical newspaper in Saigon, *La Cloche Fêlée*, and had written articles on the need for France to live up to its own ideals of liberty and justice in Viet-Nam. He never attempted an official career, but by 1927 had founded a secret society aiming to establish a socialist

Vietnamese state; for which he was arrested and imprisoned. He was again active in left-wing politics after his release, and in 1937 sought to organize an All-Indochina Congress, as well as a series of strikes. Once more imprisoned, he died in 1943 on Poulo Condore (Con-Son Island).[14] Two other prominent left-wingers, both Trotskyists, had also studied at university in France. Ta Thu Thau, who returned from France in 1932 after an active career in student politics there, was the moving spirit behind the Trotskyist newspaper *La Lutte*; his close associate was Phan Van Hum (born 1902), whose study of philosophy at the Sorbonne qualified him to be the theorist of the group, as well as author of works on Chinese philosophy.[15] Trotskyism was especially attractive to young French-educated Vietnamese, but in the event it was to play little part in an independent Viet-Nam, being unacceptable to the *Viet-Minh* and to the 'right-wing' nationalists alike.

IV

The foregoing analysis of the higher élite of 1943, together with some consideration of the limitations of the principal source used, gives rise to a number of questions about the nature of the élite which can only be answered by taking other evidence into account: for example, that provided by the French-language newspapers, whose circulation was confined to the French-educated community. In particular, one may ask how far this élite really was a homogeneous community, set apart from the rest of society. This question requires some examination of the institutional framework of the élite, which was far more elaborate in the 1930s and 1940s than it had been in the early colonial period.

The new institutions which developed during the twentieth century can be divided into three main categories: educational, economic, and political. The educational institutions actually attended by young Vietnamese seeking a French education have already been noticed. Socially, their effect would be to create the beginnings of a sense of community amongst their pupils and students, and this sense was reinforced by a number of other institutions to which former pupils could belong later in life. Especially important, perhaps, was the *Amicale des Anciens Élèves du Collège Chasseloup-Laubat which* was in existence by 1919 when Bui Quang Chieu was its president.[16] It played an important part in the emergence, about that time, of the Constitutionalist Party under Chieu's leadership. Another group, open to a wider circle of educated Vietnamese, was the *Société d'Enseignement Mutuel de la Cochinchine*, founded about 1908; by 1918 it had seven branches in different provinces, and it continued to expand in the 1920s.[17] Several of the *notabilités* of 1943 were active in it, and it was said at one time to be closely connected with the Constitutionalist Party. These associations were composed mainly, if not entirely, of Vietnamese. There was also at least one cultural association whose membership was primarily French but which by the 1930s included a number of Vietnamese: the *Société des Études Indochinoises*, founded in 1883. In 1938 it had forty Vietnamese members, including corresponding members, and two Vietnamese sat on the committee; the total number of members at that time was just under 300.[18]

Vietnamese who studied in Paris were in a different situation, in that they were never more than a tiny minority within the institutions they attended. The first move to provide an institutional framework for Vietnamese in France was the creation of an *Association Mutuelle des Indochinois* in Paris in 1920. It was reorganized in 1922, and there were 34 Vietnamese at its inaugural meeting, in addition to the emperor Khai-Dinh and his minister Pham Quynh, who were visiting France at the time. During the 1920s study in Paris became increasingly fashionable, and in 1928 moves were made to create a *Maison d'Indochine* at the University City, which still exists there.[19] One of the significant features of these institutions is that, unlike those in Cochinchina itself, they brought together Vietnamese from different regions of the country, thus to some extent breaking down the regionalism which has always existed at all but the highest social levels.

The economic institutions of the élite included some which were essentially commercial enterprises, others whose purpose was the defence of interest groups. One of the most important, existing in most provinces, was the *Syndicat Agricole*. The earliest to be founded was that of My-Tho province, in 1912. Several are mentioned in the biographies of the 1943 *notabilités*, who played a leading role in their activities: those of Long-Xuyen and Can-Tho, founded by 1919, that of Vinh-Long, created in 1922, and those of Bien-Hoa and Ba-Ria, both in existence by 1927. In 1919 there was also founded a *Syndicat National des Riziculteurs* to further the interests of landed proprietors.

Its establishment was part of a general attempt about that time, on the part of members of the Vietnamese élite, to break into the Chinese monopoly of commercial and industrial activity in Cochinchina; it included an abortive boycott of Chinese trade, and the setting up of a *Société Commerciale Annamite*.[20] The movement was not very successful, but it did give birth to a certain amount of Vietnamese business activity, and gave impetus to the attempt of Vietnamese landowners to protect their own interests as rice-producers. Truong Van Ben, whose career was mentioned earlier, was one of the most successful of those whose business activities began at this time. Later on, other economic institutions were developed, especially in the field of credit. The *Société Annamite de Crédit*, in existence by 1932, was run by a group which included several of the *notabilités* of 1943: its director was Le Van Gong (born 1896), who had gained his business experience working in French banks at Hankow and Tientsin between 1919 and 1926.[21]

The economic life of Indochina was at this period governed ultimately by the French, and it was Frenchmen who predominated in the councils which existed to regulate trade, agriculture, etc. The *Chambre d'Agriculture* and *Chambre de Commerce* each included two Vietnamese members, as against ten or more Frenchmen. In 1928 the Governor-General created a council to represent the major economic interests of the whole Indochinese Union: the *Grand Conseil des Intérêts Economiques et Financiers de l'Indochine*.[22] Of its 23 *indigène* members, as against 28 Frenchmen, there were usually about five or six from Cochinchina. In 1939 it was reformed, to exclude all nomination of members by the Governor-General and to allow for a wider range of interests to be represented. But just over a year later, in November 1940, it was suspended owing to the war situation and was never revived. Its successor, the *Conseil Fédéral*, constituted in 1941 and then reorganized in 1943, was entirely a nominated body, even though it had a majority of *indigènes* in 1943. Several of the *notabilités* of the 1943 handbook had played a part in these various bodies. A notable example was Nguyen Tan Duoc, born in Sa-Dec province in 1884, who had served in the administration from 1904 till 1918, then resigned to found a *Syndicat Agricole*, over which he presided until 1923. He belonged to the *Chambre d'Agriculture* from 1925 to 1938, and to the *Grand Conseil des Intérêts*, 1929–37. Also, from 1922 till 1939, he was a member of the Cochinchinese *Conseil Colonial*.

If any institution in Cochinchina may be said to have been a focus of political activity of the part of the élite, it was the *Conseil Colonial*.[23] Founded in 1980, shortly after the appointment of the first civilian governor of Cochinchina, its early Vietnamese members had been men on whom the French could rely for docile obedience to whatever the government proposed. Dr Osborne suggests that many of them had too limited a command of French even to follow the proceedings, let alone to participate effectively. But during the second decade of the twentieth century, a new generation of more educated Vietnamese began to develop a more critical attitude to affairs, and began to express their ideas in the council. It was in this context that a group led by Bui Quang Chieu founded the Constitutionalist Party in 1917, and organized the anti-Chinese economic movement of 1919. Their demands for economic, educational and political change met with some small successes in the next few years. In particular, in 1922 the *Conseil Colonial* itself was reformed: previously it had eighteen members, including six Vietnamese elected by a mere 1,500 people, delegates from village councils; now its membership was increased to 22, including ten Vietnamese, and the latter were to be elected on a franchise which allowed about 21,000 people to vote.[24] This gave an advantage to the new urban élite, against the previous influence of village notables, and the Constitutionalists benefited from the change. In 1926 they had all ten of their candidates elected on the first round of voting, and were able to dominate the Vietnamese side of the council from then until the election of 1939, when three Trotskyists (Ta Thu Thau, Phan Van Hum and Tran Van Thach) defeated their Constitutionalist opponents. Although the council did not give its Vietnamese members any real power, it served as a focus for some political activity simply by virtue of the fact that it involved elections, and membership conferred status if nothing else. At least fifteen of the *notabilités* in the 1943 handbook were members of it at one time or another.

Another institutional development of importance for the growth of political, as well as cultural, awareness amongst the élite was the creation of a number of French-language newspapers owned by, or written by, Vietnamese. Here too the Constitutionalists took the lead, with *La Tribune Indigène*, founded in 1917; it lasted until 1925, and was later replaced by *La Tribune Indochinoise* (1926–42). Another early newspaper with a reformist tendency was Nguyen Phan Long's *L'Écho Annamite* (1920–31). During the 1920s, there were also a number of more radical French-language newspapers, notably Nguyen An Ninh's *La Cloche*

Fêlée (1923–26); Phan Van Truong's *L'Annam* (1926–28), whose life ended in a major political trial of its editor and other journalists; and Ta Thu Thau's *La Lutte* (1934–39). But also there emerged a number of right-wing newspapers belonging to Vietnamese whose sole concern was to provide a focus of loyalty to the colonial government: for example, Le Quang Trinh's *Progrès Annamite*, founded in 1924 after a quarrel between Trinh and Bui Quang Chieu; and *L'Impartial* (1917–42), founded by the *métis* Henry Chavigny. By the 1930s, there was also an active journalism in Vietnamese, and although the *quoc-ngu* press was subject to severe censorship restrictions, the appearance of one short-lived newspaper or weekly after another showed that there was an increasing demand for literature of this kind, and an even more active desire to meet it. The seven daily (or triweekly) and nineteen weekly newspapers in Vietnamese which existed in Saigon in 1938 were the result.[25] They were, of course, not limited to a readership who knew French; therefore they are not, strictly speaking, within the scope of the present study. But both French and Vietnamese newspapers were important in helping to create a new kind of political climate, in which 'public opinion' could be a potential factor and in which a new kind of élite might begin to exercise cultural and political influence.

Yet when all this has been said, it is impossible to escape the fact that these new sorts of institution developed against the background of an older institutional framework. The imperial government and related institutions were no longer important in the South; but the traditional clan remained and may even have been strengthened by the vicissitudes of a country under alien rule. The kinship-group or clan, indeed, was so strong—even in 1943—that one is bound to confess in the end that a survey of the Vietnamese élite in terms of biographies of individuals cannot contain the whole truth about that élite. In certain respects, it is true, the individual was free to make of his life what he would or could. But his success was not exclusively his own: its fruits were expected to be shared amongst the whole of his clan, and property was traditionally a matter for clan rather than for individual decisions. Not all relatives, of course, would profit to the same degree from the success of a high official or a prosperous engineer: those closest would gain most, and others perhaps only indirectly.

Each of the 133 men and 8 women whose careers have been the principal subject of this study must be seen as a member of a kinship-group. It could well be argued that the real élite of Cochinchina consisted not of individuals so much as of a number of prominent families, within which these people were merely the most prominent individuals. Such knowledge as we have of these clans suggests that they were interrelated by marriage, usually through marriages arranged on the same economic level. Unless all this is taken into account, a mere statistical analysis of individual careers might carry with it the risk of being seriously misleading.

Notes

1 Milton E. Osborne, *The French Presence in Cochinchina and Cambodia. Rule and Response (1859–1905)*, Ithaca, 1969.

2 Hanoi, 1943; the work is very rare, the copy used for the present article being that on microfilm at the East–West Centre, Honolulu. The work is arranged alphabetically and page numbers will not be cited.

3 On this and other early educational institutions, see Osborne, *op. cit.*, pp. 105, 160.

4 Osborne, *op. cit.*, p. 4.

5 D. Lancaster, *The Emancipation of French IndoChina*, London, 1961, pp. 209, 283, 431.

6 *Annuaire Administratif d'Indochine 1938–9*, pp. 544 ff. Of the 159, however, only about twenty were of the highest grade, *doc-phu-su*.

7 Cf. Philippe Devillers, *Histoire du Viet-Nam de 1940 à 1952*, Paris, 1952, pp. 66, 173, 270.

8 For a fuller account of his career, see R. B. Smith, 'Bui Quang Chieu and the Constitutionalist Party in French Cochinchina', *Modern Asian Studies*, vol. 3:2, April 1969, pp. 131–50.

9 Bui Quang Dai, of Mo-Cay (d. 1930), *La Tribune Indochinoise*, 25 April 1930.

10 Anh Van and J. Roussel, *Mouvements Nationaux et Lutte de Classes au Viet-Nam* (Publications de la IVe Internationale), Paris, 1947?, p. 66; citing a speech by Governor-General Pasquier on 25 Nov. 1931. The same source says that Bui Quang Chieu had 1,500 ha.; and Nguyen Van Kien (referred to below), 5,500 ha.

11 Y. Henry, *Économie Agricole de l'Indochine* (Hanoi, 1932).

12 Robert L. Sansom, *The Economics of Insurgency in the Mekong Delta of Vietnam*, Cambridge, Mass., 1970, p. 24; information based on interviews in the province of Bac-Lieu.

13 On the history of Caodaism, see R. B. Smith. 'An Introduction to Caodaism; i, Origins and Early History', *Bulletin of the School of Oriental and African Studies* (London), xxxiii, 1969–70, pp. 336 ff. It includes biographical details of Nguyen Ngoc Tuong Pham Cong Tac and other leading Caodaists.

14 For details of his career, see *Avenir du Tonkin*, 5 May 1926; and the Saigon newspaper, *Dan-Quyen*, 15–16 August, 1964.

15 Cf. M. Durand and Nguyen Tran Huan, *Introduction à la Littérature Vietnamienne*, Paris 1969, pp. 125, 211–12; and I. M. Sacks, 'Marxism in Viet-Nam' in F. N. Trager, *Marxism in South-east Asia*, Stanford, 1960, pp. 127 ff.

16 *La Tribune Indigène* (Saigon), 5, 29 July 1919.

17 *Ibid.*, 27 June 1918; 5 March 1928, etc.

18 *B.S.E.I*, n.s., xiii, no. 2, 1938, pp. 253–63.

19 *Trib. Indigène*, 15 Feb. 1921, 19 Sept. 1922, and 27 Aug. 1928.

20 *Ibid.*, 5 Sept. 1919, etc.

21 *La Tribune Indochinoise*, 11 Jan. 1932.

22 Roger Pinto, *Aspects de l'Évolution Gouvernementale de l'Indochine Française*, Saigon and Paris, 1946, pp. 54 ff.

23 *Ibid.*, pp. 43 ff.

24 *Ibid*, and 'Rapport du Gouverneur de la Cochinchine, 4e trim, 1922', National Archives, Saigon, S.L. 366.

25 Counted from *Muc-Luc Bao-Chi Viet-Ngu 1865–1965*, Saigon, 1966.

Index

Printed in the United States
by Baker & Taylor Publisher Services